# ENTREPRENEURSHIP AND SMALL INDUSTRY

## (THEORY AND PRACTICE)

**NEETA BAPORIKAR**
*Professor (Entrepreneurship & Strategy)*
*Ph.D. Guide, Faculty of Management Sciences,*
*University of Pune.*



**SECOND REVISED EDITION : 2013**

Himalaya Publishing House

MUMBAI • NEW DELHI • NAGPUR • BENGALURU • HYDERABAD • CHENNAI • PUNE • LUCKNOW • AHMEDABAD • ERNAKULAM • BHUBANESWAR • INDORE • KOLKATA • GUWAHATI

**First Edition : 2010**
**Second Revised Edition : 2013**

**Published by** : Mrs. Meena Pandey for **Himalaya Publishing House Pvt. Ltd.,**
"Ramdoot", Dr. Bhalerao Marg, Girgaon, **Mumbai - 400 004.**
Phone: 022-23860170/23863863, Fax: 022-23877178
**E-mail: himpub@vsnl.com; Website: www.himpub.com**

**Branch Offices** :

**New Delhi** : "Pooja Apartments", 4-B, Murari Lal Street, Ansari Road, Darya Ganj, New Delhi - 110 002. Phone: 011-23270392, 23278631; Fax: 011-23256286

**Nagpur** : Kundanlal Chandak Industrial Estate, Ghat Road, Nagpur - 440 018. Phone: 0712-2738731, 3296733; Telefax: 0712-2721215

**Bengaluru** : No. 16/1 (Old 12/1), 1st Floor, Next to Hotel Highlands, Madhava Nagar, Race Course Road, Bengaluru - 560 001. Phone: 080-32919385; Telefax: 080-22286611

**Hyderabad** : No. 3-4-184, Lingampally, Besides Raghavendra Swamy Matham, Kachiguda, Hyderabad - 500 027. Phone: 040-27560041, 27550139; Mobile: 09390905282

**Chennai** : No. 8/2, 2nd Madley Street, Ground Floor, T. Nagar, Chennai - 600 017. Mobile: 09345345055

**Pune** : First Floor, "Laksha" Apartment, No. 527, Mehunpura, Shaniwarpeth (Near Prabhat Theatre), Pune - 411 030. Phone: 020-24496323/24496333; Mobile: 09370579333

**Lucknow** : House No 731, Shekhupura Colony, Near B.D. Convent School, Aliganj, Lucknow - 226 022. Mobile: 09307501549

**Ahmedabad** : 114, "SHAIL", 1st Floor, Opp. Madhu Sudan House, C.G. Road, Navrang Pura, Ahmedabad - 380 009. Phone: 079-26560126; Mobile: 09377088847

**Ernakulam** : 39/176 (New No: 60/251) 1st Floor, Karikkamuri Road, Ernakulam, Kochi - 682011, Phone: 0484-2378012, 2378016; Mobile: 09344199799

**Bhubaneswar** : 5 Station Square, Bhubaneswar - 751 001 (Odisha). Phone: 0674-2532129, Mobile: 09338746007

**Indore** : Kesardeep Avenue Extension, 73, Narayan Bagh, Flat No. 302, IIIrd Floor, Near Humpty Dumpty School, Indore - 452 007 (M.P.). Mobile: 09301386468

**Kolkata** : 108/4, Beliaghata Main Road, Near ID Hospital, Opp. SBI Bank, Kolkata - 700 010, Phone: 033-32449649, Mobile: 09883055590, 07439040301

**Guwahati** : House No. 15, Behind Pragjyotish College, Near Sharma Printing Press, P.O. Bharalumukh, Guwahati - 781009, (Assam). Mobile: 09883055590, 09883055536

**DTP by** : HPH, Editorial Office, Bhandup (Apte)

**Printed at** : M/s. Aditya Offset Process (I) Pvt. Ltd., Hyderabad. On behalf of HPH.

# PREFACE

The field of entrepreneurship has grown in recent decades into an interdisciplinary area of study that has found a secure niche in both humanities and business education. Credit for this development belongs to many individuals — both practioners and academicians — who have succeeded in relating entrepreneurial theory to the various problems of entrepreneurship and small industry development. Today's students, in all their wonderful diversity, are tomorrow's entrepreneurs, leaders, and managers. They are the hope of 21st century.

**Entrepreneurship and Small Industry** second revised edition is designed for this time of transformation. It is comprehensive and up-to-date discussion of the most prominent issues in the field of entrepreneurship theory and small industry developments. It is intended to be used as a text in entrepreneurship courses for both the MBA and the graduate level. This book is designed for students in colleges and universities, as well in industry and government, who seek to learn the fundamentals of entrepreneurship and small industry. Preparation of this edition has provided an opportunity to incorporate new developments and increase its value. In this revised and updated edition, the major focus is to make the learning material student-centered so as to enable them to develop entrepreneurial spirits. With this aim in mind, the third part student support consists of exercises and interesting success stories mainly to guide and support students.

## Book at a Glance

Entrepreneurship and Small Industry second revised edition presents the essentials of entrepreneurship as they apply within the contemporary work environment. Though the goal is to create entrepreneurial spirit and entrepreneurs, yet the subject matter has been carefully chosen to meet the university syllabi requirements while allowing extensive flexibility to fit various course designs and class sizes, including multidisciplinary and integrative curriculum settings. Importantly, this is done by blending the fundamentals of entrepreneurship with special attention to practical concerns.

## Features

**Preview:** Each chapter opens with a preview that outlines its contents and objectives.

**Principles:** A set of fundamental principles are developed and defined throughout the book.

**Examples:** Examples of concepts are provided wherever required.

**Chapter Sequence:** The chapter sequence represents author's best efforts to organise the material in a format that can be used in various entrepreneurship courses.

**Exercises:** Exercises are given to facilitate the training of mind for undertaking entrepreneurial activities.

**Success Stories:** Some of the world's best success stories are provided to motivate and inspire the readers.

**Model Questions and Review Exercises:** Provided to prepare the student from examination point of view.

**References:** References along with valuable sources for additional information has been provided.

## Organization

The book is organized into three parts: Entrepreneurship, Small Industry and Student Support.

Each part addresses an important issue for entrepreneurship development and project management and consists of various issue — based chapters. This is to facilitate the reader for using the book as per need and interest.

**Part I deal with ENTREPRENEURSHIP:** Introduction, The Entrepreneur, Entrepreneurial Motivation, Entrepreneurship, Entrepreneurship Development, Entrepreneurship Development Programmes and Emerging Areas of Entrepreneurship.

**Part II deals with SMALL INDUSTRY:** Role of Central and State Government, Government Procedures for Starting a Ventures, Forms of Organizations, Relevant Acts for Entrepreneurs, Government Policies – Small Scale Industries, Role of Agencies, Problems of Small Industry and Causes of Sickness in Small Industry.

**Part III deals with STUDENT SUPPORT:** Exercises, Success Stories, Appendices including Model (Review) Questions and Bibliography.


## ACKNOWLEDGEMENTS

The task of revising **Entrepreneurship and Small Industry** for second revised edition has been aided by advice of many instructors who have used it. To these contributors, whose names are too numerous to mention, I express my thanks. I also wish to express my gratitude to my student turned entrepreneurs who have been not only a constant source of inspiration but also facilitated in honing my skills — research, writing, and teaching entrepreneurship. Completed with the support of a great team at Himalaya Publishing House Pvt. Ltd., I would like to thank Mr. Anuj Pandey, Mr. Niraj Pandey and K.N. Pandey.

Finally, my deepest expression of appreciation goes to my husband Jayant and daughter Neha whose affection, patience and support have been essential for the preparation of this edition just like for earlier writing. While thanking the readers for the feedback received earlier which has helped in making this book more robust, I once again welcome feedback and comments for improving the book further.



**Neeta Baporikar**
neetajb@rediffmail.com

# CONTENTS

## PART I: ENTREPRENEURSHIP


1. Introduction 3 – 9
2. The Entrepreneur 10 – 22
3. Entrepreneurial Motivation 23 – 34
4. Entrepreneurship 35 – 53
5. Entrepreneurship Development 54 – 62
6. Entrepreneurship Development Programmes 63 – 74
7. Emerging Areas of Entrepreneurship 75 – 94


## PART II: ROLE OF GOVERNMENT


8. Introduction 97 – 101
9. Role of Central and State Government 102 – 119
10. Government Procedures for Starting A Venture 120 – 123
11. Forms of Organizations 124 – 127
12. Relevant Acts for Entrepreneurs 128 – 139
13. Government Policies — Small-Scale Industries 140 – 158
14. Role of Agencies in Entrepreneurship Development 159 – 166
15. Problems of Small-Scale Industries 167 – 178
16. Causes of Sickness in Small-Scale Industries 179 – 183


## PART III: STUDENT SUPPORT


Exercises 187 – 207

Success Stories 208 – 267

Appendices 269 – 291

Additional Reading 292 – 294

# PART I : ENTREPRENEURSHIP

1. Introduction
2. The Entrepreneur
3. Entrepreneurial Motivation
4. Entrepreneurship
5. Entrepreneurship Development
6. Entrepreneurship Development Programmes
7. Emerging Areas of Entrepreneurship

# 1

# Introduction

- *Introduction*
- *Objectives of Industrialization*
- *Plan Outlay for Small Industries, Developments*
- *Historical Development of Entrepreneur*
- *Emergence of the Entrepreneur*
- *Being an Entrepreneur*
- *Traits of a Successful Entrepreneur*

The functions of most of the people who participate in the process of producing goods and services are fairly self-evident. Inventors get the idea for new products or services. Capitalists provide the funds needed to produce them. Specialized workers provide whatever services are needed to turn an idea into a product or service for sale to public. Managers direct the workers day-to-day. One might think every role in the productive process has been listed. It is not. One role is left over: that of the *ENTREPRENEUR*. It is hard to understand as well as one of the most controversial. Some inventors have a natural talent for business, but many more of them have been people who liked to make and discover things but did not know what to do when they succeeded. Capitalists may also be business executives, but their specific function is to provide the financial resources for an enterprise and many are content to do only that. Some specialized employees sometimes do go into business, but only by ceasing to be specialized employees. Managers obviously are in business, but a manager who takes over an existing operation is usually very different from a manager who starts one up.

***Example:*** Mr. Narayan Murthy, a genius at computers applied his knowledge to the foundation of Infosys Technologies Ltd.

After the company began realizing its tremendous growth potential, jobs brought in professional managers to see the company's growth in a more structured manner. Many who start up firms find themselves with problems, if the founding entrepreneur lacks the combination of skills necessary to be both 'idea person' and 'manager' and to perceive the vital distinction between the two.

The landscape of entrepreneurism, from food service to biotechnology firms, is littered with the remains of companies/units whose founders could not function as managers or failed to enlist the services of managers when they became needed.

The primary objective of developing countries like India is to achieve rapid, balanced and sustained rate of economic growth. Hence, efforts are directed towards the creation of conditions in which a fast development of productive resources can take place. This inevitably necessitates the transformation of social and economic structures which will not restrain the potential productive forces and inhibit the development of resources. Economic development, if conceived without appropriate social changes becomes stagnated and fruitless. Social change can be achieved, only if political, technological and cultural aspects are combined and woven into the fabric of economic planning.

The objectives of planning obviously would be to ensure economic development in a balanced and equitable way. In a country like India, economic development must be consistent with the principle of democracy, ensuring that the economic task will be in full accord with the interest of the vast mass of humanity, grounded for ages in chronic and vicious poverty. Poverty obviously kills interest, initiative and enterprise. ***The greatest social tragedy in a poor country is the loss of will.*** The challenge before economic planning in countries like India lies in laying down the firm material foundations for a more equitable and equal society. There is an urgent need to overcome economic backwardness and cultural weakness and to promote intellectual advancement.

The first task, therefore, is to stimulate and arouse the people to action, aimed at improving their lot by undertaking productive, economic activity. The process of making individuals realizes that 'Self-help is the best help', then 'self-employment is the best employment' and entrepreneurship, the most exciting level of employment should be the core of economic development policies. In fact, economic development potential remains a dormant asset due to underdeveloped or undeveloped economic man. Man is much more crucial to development than other economic factors. As such, when man wants to change, economic development rolls on. Other factors though important and necessary are ancillary. Sufficiency of other resources, without the necessary human 'development will' may not lead anywhere. Hence, the creation of development will is the key factor in the process of economic development.

It is the entrepreneur, who powers the process of economic development. The strength of an economy is in one way the strength of the entrepreneur class in the society. Entrepreneurship must acquire new management skills to succeed because mere mercantile entrepreneurship may not survive in this competitive world.

Entrepreneur density, innovative propensity, and managerial ability determine the character, strength, and future of economic development. The World Bank's report, India — Poverty, Employment and Social Services, stresses that if India were to build on its improved economic performance, it would have to improve agricultural growth rate, continue her policy of industrial deregulation and rationalization of trade policies, improve public sector finances and increase efficiency in the social sectors.

In India, agricultural growth is still governed by seasonal rains. The phenomenal growth in agriculture is attributed to the entrepreneurial skills and hard work. Yet, industrialization is a *sine qua non* of economic progress effective instrument of growth and welfare and is recognized as one of the important means to usher individual and country in economic and social transformation.

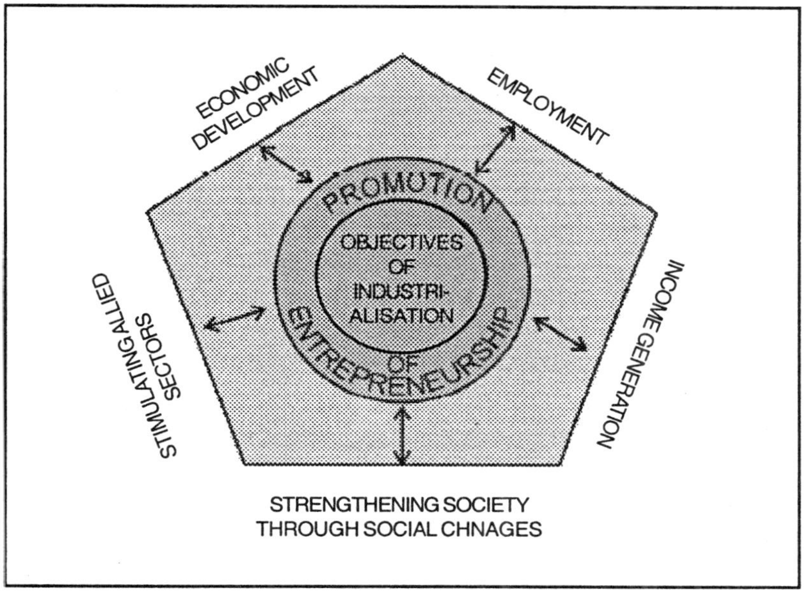


*Fig. 1.1: Objectives of Industrialization*

Industrial development or industrialization depends on a number of factors. The important factors are:

(1) Government policies.

(2) Natural resources which include: *(a)* Mineral resources, *(b)* Energy resources, *(c)* Forest resources, *(d)* Marine resources, and *(e)* Water resources.

(3) Natural factors: *(a)* Geographical, *(b)* Climatic, and *(c)* Technical.

(4) Entrepreneurship.

(5) Human resources.

(6) Finance and capital.

(7) Market and infrastructure.

## CLASSIFICATION OF INDUSTRIES

Indian Industries can be classified into following ways:

(*a*) *Ownership basis:* (*i*) Public sector, and (*ii*) Private sector.

(*b*) *Size basis:* (*i*) Tiny sector, (*ii*) Small sector, (*iii*) Medium sector, and (*iv*) Large sector.

(*c*) *Nature of operation basis:* (*i*) Manufacturing, (*ii*) Trading, (*iii*) Distribution, (*iv*) Infrastructure, and (*v*) Service sectors.

(*d*) *Jobs done basis:* (*i*) Artists, (*ii*) Agents, (*iii*) Professionals, and (*iv*) Agriculturists, etc.

Apart from the most important reason of self-employment through entrepreneurship, there are many reasons which substantiate the advantages of being an entrepreneur, which are given below:

(1) It provides an opportunity to enter into a process which leads to the realization of an individual's passion for innovation and development.

(2) To find a suitable employment, one has to knock many doors and soak many shocks and even then, one may not succeed. But to be an entrepreneur one has to knock only one door, that is one's own self and if the qualities and competencies are therein whatever small quantity, the prospects to succeed are there. The shocks are there in entrepreneurship too, but they can be absorbed if one has decided to be an entrepreneur.

(3) The Government of India and the states offer so many facilities, incentives, and schemes to help new entrepreneurs and particularly qualified individuals, be it technical, managerial or otherwise in taking up entrepreneurial career. This career path is not as thorny as it used to be years ago.

(4) As an entrepreneur, one is not only employed but also creates employment for others, one is not only realizing the goal in his life but is also a source of livelihood for so many. The pride of being a lord of one's own destiny is coupled with the satisfaction of being the benefactor of so many.

It is not enough to be qualified and experienced, one has to let the society, nation at large benefit from one's competence and experience. Entrepreneurship provides an excellent opportunity to realize both the goals — the individual status as well as individual's contribution to the society.

Entrepreneurship is not a matter of heritage, it is entirely a manifestation of such potentialities that any individual born in any caste, community and class can have. As such, any person having a certain set of behavioural traits and mental aptitudes in him/her can become an entrepreneur.

Besides, there is no need for such a person to be groomed from the very childhood for becoming an entrepreneur. Even if he is grown up, has worked on a different line and has developed these traits or aptitudes, he or she can be groomed and developed as an entrepreneur through counselling and motivational measures.

Thus, a pool of capable people keeps the economic development on growth track. Industrialization is one of the important means to usher individuals and nations towards economic and social transformation. More so, when agriculture cannot sustain the burden of population growth, it is industry and the public sector which have to shoulder the responsibility and sustain as well as accelerate the rate of growth. Industrialization results from the interaction of technological change, innovation, entrepreneurial growth, specialization, and trade. Large industrial units and business houses also have an important role to play in developing and sustaining new entrepreneurship.

Inspite of India having abundant natural and human resources, we are not a prosperous country because of *Entrepreneurship* being still a comparatively scarce factor, as indeed in all developing countries. In this connection, government's economic policies have an important impact on the growth of entrepreneurship. Among the prominent economic policies, to develop entrepreneurship has been the strategy by stimulating Small-Scale Industry (SSI) and to use it as a tool for economic growth.

The pivotal role the small industries played in the economic development of the country to rank India among the 10 most industrial countries in the world can be judged by looking at the plan outlays provided in different five-year plans.

Thus, the entrepreneurship development in India has received significant attention: borne out by the fact that small units/enterprises have made phenomenal progress during the last five decades and today occupy an important position in the industrial economy of India. Every new Industrial Policy Resolution (IPR) aims at entrepreneurship development through small-scale industry/sector development.

## HISTORICAL DEVELOPMENT OF ENTREPRENEUR

The classical economists led by Adam Smith recognized the importance of organizing land, labour and capital in a meaningful way to get the best out of them. By themselves these three factors had a tendency to be dormant. However, these economists give the organizer of these factors the dictum 'factor of production.' In fact, Ricardo had dealt in length about the capitalist farmer and his role in improving the 'art of agriculture.' But nowhere has the entrepreneur been recognized as a full-fledged factor of production in the writings of the English classical school.

## EMERGENCE OF THE ENTREPRENEUR

The Industrial Revolution can be cited as the single big reason for the emergence of the entrepreneur. Nicholas Kaldor has observed that the Industrial Revolution was the result of 'the displacement of production units governed by traditionalist outlook by business enterprises led by men who found risk taking and money making their chief interest in life'.

These entrepreneurs did not suddenly appear in the British economy. The British society was slowly preparing a class of industrial leaders capable of leading the process of development. These persons came primarily from the wealthy merchant and trading classes that the 17th and 18th centuries produced. These merchants were highly prosperous and were great organizers combining in them the functions of the capitalist, financier, manager, merchant, and salesman. It was from this class that men came who commercialized the great inventions of the 18th and 19th centuries. Thus, 'the entrepreneur had arrived and had come to stay'. The economists of the latter half of the 19th century and the 20th century made 'entrepreneur' the 'fourth factor of production'.

In the emergence of the entrepreneur, it must be clarified that the entrepreneur is not an inventor. What he did was to use his immense wealth in putting new ideas into practice. The large number of inventions would have all gone waste, had they not been made commercially viable by these entrepreneurs. That is why the entrepreneurs are given the credit for the success of the Industrial Revolution. In Britain, the entrepreneurs did not confine themselves to industry alone, it was widespread and made its impact felt, in every branch of activity — manufacturing, agriculture, transportation and finance.

## BEING AN ENTREPRENEUR

What qualities and traits are required to be a successful entrepreneur? While it is difficult to answer this question definitively, it appears that a successful entrepreneur has the following qualities and traits:

1. **Willingness to make sacrifice:** A new venture is often plagued with numerous difficulties and unanticipated problems. To nurture it in such an inhospitable environment, the entrepreneur has to be prepared to sacrifice his time, energy and resources. He must be willing to struggle, sacrificing personal comforts and conveniences, against seemingly endless odds. An entrepreneurial job is not like a typical nine-to-five job, it tends to be far more demanding, requiring total commitment and sometimes, even an obsessive preoccupation — on the part of the entrepreneur.
2. **Leadership:** Successful entrepreneurs generally have strong leadership qualities. They are able to inspire ordinary persons to accomplish great feats , even though outwardly they may show bizarre signs (they may be whimsical, timid, or even cantankerous), they are able to fire people with their zeal. They have the flair of galvanizing their team to successfully cope with the challenges and frustrations inherent in a new venture.
3. **Decisiveness:** A fledging enterprise has to accomplish many things in an atmosphere of uncertainty. Numerous decisions have to be taken in quick succession on the basis of limited information. The firm does not have a history to fall back on or a well — organized data-base to rely upon. Unless the entrepreneur is decisive by nature, he would not be able to cope with the enormous burden of decision-making. If he procrastinates, he may court disaster, if he dillydallies, he may miss valuable opportunities. The fluid situation of a new enterprise calls not only for an ability to

decide quickly but also an ability to revise the decisions to adopt the enterprise to an environment in which it has not established proper moorings.

4. **Confidence in the project:** An entrepreneur should have unbounded faith in his project. This helps him in instilling confidence in suppliers, creditors, customers, employees and others. Without unflinching conviction in the project, it would be difficult for the entrepreneur to withstand the failures and frustrations that form the new venture diet.

5. **Marketing orientation:** A strong marketing orientation is critical to a new venture. An entrepreneur who is skilful in exploiting market opportunities has the best chance of success. Irrespective of the professional guise he wears (whether it be that of an engineer, inventor, production technologists, accountant or any other) the entrepreneur must have marketing talent. Edwin Land of Polaroid is widely recognized as an ideal example of distinguished marketing talent. Edwin Land had superior marketing skills and perhaps this was the most critical factor in the outstanding success of Polaroid. He could inspire the technical and financial world. If an entrepreneur lacks marketing skills, he must find a partner who can remedy this deficiency; otherwise the venture will be severely handicapped because of its inability to exploit the marketing opportunities.

6. **Strong ego:** Setting up a new enterprise is like riding on an emotional roller coaster. There are days which bring jubilation and there are days which cause despondency, as the enterprise is buffeted by environmental forces, which tend to have a strong influence on the nascent venture. The entrepreneur needs a strong ego to bear up with such ups and downs. To endure periods of adversity and to maintain proper perspective when events cast their shadow over the enterprise, the entrepreneur needs a strong identity and self-image.

*****

# 2

# The Entrepreneur

- *Definitions*
- *Characteristics of an Entrepreneur*
- *Significance of an Entrepreneur*
- *Entrepreneur vs. Entrepreneurship*
- *Qualities of an Entrepreneur*
- *Discussion 'Entrepreneurs are born and not made'*
- *Entrepreneur and Enterprises*
- *Intrepreneur*
- *Classification of Entrepreneur*
- *Examples of Entrepreneurs*
- *Do's and Don'ts of an Entrepreneur*
- *The Entrepreneur and Economic Development*
- *Who can be an Entrepreneur?*
- *A Doer not a Dreamer*
- *The New Entrepreneur: Myths vs. Reality*

The word 'Entrepreneur' is derived from the French word 'Enterprendre' meaning 'to undertake.' In 16th century, the Frenchmen who undertook military expeditions were referred to as an 'Entrepreneur'. Later the word 'entrepreneur' got associated with person who starts his own enterprise, *i.e.,* risks for establishing a venture which is one's own. Hence, all new business units which come into existence are by entrepreneurs and can be called as enterprises, but all entrepreneurs need not, start/establish business enterprises. Entrepreneurship can be in other areas also, which may not be dominated only by business concerns.

## DEFINITIONS

**Quesnay:** 'A rich farmer is an entrepreneur who manages and makes his business profitable by his intelligence and wealth'.

**Adam Smith:** 'Entrepreneur is a person who provides capital without taking active part in the leading role in an enterprise'.

**Richard Cantillon:** 'All persons engaged in economic activity are entrepreneurs'.

**J.B. Say:** 'Entrepreneur is a person endowed with the qualities of judgment, perseverance and knowledge of the world as well as of the business'.

**J.A. Schumpeter:** 'A person who introduces innovative changes is an entrepreneur and he is an integral part of economic growth'.

**Frank Young:** 'Entrepreneur is a change agent'.

**Webster:** 'Entrepreneur is one who assumes risks and management of business.

**Walker:** 'True entrepreneur is one who is endowed with more than average capacities in the risk of organizing and co-coordinating various factors of production'.

**Peter Drucker:** 'Entrepreneur is one who always searches for change, responds to it and exploits as an opportunity. Innovation is a specific tool of entrepreneurs, the means by which they exploit change as an opportunity for different business or service'.

**Dewing:** 'The function of entrepreneur is one that promotes ideas into business'.

**Dantrof:** 'Entrepreneur is a person who makes decisions under alternative courses of action'.

From the above definitions given by various experts in the field of economics and management, etc., it is clear that entrepreneur has become the focal point in economic activities. Entrepreneur is, viewed as an initiator of action, stimulator of social economic change and a harnesser of resources and factors of production to create wealth. Entrepreneur is one who distinguishes as a person and must be a visionary carrying dream and desires to achieve and lead his enterprise and men for success. Entrepreneurship is neither a science nor an art, it is a practice, it has a knowledge base.

Knowledge in entrepreneurship is a means to an end. Indeed, what constitutes knowledge in practice is largely defined by ends, *i.e.*, by practice. Martin Luther King was not far from truth when he said, 'I have a dream', thousands followed in spite of overwhelming obstacles. In order to establish a successful new business venture, the entrepreneurial leader must have a dream and work against all obstacles to achieve it. To conclude, an entrepreneur is the one who can dream, desire, change, and succeed, in spite of adversities for establishment of his venture.

## CHARACTERISTICS OF AN ENTREPRENEUR

The characteristics of an entrepreneur that contribute to success are the result of his achievement and motivation.

The characteristics of achievement motivated persons as identified by McClelland are:

(1) Technical competence.

(2) Initiative.

(3) Good judgment.

(4) Intelligence.

(5) Leadership.

(6) Confidence.

(7) Energy.

(8) Attitude.

(9) Creative.

(10) Fair.

(11) Honest.

(12) Tact.

(13) Emotionally stable.

An entrepreneur who has high level of administrative ability, mental ability, human relation ability, including communication skills, stands better chances of success than who has low levels of these basic qualities. Robert Hirsch identified few more capabilities or characteristics which could make an entrepreneur successful. Those are:

(1) Motivator.

(2) Self-confidence.

(3) Long-term involvement.

(4) High energy level.

(5) Persistent problem solver.

(6) Initiative.

(7) Goal setter.

(8) Moderate risk taker (calculated risks).

## SIGNIFICANCE OF AN ENTREPRENEUR

Entrepreneur is one of the most important inputs in the economic development of a country or of regions within the country. Entrepreneurial talents and competence makes all the difference in the rate of economic growth.

In India because of mixed economy pattern of society both state and private enterprises co-exist. The small-scale sectors and business are left completely too private entrepreneurs. It is therefore, important to identify and promote entrepreneurs. The need for broad — based entrepreneurial class in India arises both in the government and private sector since there is a dire need to speed up the process of activating the factors of production, leading to a higher rate of economic growth, dispersal of economic activity so as to ensure balanced regional development, creation of employment opportunities and improving existing standard of living through eradication of poverty.

In view of India, being a large democratic country with abundant natural resources but having unique problems like huge population, low employment opportunity, poor standard of living, low literacy level, poor health conditions, lack of medical facilities, an entrepreneur who would harness the resources for minimizing some of the above problems would certainly be of importance. The significance of entrepreneur, entrepreneurship, and entrepreneurship development needs no emphasis since all the three would work for economic development of an individual and country.

## ENTREPRENEUR VS. ENTREPRENEURSHIP

Both the terms 'entrepreneur' and 'entrepreneurship' are often used interchangeably, but conceptually they are different yet they are like two facets of the same coin. The differences which exist are:

**Table 2.1**

**Entrepreneur Vs. Entrepreneurship**

| *Entrepreneur* | *Entrepreneurship* |
|---|---|
| is a person | is a process |
| a visualizer | a vision |
| a creator | a creation |
| an organizer | an organization |
| an innovator | an innovation |
| a planner | planning |
| a risk taker | risk taking |
| a communicator | communication |
| a leader | leadership |

**Source:** 'Small Scale Industries and Entrepreneurship' by Vasant Desai.

From the above, it is clear that entrepreneur refers to a person and entrepreneurship refers to a process. However, the importance of the person cannot be over emphasized, since individuals place themselves in a particular capacity for rational reasons relating their own lives, for the firms with a desire to build an enterprise.

## QUALITIES OF AN ENTREPRENEUR

A true entrepreneur besides possessing functional qualities must also possess personal qualities which help him in developing initiative and drive to accomplish great tasks and face challenges squarely.

James J. Berne has traced the following qualities of a good entrepreneur:

(1) He is an enterprising individual. He is energetic, hard working, resourceful, alert to new opportunities, able to adjust himself to changing conditions with ease and willing to assume risks involved in change.

(2) He is interested in advancing technologically and in improving the quality of his product or service.

(3) He is interested in expanding the scale of his operations by reinvesting his earnings.

(4) He visualizes change and adapts.

(5) He is a firm believer in planning and systematic work.

(6) He works for the society at large and for the good of his fellow beings.

These qualities sum up what is usually implied from the phrase 'Spirit of Enterprise'. Entrepreneurship appears as a personal quality which enables certain individuals to make decisions with far-reaching consequences.

## DISCUSSION: 'ENTREPRENEURS ARE BORN AND NOT MADE'

'Entrepreneurs are born and not made' *vs.* 'Entrepreneurs can be developed' are two statements which calls for a discussion. Since entrepreneurial qualities are to some extent innate, *i.e.*, inborn, hence entrepreneurs are born is partially true, however all qualities entirely are not inborn, some can be enhanced by training and some can be acquired by experience.

*Example:* Analytical ability and computational skills can be enhanced by education at school and university, while practical knowledge and foresight skills can be enhanced by experience. Technical capabilities can be developed and skill can be acquired with practice, patience and perseverance.

Entrepreneurial careers are strongly influenced by the desire to enhance qualities which are scarce, yet difficult to obtain through opportunities. Of the two indispensable qualities of the entrepreneur, imagination is almost entirely innate, while foresight, though to some extent innate, can be enhanced by varied experience. Imagination and insight are scarce qualities which are difficult to analyze and quantify. Hence, entrepreneurs need to have some innate qualities and rest can be developed.

To conclude, both the statements are partially true and the real fact is, persons desiring of becoming entrepreneurs need to have innate qualities, *e.g.*, imagination, foresight and other qualities required need to be acquired/developed, *e.g.*, analytical skills, logic, etc.

## ENTREPRENEUR AND ENTERPRISE

Entrepreneur is the fourth factor of enterprise. According to Webster, Entrepreneur is one who assumes the risk and management of business. The Enterprise is the basic unit of an economic organization. It produces goods and services whose worth is more than the resources used. The factors of production which aid or put the resources to use are land, labour, capital and organization.

Enterprise is an undertaking which involves risk taking and decision making, unless an individual involves oneself for the activities with courage and energy backed by willingness to take risk and assume responsibilities, enterprises cannot come into existence and neither grow. Hence, entrepreneur and enterprise are so closely connected and inter-linked so much that one cannot exist without the other. Enterprise is the off-shoot of an entrepreneur and its success is dependent on the entrepreneur.

## INTREPRENEUR

They are entrepreneurs who catch hold of a new idea for a product, service, or process and work to bring their vision to fruition within the framework of the organization. Intrepreneurs with their innovations and dedicated product are perceived as a valuable asset by the organization, inspiring others. In other words, intrepreneur refers to an enterprising person within the boundaries of his job. The concept of the intrepreneur needs to be understood in its broader sense and that he is a person who acts as an agent of change for the good of the people. He tries to make a better society, a healthy economy, hence, he is considered as a critical input for socio-economic development.

## EXAMPLES OF ENTREPRENEURS

**1. Uday:** A fresh science graduate:

After Uday's graduation from a science college in Belgaum, in 1970, his father an agriculturist wanted him to look out for a job. Incidentally, he cleared the first interview for the post of Medical Representative in Alembic India Limited. He went to Mumbai for the final interview. On account of delay in getting his final B.Sc. results he could not get selected in Alembic. He could have returned back to Belgaum, but circumstances made him take up a job as stores supervisor in a small company called United Potteries. He served there sincerely and honestly for 10 long years. During the same time, he acquired additional qualifications in management and cost accounting.

Seeing his sincerity, honesty and commitment, one of the major dealers of United Potteries offered him a good opening as working partner with a percentage in profit sharing (on sales) at Kolhapur. He took this opportunity and joined Shri OM Traders in 1980. Within 3 years, the sales were fourfold. By now he had become confident about his capacity to work and also saved a tiny sum. In 1983, he took up a small shop and began his own business (Quality Traders) dealing in sanitary-ware and allied items with his savings.

Today, Uday is an established sole trader, happy with himself and also has been able to provide quality materials to the middle class society of Belgaum.

**2. Tirupati:** An ITI Welder:

Tirupati, a young lad of 17 came to Baroda in 1986 and joined one of the Defence mess to earn his livelihood. Tirupati had done a welding course from ITI but did not get any opportunity/job. During his job in helping officers in the mess he got acquainted with one of the technical officers. Seeing Tirupati's urge, and desire to learn, the technical officer taught him some basic technical skills including repairing of scooters, vehicles, etc. After the officer got posted out of Baroda, Tirupati's future was uncertain.

The officer recommended him and through one of his friends was able to place Tirupati in Apple Computers at New Delhi as a helper-cum-technician in 1989. He worked there for 2 years and with sheer determination, urges and interest rose up to the level of technician and undertook installation of computers. During this course, Tirupati had picked up sufficient knowledge and understanding of computers and its market. So in 1993, with a small capital (out of his savings) he started his own business dealing in assembling of computers and selling hardware items. Within few years, young Tirupati was established as a businessman in New Delhi. He is also serving the society through his policy, *i.e.*, anybody coming from his hometown without two square meals, is provided with an opportunity to work and sustain till the individual finds a means of livelihood.

## CLASSIFICATION OF ENTREPRENEURS

There are various ways in which entrepreneurs have been classified. Table 2.2 below shows the various types of entrepreneurs under each classification. The types given under each classification are also not rigid, *e.g.*, there can be women technical entrepreneur or old unskilled entrepreneur. In short, whatever the type of classification, as long as they serve the economic purpose of the nation they have to be hailed as entrepreneurs.

**Table 2.2**

**Classification of Entrepreneur**

| *Classification* / *Types* | *Business* | *Technology* | *Motivation* | *Growth* | *Stages of development* | *Gender and age* | *Other* |
|---|---|---|---|---|---|---|---|
| 1. | Business entrepreneur | Technical entrepreneur | Pure entrepreneur | Growth entrepreneur | Classical entrepreneur | Men entrepreneur | Immigrant entrepreneur |
| 2. | Trading entrepreneur | Non-Technical entrepreneur | Induced entrepreneur | Super growth entrepreneur | Modern entrepreneur | Women entrepreneur | Urban entrepreneur |
| 3. | Industrial entrepreneur | Professional entrepreneur | Spontaneous entrepreneur | | | Young/old entrepreneur (Men and Women) | Rural entrepreneur |
| 4. | Corporate entrepreneur | Hi-tech entrepreneur | | | | | Bureaucratic entrepreneur |
| 5. | Agricultual entrepreneur | | | | | | Intrepreneur entrepreneur |
| 6. | Service entrepreneur | | | | | | |

Table 2.3
Dos and Don'ts for an Entrepreneur

| *Dos* | *Don'ts* |
|---|---|
| 1. Do take decision, keeping in mind the fact that an entrepreneur should be moderate and calculated risk taker. | 1. Don't overburden from the beginning. |
| 2. Do proper and planned utilisation of time. | 2. Don't do all the work by self, delegate. |
| 3. Do keep oneself fully informed about the market developments and think about the adjustments in advance. | 3. Don't avoid or run away from problems, be it creditors/money/lenders. |
| 4. Do know more about competitors. | 4. Don't promise immediate repayments of private borrowings, from your relatives or friends, especially if they have been put into long-term assets. |
| 5. Do take help/advise from experts to develop all round managerial understanding. | 5. Don't hesitate and be afraid to take hard and unpleasant decisions. |
| 6. Do weign implications of short-term and long-term decisions. | 6. Don't depend too much on memory. Make habit of writing and recording, a regular practice. |
| 7. Do have information system to know where one's business is leading. | 7. Don't assume finance is the only cause or factor for performance. |
| 8. Do anticipate changes and problems and prepare to face them. | 8. Don't keep yourself totally busy and involved in day-to-day work, but keep adequate free time to think, plan, and work for future. |
| 9. Do keep oneself updated about technology. | 9. Don't worry about uncertainty beyond control. |
| 10. Do be careful in the initial periods. | |

## THE ENTREPRENEUR AND ECONOMIC DEVELOPMENT

**Economists' View:** The position of the entrepreneur in modern production is like that of the director of a play. Modern economic development is closely linked with production. Modern production is highly complex. The entrepreneur directs production and he must do whatever is necessary for its success.

His role in modern economic development has at least three aspects:

(a) *The entrepreneur co-ordinates the other factors of production.* This involves not only assembling the factors, but also to see that the best combination of factors is made available for the production process. Co-ordination involves selection of the right type of factors, employment of each factor in the right quantity, use of the best technical devices, division of labour, reduction of waste, etc.

(b) *The entrepreneur takes risks.* In Hawtrey's view, this is the most important function of the entrepreneur and the quantum of profit he receives is directly proportionate to the risks he takes. Risks are generally based on the anticipation of demand. Prof. B.R. Knight has gone one step forward in his opinion — risks are of two types — insurable and non-insurable. He calls non-insurable risks by the term 'uncertainty'. In his view uncertainty-bearing is the primary function of an entrepreneur which enables him to get profit. This function has assumed great importance with the increasing complexities of modern production.

(c) *Finally, the entrepreneur innovates.* Innovation is different from invention. Invention is the work of scientists. Innovation implies the commercial application of an invention. As an innovator, the entrepreneur assumes the role of a pioneer and an industrial leader. Joseph Schumpeter and his followers believed that the entrepreneur is one who innovates and innovation makes the entrepreneur the hero in the drama of economic development.

Modern economists tend to agree with the view expressed by Schumpeter since the process of economic development is characterized by the presence of discontinuous disturbance, economists tend to agree to the view that this disturbance comes in the form of innovation.

The entrepreneur can undertake any one type of the following five categories of innovation:

(a) The introduction of new goods or new quality of goods.

(b) The introduction of a new method of production.

(c) The opening of a new market.

(d) The conquest of a new source of supply of raw materials.

(e) The carrying out of a new organization of any industry.

The innovational activity raises the productive efficiency of the economy resulting in greater output and income. Schumpeter finds in rising productivity the secret of economic development as distinguished from economic growth. Economic growth occurs when more resources are available in the economy. But economic development is an entirely different phenomenon it occurs when output increases as a result of entrepreneurial activity. Schumpeter therefore defines development as, 'the carrying out of new combinations'.

The entrepreneur is the central figure in the process of development. He introduces new combinations of factors thereby channelizing the economy's resources along productive lines. He is not a producer, for the latter chooses any one of the available methods, the entrepreneur is constantly engaged in introducing newer methods of production. The entrepreneur is not a capitalist.

The capitalist provides the funds for production, the entrepreneur divests the funds to new production. The entrepreneur is thus, always on the look out of making the economic system at its dynamic best. Thus, entrepreneurial activity stimulates progress and forms the mainspring of economic development.

## WHO CAN BE AN ENTREPRENEUR?

Anyone who wants to become an entrepreneur can become one. All he or she has to do is keep an open mind, search, understand, and analyze the implications of changes all round. A systematic search for changes will throw up many valuable opportunities. Innovations are the key to entrepreneurship. Entrepreneurship is not a matter of heritage, it is entirely a manifestation of such potentialities that any individual born in any caste, community, and creed can have. As such, any person having a certain set of behavioural traits and mental aptitude in him/her can become an entrepreneur.

Besides there is no need for such a person to be groomed from the very childhood for becoming an entrepreneur, even if he is grown up, has worked on a different line and has developed these traits or aptitude, he or she can be groomed and developed as an entrepreneur through counselling and motivational measures. The success of an entrepreneur depends on the intelligence, imagination and strength of purpose of the individual. Turning visions into realities is more about hardwork than good luck. Jamshedji Tata, Jamnalal Bajaj, Laxmanrao Kirloskar, G.D. Birla, and Dhirubhai Ambani are some of the Indian entrepreneurs, who have proved their entrepreneurial abilities.

## A DOER NOT A DREAMER

Most people believe that to be an entrepreneur one requires a professor's intelligence, a fortune teller's capacity to foresee the future, a rich man's bank roll, a salesman's persuasiveness, a financial talent for manipulating funds, an auditor's precision, a political leader's power, and the magnetic personality of a film star. Since very few people possess even one or two of these qualities, no one believes he can be an entrepreneur. In fact, the only capacity essential for becoming an entrepreneur, is willingness to work hard.

Before you set out to be an entrepreneur, take this test and see if you are cut out to be one:

(1) Do you find yourself 'selling' others your own ideas?

(2) Do you enjoy working independently?

(3) Can you handle a lot of things at the same time?

(4) Do you often come up with more than one solution to a problem?

(5) Do you consider yourself smarter than your boss?

(6) Are you willing to work long hours?

(7) Do you have skills or interests that others admire?

(8) Are you always willing to learn?

(9) Are you persistent?

(10) Do you feel that most events in your life are determined by you?

If you have seven or more 'Yes' answers, you fit the entrepreneurial profile and you have probably thought a lot about owning a business. You are independent, creative and not afraid of commitment. You are willing to work hard in return for personal and financial rewards. You are self-motivated and determined.

If you have less than seven 'Yes' answers, chances are that you are more of a team player than an entrepreneur. The responsibility of owning a business may not appeal to you, but in fact you are not alone, many prefer the nine to five routine and the security of working for someone else.

The five words a potential entrepreneur often says are 'I think I will wait'. But more opportunities are lost, more years wasted and more lives unfulfilled by these five words. But rest assured, if you do not like the freedom and the rewards of being your own boss, you can always go back to where you were. But chances are you will be having too much fun to even look back.

The new enterprise equalizers are the intangible talents of the entrepreneur — enthusiasm, endurance, conclusiveness, leadership, product pride, marketing skills, nerve, and shrewdness. The key to make money is not to think about it at all. Do not become an entrepreneur with the sole intention of making money. Then it becomes tension ridden. Learn to enjoy your business, and things will automatically fall into place.

But do not harbour delusions. It is a tough battle out there. If you develop cold feet, take shelter under the corporate umbrella then stay put. One has to be mentally strong, have tremendous patience, endurance power and also be equipped to deal with a lot of harassment, if it occurs. Above all, one should be familiar with all commercial and legal aspects of one's own enterprise.

For an individual who dreams of becoming an entrepreneur, it's worthwhile to remember the following lines:

'Heights have been achieved by great men,
Not by sudden flight;
But while their companions slept,
They toiled and soiled at night'.

## THE NEW ENTREPRENEUR

In his monumental work: 'Searching for the Spirit of Enterprise,' Larry C. Farrell has introduced a new classification of entrepreneurs, whom he refers to as 'The New Entrepreneurs'. Farrell points out that except, for certain occasional super stars most self-inspired entrepreneurs are very ordinary persons. New entrepreneurs have emerged only due to circumstances like being very poor, or full of frustration, or losing a job, normally the number one reason is why people go into business. In fact, the 'new entrepreneurs' are very ordinary people who find themselves in extraordinary situations.

Larry C. Farrell gives the analysis wherein he tries to break certain myths about an entrepreneur in the following table:

| *Myths* | *Reality* |
|---|---|
| 1. Entrepreneurs are born, not made. | 1. The average entrepeneur is, 35-40 years old, has atleast 10 year's experience in a large company and only has an average education and intelligence. Contrary to popular myth, the entrepeneur has a surprisingly normal psychological profile. |
| 2. The entrepreneurs has a great ambition to become a millionaire. All his creations are for money and nothing else. | 2. The money earned by entrepeneurs is not much. Most chief executives of firms earn much more than the entrepeneurs. Research studies have revealed that the main obsession of the new entrepeneurs is to purpose his vision about a product. Money is necessary fueld to do this. |
| 3. Entrepeneurs are prepared to follow any type of method the legal or illegal and are ready to take any shortcut to maximise the benefits of business. | 3. Studies reveal that most entrepeneurs work within the limits prescribed by the law. It is true that they make full use of the loopholes in the system but that does not mean that lower ethics and illegal tactics are used by entrepeneurs. |
| 4. Entrepeneurs are high risk takers. | 4. Entrepeneurs are innovative and each innovation is accompanied by a certain degree of risk. The reality is that, big company executives regularly take greater risks with shareholders money than entrepeneurs are willing to take with their own. The only risk that can be aassociated with entrepeneurship is leaving a secure job and starting a venture of their own. |
| 5. The giant corporations are size engines of prosperity, and smaller entrepeneurial companies do not faster growth. | 5. The advantages of smaller size are becoming very great. Big companies are suffocating under — growth their own weight. These large corporate bodies made their strategic decisions half a century age, since that time it has been impossible for them to grow any further and dismanting their present structure is out of question, on the other hand, the small units are compact and are amenable to new and modern technology. |
| | Restructuring them to imbible is easier and this has prompted Larry Farrell to remark 'Most real growth comes from smaller, more entrepeneurial companies'." |

*****

# 3

# Entrepreneurial Motivation

- *Introduction*
- *Motivation Theories*
- *Maslow's Need Hierarchy Theory*
- *McClelland's Acquired Needs Theory*
- *Motivating Factors*
- *Achievement Motivation*
- *Kakinada Experiment*

## INTRODUCTION

The term 'motivation' has been derived from the word 'motive'. Motive may be defined as an inner state of our mind that moves or activates or energizes and directs our behaviour towards our goals. Motives are expressions of a person's goals or needs. In simple terms, motives or needs are ways of behaviour. They give direction to human behaviour to achieve goals or fulfill needs.

Motivation may be defined as the process that motivates person into action and induces him to continue the course of action for the achievement of goals. It is an ongoing process because human needs/goals are never completely satisfied.

According to Dalton E. McFarland, 'Motivation refers to the way in which urges, drives, desires, striving, and aspirations or needs direct, control or explain the behaviour of human being'.

The basic elements of the process of motivation are: *(i)* motive, *(ii)* behaviour and *(iii)* goal.

This is shown in Figure 3.1.

## Enterpreneurial Motivation

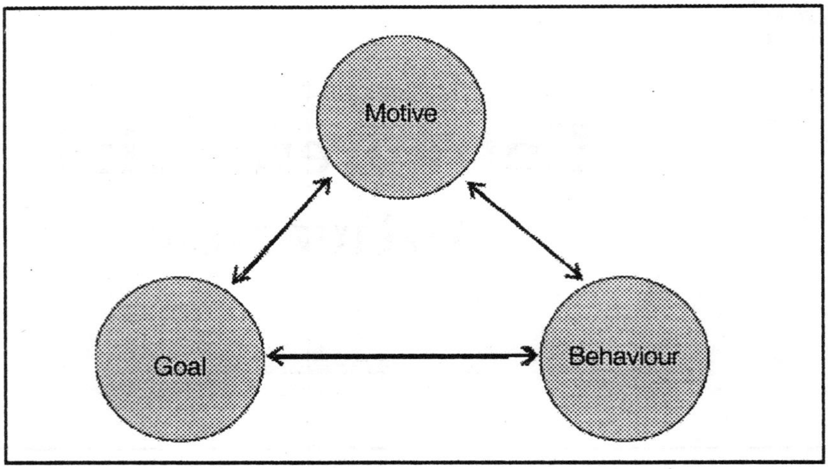


*Fig. 3.1: Process of Motivation*

## MOTIVATION THEORIES

The number of theories that have been propounded to explain people's behaviour reflect the importance of motivation to human life and work. They explain human motivation through human needs and human nature. Prominent among these theories and particularly relevant to entrepreneurship are Maslow's Need Hierarchy Theory and McClelland's Acquired Needs Theory.

## MASLOW'S NEED HIERARCHY THEORY

Maslow's theory is based on the human needs. These needs are classified into a sequential priority from the lower to the higher.

According to Maslow, all human needs are classified into the five need clusters as shown in Figure 3.2.

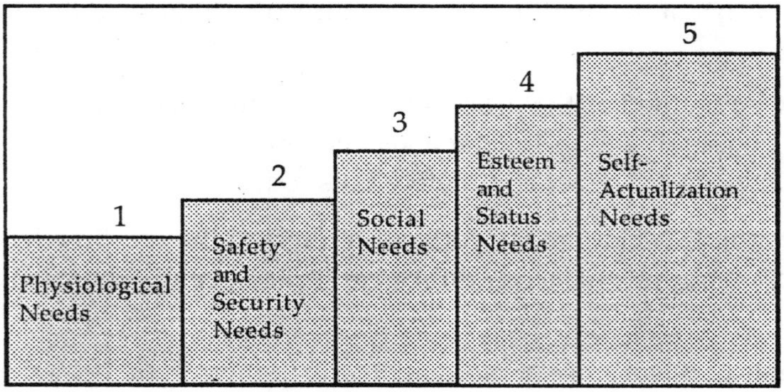


*Fig. 3.2: Maslow's Need Hierarchy*

**1.** ***Physiological Needs:*** These needs are basic to human life and include food, clothing, shelter, air, water, and other necessities of life. They exert tremendous influence on human behaviour. Entrepreneur also being a human being needs to meet physiological needs for survival. Hence, he/she is motivated to work in the enterprise to have economic rewards to meet the basic needs.

**2.** ***Safety and Security Needs:*** After satisfying the physiological needs, the next needs felt are called safety and security needs. These needs find expression in such desires as economic security and protection from physical dangers. Meeting these needs requires more money and hence, the entrepreneur is prompted to work more in his/her enterprise. Like physiological needs, these become inactive once they are satisfied.

**3.** ***Social Needs:*** Man is a social animal. These needs, therefore, refer to belongingness. All individuals want to be recognized and accepted by others. Likewise, an entrepreneur is motivated to interact with fellow entrepreneurs, his employees and others.

**4.** ***Esteem Needs:*** These needs refer to self-esteem and self-respect. They include such needs that indicate self-confidence, achievement, competence, knowledge, and independence. In case of entrepreneurs, the ownership and self-control over the enterprise satisfies their esteem needs by providing them status, respect, reputation and independence.

**5.** ***Self-Actualization Needs:*** The final step under the need hierarchy model is the need for self-actualization. This refers to self-fulfillment. Kurt Goldstein means, to become actualized in what one is potentially good at and coined the term 'self-actualization'. An individual may self-actualize in being a successful entrepreneur.

In Maslow's theory, needs are arranged in a lowest to the highest hierarchy. The second need does not dominate unless the first is reasonably satisfied, and the third need does not dominate until the first two needs have been reasonably satisfied. This process goes on till the last need. Once a need is satisfied, it ceases to be a motivating factor. For entrepreneurs, it is mainly social, esteem, and self-actualization needs that motivate them to work more and more for satisfying them.

## McCLELLAND'S ACQUIRED NEEDS THEORY

According to David McClelland, a person acquires three types of needs as a result of one's life experience. These three needs are:

(i) *Need for Affiliation* — These refer to needs to establish and maintain friendly and warm relations with others.

(ii) *Need for Power* — These mean that one's desire to dominate and to influence others by using physical objects and actions.

(iii) *Need for Achievement* — This refers to one's desire to accomplish something with own efforts. This implies one's will to excel in his/her efforts.

McClelland also suggests that these three needs may simultaneously be acting on an individual. But, in case of an entrepreneur, the high need for achievement is found as the dominating one. In his view, the people with high need for achievement are characterized by the following:

- They set moderate, realistic, and attainable goals for them.
- Prefer situations in which they can find solutions for solving personal responsibility.
- They need concrete feedback on how well they are doing.
- They have need for achievement for attaining personal accomplishment.
- They look for challenging tasks.

## MOTIVATING FACTORS

Now let us address the larger question what factors motivate entrepreneurs to start enterprises. Several researchers have tried to answer this question by conducting research studies to identify the factors that motivate people to start business enterprises. Here, we are presenting the findings of some of these studies.

In his study, Sharma classified all the factors motivating the entrepreneurs into two types as follows:

1. ***Internal Factors:*** These include:
   (a) Desire to do something new.
   (b) Educational background.
   (c) Occupational background or experience.
2. ***External Factors:*** These include:
   (a) Government assistance and support.
   (b) Availability of labour and raw material.
   (c) Encouragement from big business houses.
   (d) Promising demand for the product.

While studying entrepreneurial motivation, Murthy studied and classified the motivating factors on different bases. According to them, entrepreneurs are motivated to start business enterprises due to the following three types of factors:

1. Ambitious factors.
2. Compelling factors.
3. Facilitating factors.

In another study on motivational factors, it was found that out of a sample of 264 small-scale entrepreneurs, 98 (37.12 per cent) wanted to do something pioneering and innovative. For 74 (28.03 per cent) entrepreneurs, the principal motivating factor was the desire to be free and independent. Those who were motivated due to bright demand prospects for the product accounted for 56 (21.21 per cent). For 36 (13.64 per cent), the main motivating factor to start enterprises was availability of sub-contracting facilities from large units. By and large, similar findings are reported in yet another study of 50 small-scale entrepreneurs in Kumaun division of Uttar Pradesh. The findings are summed up in Table 3.1.

**Table 3.1**

**Factors which Prompted Individuals to Enter Entrepreneurship**

| *Factors* | *No. of Entrepreneurs* |
|---|---|
| I. Factors intrinsic to Entrepreneurs: | |
| 1. Enterprising Attitude | 7 (14) |
| 2. Training/education in such kind production | 3 (6) |
| 3. Previous experience in the same or related line | 12 (24) |
| II. Factors Extrinsic to Entrepreneurs: | |
| 1. Shortage of demand for product | 10 (20) |
| 2. Government and institutional assistance | 9 (18) |
| 3. Advice of business friends | 4 (8) |
| 4. Profit earned by friends in similar concern | 2 (4) |
| 5. Contact with others | 2 (4) |
| 6. Unsound units available at cheap price | 1 (2) |
| Total | 50 (100) |

*Note.* Figures in brackets denote percentage to total.

Table 3.1 reveals that one's previous experience gained in the same and/or related line has been the most motivating factor to plunge into industry.

The next important factor that brought people to industry is heavy demand for the particular product in the market. Many individuals (18 per cent) are attracted by extrinsic factors as well, like government.

**Assistance in one form or other:** In fact, an overriding inclination with them may not be their strong desire to do something independent in life nor any kind of experience gained, rather it may be availability of financial assistance from the institutional sources, which can kindle their entrepreneurial spirit.

There were some stray cases also induced by varied factors like 'advice of business friends', the fabulous profits earned by others in similar concerns, contact with others, etc. Now, it is crystal clear from the foregoing analysis that the majority of entrepreneurs are motivated to enter industry mainly because of four factors —

*First,* they possessed technical knowledge or manufacturing experience in the same or related line.

*Second,* there was heavy demand for the particular product.

*Third,* the Governmental and institutional assistance available facilitated individuals to enter industry.

*Fourth,* they have enterprising attitude, what McClelland designates 'an achievement motive', to do something independent in life.

Our understanding about what motivates the entrepreneurs will be clearer by going through the sources of entrepreneurial supply and motivation reported by some behavioural experts. These are juxtaposed in Table 3.2.

**Table 3.2**

**Entrepreneurship: Sources of Supply and Motivation**

| *Author/Expert* | *Entrepreneurial Phenomenon* | *Sources of Entrepreneurial Supply* | *Motive Force or Triggering Factor* |
|---|---|---|---|
| Schumpeter<br>Weber<br>McClelland<br>Hagen | Individual<br>Status<br>Groups<br>Religious and<br>Social | Extraordinary<br>Individuals<br>Extraordinary<br>Individuals with<br>high N-achievement<br>creative | Innate urge to<br>achieve success<br>Religious beliefs<br>Calvinist ethic<br>Child-rearing<br>practice and climate |
| Cochran | Groups<br>subordinated | Individuals in<br>the society | Status<br>withdrawal and<br>relative social blockage |
| Younng<br><br>Kunkel<br>Hoeselitz | Groups<br>Individual<br><br>Homogeneous<br>Group | Driven by a duty<br>to achieve Society's<br>model personality<br>determined by its<br>cultural values | Social acceptance of<br>entreprenurial role<br><br>Development view of<br>the world strengthened<br>by group solldarly |
| | | Relative Sub-groups,<br>occupational groups or<br>politically oriented<br>function | Re-enforcing stimuli<br>Gaining social<br>recogntion |
| | | Operant conditioning<br>procedures in a society<br>Culturally marginal<br>groups | |

## ACHIEVEMENT MOTIVATION

The need for achievement plays an important role in making an entrepreneur as successful. It is an inner spirit that activates an entrepreneur to strive for success. In simple terms, need for achievement is the desire to do well. The empirical evidences support the hypotheses that need for achievement contributes to entrepreneurial success. Hence, there is the need for developing achievement motivation for developing entrepreneurship in an economy.

How to develop achievement motivation? David C. McClelland, a well-known behavioural scientist of USA holds the view that achievement motivation can be developed through training and experience.

For this, McClelland conducted his experiments with groups of businessmen in three countries, *i.e.*, Malawi, India and Ecuador. He carried out a separate full-fledged training programme in India to instill achievement motivation in the minds of entrepreneurs. This successful experiment is popularly known as 'Kakinada Experiment'. Following is a brief description of the same:

## KAKINADA EXPERIMENT

Kakinada is an industrial town in Andhra Pradesh. The experiment started in January 1964. The main objective of the experiment was to break the barrier of limited aspirations by inducing achievement motivation. A total of 52 persons were selected from business and industrial community of the town. They were given an orientation programme at Small Industry Extension Training Institute (SIET), Hyderabad. The participants were grouped into three batches. They were put under training for 3 months.

The training programme was designed in such a way that it could help the trainees improve imagination and enable them introspect their motivation.

Accordingly, the programme included the following items in its syllabi:

1. The individuals strived to attain concrete and regular feedback.
2. The participants sought models of achievement to emulate.
3. The participants thought of success and accordingly set plans and goals.
4. The participants were encouraged to think and talk to themselves in a positive manner.

The impact of this training programme on the participants' behaviour was observed after a period of 2 years. The observations were encouraging. It was found that those who attended the programme performed better than those who did not. Using Thematic Appreciation Test (TAT) assessed the participants' need for achievement. In this TAT, ambition related pictures were displayed to the trainees and then they were asked to interpret the picture and what is happening in the picture. Thereafter, all the themes related to achievement were counted and, thus, the final score represented one's need for achievement. McClelland reached to this conclusion that the training programme positively influenced the entrepreneurial behaviour of the participants.

As regards caste, the traditional beliefs and imitation of Western culture, they did not determine one's behaviour as an entrepreneur. That the need for achievement motivation can be developed more especially in younger minds is well supported by the cross-country experiments. For example, a 'Junior Achievement Programme' is started in the United States of America with a view to instill achievement motivation in the minds of younger generation. Similarly, in United Kingdom, 'Young Enterprise' programme has been started with the same objective of inducing achievement motivation in younger minds.

The above said experiments/programmes have made us to realize that entrepreneurship is to be developed from a very young age. Accordingly, efforts have been made to develop a school curriculum that would result in a high need for achievement among the students. For this purpose, the success stories drawn from history and legends of the indigenous culture are introduced in course curriculum to induce in young minds the 'need for achievement' and strong desire to do something good/great they grow up. This is because the younger minds are more susceptible to change.

## CURRENT THEORIES OF ENTREPRENEURSHIP

Entrepreneurship is a constructive response to an environment, identified as favourable by an individual or a group which results in establishing and managing an organization aiming at converting opportunities into business prospects, expected to yield an uncertain surplus (profit) and to generate wealth, through maintaining the continuum, characterized by risk bearing. A successful entrepreneur is the one who begins as a creature of the (given) environment and grows into a creator of the environment.

Entrepreneurship is derived from the French word 'Entreprendre', refers to individuals who were 'undertakers' meaning those who 'undertook' the risk of new enterprise.

## PSYCHOLOGICAL THEORIES AND THE NEED FOR ACHIEVEMENT

Psychological theories such as those developed by McClelland pay attention to personal traits, motives and incentives of an individual and conclude that entrepreneurs have a strong need for achievement (McClelland & Winter, 1971). A similar focus is found in locus of control theories that conclude that an entrepreneur will probably have strong internal locus of control (Low & MacMillan 1988, 147; Amit *et al.*, 1993, 821). This means that an entrepreneur believes in his or her capabilities to commence and complete things and events through his or her own actions. Brockhaus (1982, 423 – 45), suggests that an internal locus of control, even if it fails to distinguish entrepreneurs, may serve to distinguish the successful entrepreneur from the unsuccessful one.

How do we measure success of entrepreneur? Success is a relative concept that can also be measured differently in different contexts. If success is measured in relation to the fulfillment of the goals and objectives of a particular entrepreneur, self-employed could also be classified as successful if their businesses generate continuously a satisfactory (in relation to their goals) level of living. On the other hand, high-growth ventures may be considered unsuccessful if they are not able to offer high enough ROI to their investors.

Davidson (1989, 210 – 211), states that achievement motivation is the most important factor contributing in explaining variation of growth rates and entrepreneurship. Shaver & Scott (1991, 31) believe that achievement motivation is perhaps the only convincing personal logical variable associated with new venture creation. Why is it convincing? If the concept will be defined broadly as Murray (1938 'Explorations in Personality') it is no wonder, why Johnson (1990) found a relationship between achievement motivation and entrepreneurship in 20 of 23 studies. According to Shaver & Scott (1991, 31) Murray (1938) saw a need as a force 'in the brain region' and the specific need for achievement was defined as: 'To accomplish something difficult. To master, manipulate, or organize physical objects, human beings, or ideas. To do this as rapidly, and as independently as possible. To overcome obstacles and attain a high standard. To excel one's self. To rival and surpass others. To increase self-regard by the successful exercise of talent'.

This definition compared with the others includes the most characteristics listed above.

Internal locus of control is included in 'To master and manipulate physical objects, human beings, or ideas,' in 'To overcome obstacles and attain a high standard,' and in 'To excel one's self.' High risk-taking propensity is connected with 'To overcome obstacles and attain a high standard'. Tolerance of ambiguity is associated with 'To accomplish something difficult'. High needs for autonomy, dominance, and independence coincide with 'To master, manipulate, or organize physical objects, human beings, or ideas as independently as possible'. The capacity for endurance or capability for intense effort is parallel to 'To overcome obstacles and attain a high standard .... To accomplish something difficult .... To rival and surpass others'. 'To do this as rapidly,' and to 'To excel one's self'.

In addition to the above traits, the definition of need for achievement includes traits as competitive mind ('To rival and surpass others'), self-consciousness, and an itch to self-development and learning ('To increase self-regard by the successful exercise of talent') (Sexton & Bowman 1985,134; Low & MacMillan 1988, 147; Amit *et al.*, 1993, 821).

In analyzing entrepreneurial behaviour, we should pay more attention to expectations, motives, and incentives. 'The forces in the brain region' (needs) foster expectations, motives, and incentives to take some action. What kind of motives and incentives are required to enforce entrepreneurial activity? Why would someone start a new venture? The reasons, as well as the businesses, may differ from case to case. Thus, to systematically approach the question we should conceptualize the phenomenon into some controllable pieces and to define the concepts.

## DEFINITIONS OF ENTREPRENEURSHIP

In conceptualizing entrepreneurship we could differentiate between concepts:

1. Entrepreneur = individual actor in the market,
2. Entrepreneurial = behaviour in the market,
3. Entrepreneurship = combines the actor (entrepreneur) and the behaviour in the market,
4. Entrepreneurial process = combines time dimension and behaviour in the market. No commonly accepted definitions of the entrepreneur, entrepreneurial or entrepreneurship exist.

## ENTREPRENEUR

Gartner (1989, 48) considers the search for definition in trait approaches to be unfruitful and suggests that we should use behavioural theories. Since a definition is important, we have reasons for not accepting simplistic statement that 'the entrepreneur is the one who creates an organization'.

*First,* organizations are created all the time by people who are not entrepreneurs (*e.g.,* political parties, associations, and social groups). *Second,* when evaluating the ability to act as an entrepreneur, no signs suggest that creation of organization would be any kind of differentiating criteria. On the other hand, if certain traits imply and predict the behaviour what difference does it make if we apply only behavioural theories? Traits and characteristics may be those intermediating variables that explain and predict entrepreneurial activity and behaviour. Several contributors in entrepreneurship literature have tested the existence of personality traits concluding that the traits are common also to several other groups of people (Low & MacMillan 1988, 147). For example, Amit *et al.,* (1993, 821 – 822) report problems of these studies and suggest that observed traits could be the result of learning through experience. They conclude that the interpretation of the outcome is difficult since these psychological traits do not distinguish the entrepreneur from the manager.

My argument is that if trait theories — even if they do not predict entrepreneurship — present characteristics common to most entrepreneurs, those individuals who do not possess these characteristics could be excluded (cf. Miller 1988). Gartner (1989), argues that trait approach seeks to answer the wrong question: 'Who is an entrepreneur?' He criticizes Carland *et al.,*'s (1984, 358) definition of entrepreneur: 'An entrepreneur is an individual who establishes and manages a business for the principal purposes of profit and growth'. However, a closer look reveals that the question could actually be stated as: 'Why does an entrepreneur start a venture?' — which was stated as a failure of trait theoretic approaches in Gartner (1989, 47). Since the principal purpose of a venture is to add value through profit and growth, it has to be innovative to gain the so-called abnormal profit or economic rent that may simultaneously be a necessary condition for growth. Thus, the answer to why question is clear cut: an entrepreneur expects economic rents to be available in the future.

Hebért & Link (1989, 47) conclude that entrepreneur is a person, not a team, committee or organization. Their view is that this person has some comparative advantage in decision-making either because he or she will have better information or different perception of events or opportunities. They also argue that individuals whose judgment differs from the norm perform entrepreneurial actions in all societies. Pickle & Abrahamson (1990, 5 and 9) introduced a compact definition of an entrepreneur: 'An entrepreneur is one who organizes and manages a business undertaking, assuming the risk, for the sake of profit. The entrepreneur evaluates perceived opportunities and strives to make the decisions that will enable the firm to realize sustained growth'. The latter sentence emphasizes the decision-making ability and growth objective of an entrepreneur. However, Pickle & Abrahamson's definition does not include any process characteristics thought to be important at least in high growth ventures. According to Timmons (1994, 24) entrepreneurial mind, means the attitudes and behaviour of successful entrepreneurs, almost similarly as Murray (1938): 'They work hard and are driven by an intense commitment and determined perseverance; they see the cup half full, rather than half empty; they strive for integrity; they burn with competitive desire to excel and win; they are dissatisfied with the status quo and seek opportunities to improve almost any situation they encounter; they use failure as a tool for learning and eschew perfection in favour of effectiveness; and they believe they can personally make an enormous difference in the final outcome of their ventures and their life'.

## ENTREPRENEURSHIP

From the viewpoint of growth-oriented innovative companies, one of the best definitions of entrepreneurship is found in Ronstadt (1984, 28): 'Entrepreneurship is the dynamic process of creating incremental wealth. Individuals who assume the major risks in terms of equity, time and/or career commitment or provide value for some product or service create the wealth. The product or service may or may not be new or unique but value must somehow be infused by the entrepreneur by receiving and allocating the necessary skills and resources'.

The most essential part of this definition is how it defines incremental wealth of value creation as a result or goal of the process. This result is also parallel to need for achievement. While Ronstadt's definition above includes such other trait theoretic characteristics of entrepreneurship as risk taking propensity and responsibility, a more complete view of these could be achieved by including the need for achievement as defined by Murray (1938) in the definition.

Thus, the best definition is the multidimensional definition of entrepreneurship with specific emphasis on the entrepreneur as the main actor in the process: 'Entrepreneurship is a dynamic process created and managed by an individual (the entrepreneur), which strives to exploit economic innovation to create new value in the market. An entrepreneur is a person, who has entrepreneurial mind with a strong need for achievement' defined as in Murray (1938). The most interesting points of this definition are the purpose of value creation and the exploitation of economic innovation. The definitions of entrepreneurial process given below by Bygrave (1989) and by Bygrave & Hofer (1991) include some of the important characteristics, but lack perhaps the most important ones, namely, the goal and purpose. Why does the entrepreneurial process take place? What is the purpose of entrepreneurial process or activity?

The goal of entrepreneurial activity is to create value. Creating value and exploiting innovation process — likely also implies the growth of a venture. Thus, it should be emphasized that without any further attributes, this definition does not suit for stable or declining companies. It could be argued that Bygrave (1989, 9) supports the simple definition that 'entrepreneurship is creating of organizations' by describing entrepreneurship as a dynamic rather than a static system, hence a process of becoming rather than a state of being, which includes non-linear and unstable discontinuities. But he argues also that this process is a holistic one that cannot be analyzed partially by studying different pieces of the entity. Thus, when considering holistic process of entrepreneurship, we should be aware of that discontinuities does not happen all the time and able to identify discontinuous quantum jumps and their causes to understand entrepreneurship. Even if entrepreneurship were a science of turbulence and change, such would not necessarily mean continuous discontinuity.

But compared with conceptual frameworks of institutional economics and transaction cost approaches, chaos and catastrophe theories emphasize characteristics of entrepreneurship. As Bagby (1988, 5) notes: 'Entrepreneurs capitalize on change, or even create it'. Instability, turbulence and change would suggest entrepreneurship to be rather becoming than existing. The importance of both aspects should be pointed out in analyzing the entrepreneurial process.

Richard Cantillon, a French economist describes an Entrepreneur as a person who pays a certain price for a product to resale it at an uncertain price thereby making decisions about obtaining and using the resources while assuming the risk of enterprise.

Adam Smith spoke of the 'enterpriser' in his '1776 Wealth of Nations' as an individual who undertook the formation of an organization for commercial purposes. He ascribed to the Entrepreneur the role of industrialist, but he also viewed the entrepreneur as a person with unusual foresight who could recognize potential demand for goods and services. In Smith's view, entrepreneurs reacted to economic change, thereby becoming the economic agents who transformed demand into supply. In 1848, British economist John Stuart Mill elaborated on the necessity of Entrepreneurship in private enterprise. The term entrepreneur subsequently became common as a description of business founders and the fourth factor of economic endeavour and he recognized entrepreneurship as a central to economic theory.

In Schumpeter's words 'Entrepreneurship' is to reform or revolutionalize the pattern of production by exploiting an invention or more generally, an untried technological possibility for producing a new commodity or an old one in a new way, by opening up a new source of supply materials or a new outlet for products. Entrepreneurship defined essentially consists of doing things that are not generally done in the ordinary course of business routine.

Robert Ronstadt defines entrepreneurship as the dynamic process of creating incremental wealth. Individuals who assume the major risk in terms of equity, time and career commitment providing value for some product or service create this wealth. The product or service itself may or may not be new or unique but the entrepreneur must somehow infuse value by securing and allocating the necessary skills and resources.

*****

# 4

# Entrepreneurship

- *Entrepreneurial Continuum*
- *Entrepreneurial Roles*
- *Functions of an Entrepreneur*
- *Entrepreneurship*
- *Process of Entrepreneurship*
- *Definitions*
- *Causes for Slow Growth of Entrepreneurship in India*
- *Entrepreneurship Stimulants*
- *Entrepreneurship and Economic Development*
- *Entrepreneurship and Economic Systems*
- *Obstacles Inhibiting Entrepreneurship*
- *Factors Affecting Entrepreneurship Growth*
- *Factors Affecting Entrepreneurship*
- *Economic Factors*
- *Social Factors*
- *Cultural Factors*
- *Personality Factors*
- *Psychological and, Sociological Factors*

In the previous chapter, we have covered who an entrepreneur is. Most of the definitions of entrepreneur throw light on the role played by him. They also state the various functions which a person as an entrepreneur will have to perform.

An entrepreneur is a person who initiates and establishes an enterprise. Entrepreneurship refers to the decisions one takes in setting up and running a new enterprise. The individual constitutes the most important element in entrepreneurship. It is an individual who takes a decision to start or not to start an enterprise. It is 'HE' or 'SHE' who strives, to make it a success. Entrepreneurship involves a few major decisions. They are:

(1) Decision to become an entrepreneur.

(2) Identification and selection of an opportunity.

(3) Business plan formulation and its implementation.

(4) Entrepreneurial continuum.

**1. Becoming an Entrepreneur:** Decision to be one's own master is the first major step. The motivational factor, hence, should be, considered crucial to entrepreneurship. The inner urge of the individual to do something new, to be on one's own has been found to be and is an important factor.

This may be reinforced by one or more of the following:

*(a)* To prove oneself.

*(b)* To be independent.

*(c)* To do something unique.

*(d)* To utilize skills.

*(e)* To acquire greater economic reward.

*(f)* To excel.

**2. Finding an Opportunity:** For effective coping with inner desire, to be an entrepreneur the individual starts searching for an 'opportunity', the focus of his entrepreneurial desires. He looks around for different possibilities of business, reads about them, and meets people who could give ideas and inspiration and collects information and data on various/several possibilities.

**3. Business Plan Formulation and Implementation:** This function refers to making of a project report and subsequent implementation of it. The efforts of the entrepreneur are directed towards visualizing the establishment of the enterprise. He studies the feasibility and profitability of the project. He has to take crucial decisions, which have a far reaching effect, at this juncture.

**4. Entrepreneurial Continuum:** Once the entrepreneur establishes the enterprise, he has to manage it well by translating problems into opportunities and must endure to mobilize relevant production factors such as capital and human resources.

Entrepreneurial Continuum as shown in Fig. 4.1 can be achieved through a series of decisions, actions, and functions directed towards the following factors:

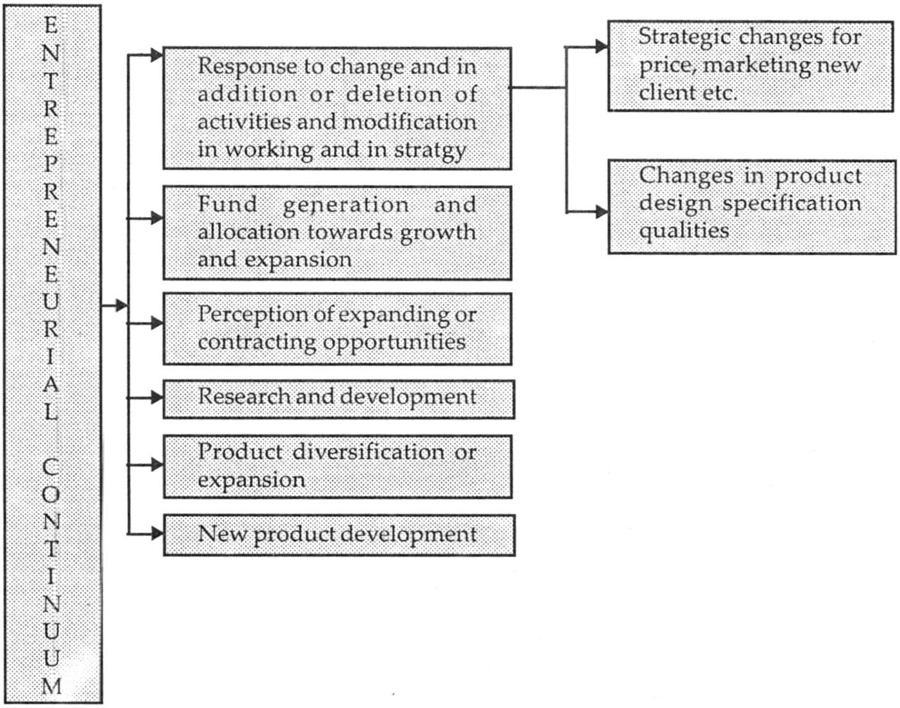


*Fig. 4.1 Entreprenerial Continuum*

## ENTREPRENEURIAL ROLES

Entrepreneurship is different from management, as Paul H. Wilken states: 'Entrepreneurship involves combining to initiate changes in production where management involves combining to produce.

Management therefore refers to the ongoing co-ordination of the production process, which can be visualized as a continual combining of the factors of production. But entrepreneurship is a discontinuous phenomenon, appearing to initiate changes in the production process and then disappearing until it reappears to initiate another change.

Entrepreneurs often play roles especially those of capitalists and managers, while people who primarily act as capitalists or managers may at times become entrepreneurs. Many people, who want above all to be entrepreneurs, find that they must eventually leave the new ventures, they create because they do not have the proper state of mind to run an established business.

Entrepreneurship is above all about change. In chart 4.1, Wilken's categorization of 'Types of changes' initiated by entrepreneurs is given.

'Entrepreneurs see change as the norm and as healthy. Usually, they do not bring about the changes themselves (*i.e.*, they are usually not inventors) and this defines, entrepreneur and entrepreneurship, the entrepreneur always searches for change, responds to it and exploits it as an opportunity.' These words were written by Peter Drucker, a well-known contemporary management writer. But they might just as easily have come from the pen of Joseph Schumpeter,

**Chart 4.1: Types of Changes**

1. Initial expansion — original production of goods.
2. Subsequent expansion — subsequent changes in the amount of goods produced.
3. Factor innovation — increase of supply or productivity of factors.
   (a) Financial — procurement of capital from new source or new form.
   (b) Labour — procurement of labour from new source or of new type: or upgrading of existing labour.
   (c) Material — procurement of old material from news source or use of new material.
4. Product innovations — changes in the production process.
   (a) Technological— use of new production techniques.
   (b) Organizational — change of form of structure of relationships.
5. Market innovations — changes in the size or composition of market.
   (a) Product — production of new goods or change in quality or cost of existing goods.
   (b) Market — discovery of a new market.

the Austrian economist who assigned the term 'Entrepreneurship'. For Schumpeter, indeed, the whole process of economic change hung ultimately on the person who makes it happen, the entrepreneur.

A successful entrepreneur recognizes the commercial potential of a product or service and designs operating policies in marketing, production, product development, and the organizational structure. He carries out the whole set of activities of the business. He has a high capacity of taking calculated risk and has faith in his own capabilities.

## FUNCTIONS OF AN ENTREPRENEUR (ROLES)

According to some writers the functions of an entrepreneur is co-ordination of the business, management of the enterprise, risk taking, controlling the enterprise, innovation for change, motivation and other related activities.

In reality, an entrepreneur has to carry-out a combination of these, keeping in tune with time and environment. Figure 4.2 gives the functions of an entrepreneur in modern economy.

Truly entrepreneurship calls for the ability to react to new ideas, demands and exploit the opportunities and thereby contribute to progress. An entrepreneur is expected to perform the following functions/roles:

(1) Assumption of risk.

(2) Business decisions.

(3) Managerial functions.

(4) Function of innovation.

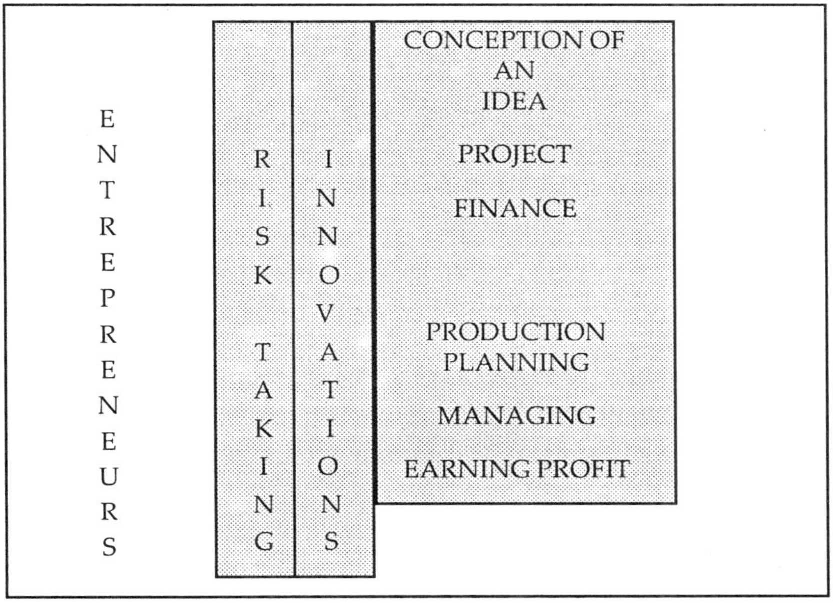


*Fig. 4.2 Process of Entrepreneurship*

**1. Assumption of Risk:** The entrepreneur assumes all possible risks of business. A business risk also involves risk due to the possibility of changes in the taste of consumers, techniques of production and new inventions. Such risks are not insurable. If, they materialize, the entrepreneur has to bear the loss himself. Thus, risk bearing or uncertainty still remains the most important function of an entrepreneur. An entrepreneur tries to reduce the uncertainties by his initiative, skill, and good judgment.

**2. Business Decisions:** The entrepreneur has to decide the nature and type of goods to be produced. An entry into a particular industry is due to his judgment as it offers him the best prospect and whatever commodities produced would pay him well and would employ those methods of production which seem to him the most profitable. He effects suitable changes in the size of business, its location, techniques of production and does everything that is needed for the development of business.

**3. Managerial Functions:** The entrepreneur also has to perform the managerial functions, though the managerial functions are different from entrepreneurial functions. Formulation of production plan, arranging finance, purchasing raw materials, providing production facilities, organizing sales, and assuming the task of personnel management are all managerial functions performed by the entrepreneur in case of small enterprises. Otherwise in a large establishment, these management functions would be delegated to paid managerial personnel.

**4. Function of Innovation:** An important function of an entrepreneur is 'INNOVATION.' An entrepreneur conceives the idea for the improvement in the quality of production line or considers the economic viability or technological feasibility in bringing about improved quality. The introduction of different kinds of electronic gadgets is an example of such an innovation of new products. Innovation is an ongoing function, rather than once and for all or possibly intermittent activity. Thus, the functions of entrepreneur can be performed by different kinds of people under different economic systems.

Arthur H. Cole described an entrepreneur as a decision-maker and attributed the following functions:

(1) Determination of the objectives of the enterprise and the change in those objectives as conditions require.

(2) Development of an organization, including efficient relation with subordinates and employees.

(3) Securing adequate financial resources and maintaining good relations with the existing and potential promoters.

(4) Requisition of efficient technological equipment and the revision of it.

(5) Development of a market for the products and the devising of new products to meet or anticipate consumer's demand.

(6) Maintenance of good relations with public authorities and with the society at large.

Modern writers have outlined the following three broad functions of an entrepreneur, namely:

(1) Innovation — 'Doing new things or doing of things that are already being done in a new way'.

*Example:* E-mail vs. Postal correspondence.

(2) Risk taking.

(3) Organization and management of business.

## ENTREPRENEURSHIP

Entrepreneurship refers to a process of action an entrepreneur (person) undertakes to establish his/her enterprise. It is a creative and innovative response to the environment. Entrepreneurship is a cycle of actions to further the interest of the entrepreneur. Entrepreneurship is the composite skill, the resultant mix of many qualities and traits. It involves taking of risk, making the necessary investments and the ability to put other factors of production (land, labour, capital) into productive use through scientific and technological methods for creating wealth for an individual and economy. Entrepreneurship perhaps lies more in the ability to maximize resources. Figure 4.3 gives the process of entrepreneurship.

Entrepreneurship is 'the propensity of mind to take calculated risk with confidence to achieve a pre-determined business/industrial objective'.

Entrepreneurship, equals ability to take risk and take correct decisions.

Hence, Entrepreneurship = R + D + O + E

where, 'R' stands for Risk taking.

'D' stands for Decision making.

'O' stands for Opportunities.

'E' stands for Environment.

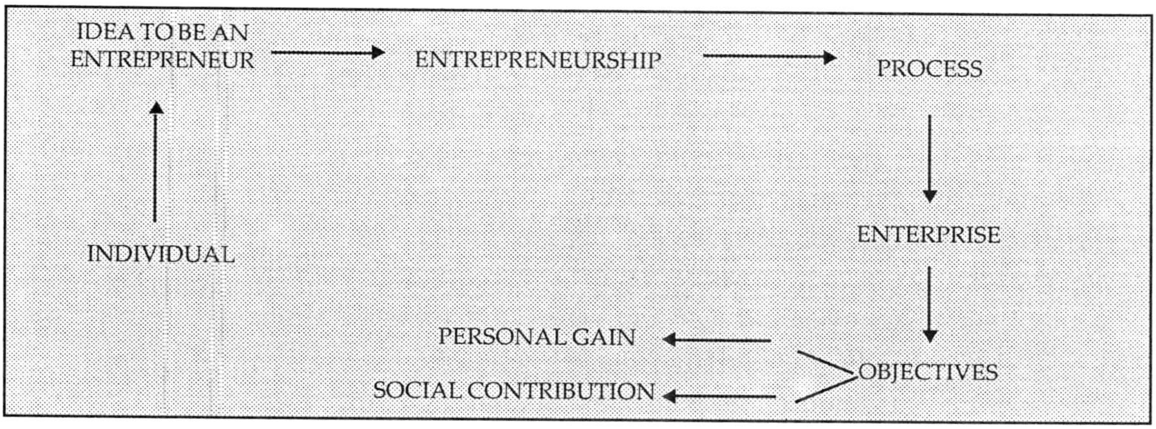


*Fig. 4.3 Process of Entrepreneurship.*

## CHARACTERISTICS OF ENTREPRENEURSHIP

Entrepreneurship means the function of creating something new, organizing and coordinating, undertaking risk and handling economic uncertainty.

### DEFINITIONS

**Higgins:** 'Entrepreneurship is meant the function of seeing investment and production opportunity, organizing an enterprise to undertake a new production process, raising capital, hiring labour, arranging for the supply of raw materials and selecting top managers for the day-to-day operation of the enterprise'.

**A.H. Cole:** 'Entrepreneurship is the purposeful activity of an individual or a group of associated individuals, undertaken to initiate, maintain or organize, a profit oriented business unit for the production or distribution of economic goods and services'.

**McClelland:** 'Entrepreneurship involves doing things in a new and better way. It calls for decision-making under uncertainty. If there is no significant uncertainty and the action involves applying known and predictable results, then entrepreneurship in not at all involved'.

**Peter Drucker:** 'Entrepreneurship is neither science nor art, it is a practice. It has a knowledge base. Knowledge in entrepreneurship is a means to an end. Indeed, what constitutes knowledge in practice is largely defined by the end, which is by the practice'.

From the above definitions, following are the characteristics of entrepreneurship emerging:

(1) Innovation.

(2) Risk taking.

(3) Decision making.

(4) Accepting challenges.

(5) Organization and management.

(6) Ensuring the success of enterprise.

Reasons for increase in entrepreneurship are:

(1) An increasing focus on capital formation. Availability of capital is one of the reasons why individuals get ideas to start new firms/enterprises.

(2) Ability to transform scientific and technical developments.

(3) Supportive government programmes.

(4) Availability of required training and inputs.

(5) Collaborative relationship between business and research and their direct attempts to transfer technology to market.

*Example:* Tata Institute of Fundamental Research.

(6) Environment conducive to innovation and entrepreneurial activities.

## CAUSES FOR SLOW GROWTH OF ENTREPRENEURSHIP IN INDIA

Inspite of all the policies, government support, change in the attitude of the society, the growth of entrepreneurship in India is slow. The three main factors to cause slow growth of entrepreneurship are:

1. Discouraging social factors, namely unfavourable family background, family burden, lack of education, dual role of women, influence of sex, caste, custom, lack of attitudes, spirits, urge, etc.
2. Discouraging economic factors, which consist of inadequate infrastructural facilities, shortage of capital, shortage of technical labour, lack of transportation and communication facilities, absence of regular and cheaper supply of power and raw materials, etc.
3. Discouraging environmental factors, which include unstable government, lack of security, absence of ideal market conditions, red-tapes in administration, complicated statutes, etc.

Entrepreneurship is thus an attitude of mind which can take risk but calculated ones, a true entrepreneur is one who can see possibilities in a given situation where others see none and has the patience, perseverance and optimism to work out the idea into a scheme for which financial support can be provided. The stimulation of entrepreneurship is a function of both internal and external variables.

Inspite of the slow growth in entrepreneurship, India still has a proud record of entrepreneurship. Its present status among the ten industrialized countries in the world is its proof. However, it has to prepare itself for entrepreneurship of a different order. Tremendous advancement of science and technology will have to be harnessed since industrial growth in the country can only be achieved through a mix of science, technology, large and small industry.

In fact, the SSI sector is considered as an ideal nursery for testing out new technologies and for enhancing the industrial growth and development of entrepreneurship. Entrepreneurship is thus the cornerstone of emerging economic scene in the world.

David McClelland was not far from truth when he stated, 'What accounts for the rise in civilization is not the external resources such as markets, minerals or factories but the entrepreneurial spirit which exploits the resources — a spirit found most often among businessmen'.

## ENTREPRENEURSHIP STIMULANTS

A variety of factors have, helped to stimulate entrepreneurial activity and generate economic development. Figure 4.4 gives the stimulants of entrepreneurship.

These stimulants are the following:

(1) Increasing focus on capital formation, making capital available to the entrepreneur to start a new enterprise.

(2) The environment to transform scientific and technical developments into economically viable projects.

(3) Supportive government programmes.

(4) Availability of sufficient training facilities.

(5) A collaborative relationship between business and research and the easy transferability of technology to the market place.

(6) Finally, the endeavour to create the ideal climate for innovation and the entrepreneurial activities.

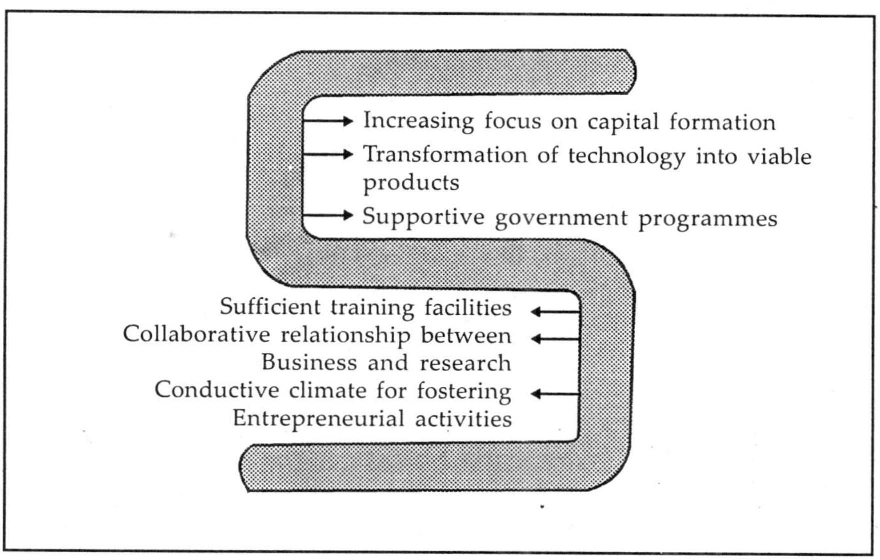


*Fig. 4.4: Stimulants of Entrepreneurship*

## ENTREPRENEURSHIP AND ECONOMIC DEVELOPMENT

Only purposeful human activity can bring about economic development. Man stands at the centre of the whole process of economic development. Schumpeter feels that economic development will be a reality if new combinations of the means of production are undertaken. This is the work of the entrepreneur, he locates ideas and puts them into effect in the process of economic development.

Thus, the entrepreneur occupies a crucial place in the process of economic development. Schumpeter further states that economic progress depends on the rate of applied technical progress or innovation. The rate of applied technical progress in turn depends on the supply of entrepreneurs in the society. Therefore, entrepreneurial activity or entrepreneurship is the agency which brings about change in the society.

David McClelland has introduced a new dimension to the importance of entrepreneurship in economic development. He says that the development of entrepreneurship depends on human motivation to achieve or need for achievement. McClelland's hypothesis is that a society with a generally high level of achievement will produce more energetic entrepreneurs who in turn would accelerate the process of economic development. That is why there is a steady stream of entrepreneurs in developed countries where the motivation to achieve is very high. Similarly, in the underdeveloped regions this motivation is either lacking or low, causing short supply of entrepreneurs.

Here it will be worth looking into this aspect in the context of India. The typical Indian entrepreneur is not an 'innovator' but an 'imitator'. He copies the organization, technology and the products of innovation from other developed regions. But as an imitator the Indian entrepreneur is able to adapt the innovative technology in the conditions prevailing in the country. This type of imitative entrepreneurship is playing a crucial role in India's progress especially in the industrial and service sectors.

This analysis goes to establish that entrepreneurial activity or entrepreneurship is an important source of economic development. It is a must that motivational training programmes are conducted to stimulate entrepreneurship in developing countries. Innovative entrepreneurship can alter the production function of nations and bring about rapid development. Entrepreneurship appears to be the best medicine for underdeveloped countries to overcome their ills and bring about substantial economic development.

## ENTREPRENEURSHIP AND ECONOMIC SYSTEMS

Entrepreneurship can be analyzed with reference to different types of economic systems. In fact, entrepreneurship and the economic system complement each other. An economic system determines the nature and scope of entrepreneurship. Entrepreneurship gives a fillip to new organizational forms and the economy has to adjust to these demands. Entrepreneurship can bring about changes in the very structure of the economy thus strengthening the economic system.

## ENTREPRENEURSHIP IN DIFFERENT ECONOMIC SYSTEMS

**Capitalism:** Capitalism has freedom as its hallmark. A capitalist economy is characterized by free enterprise, freedom to save, invest competition, consumer sovereignty and minimum interference from the government. The price mechanism solves the problem of 'What to produce'? The forces of demand and supply determine the price with reference to the cost of production. The entrepreneur controls the process of production and distribution and entrepreneurship has a place of prominence. Entrepreneurship in the domestic market is characterized by the entrepreneur assuming the role of a competitor or a monopolist or a monopolistic competitor. In the overseas market, there is a cut-throat competitor where the price of his product is determined by his capacity to unload goods, a special case of discriminating monopoly.

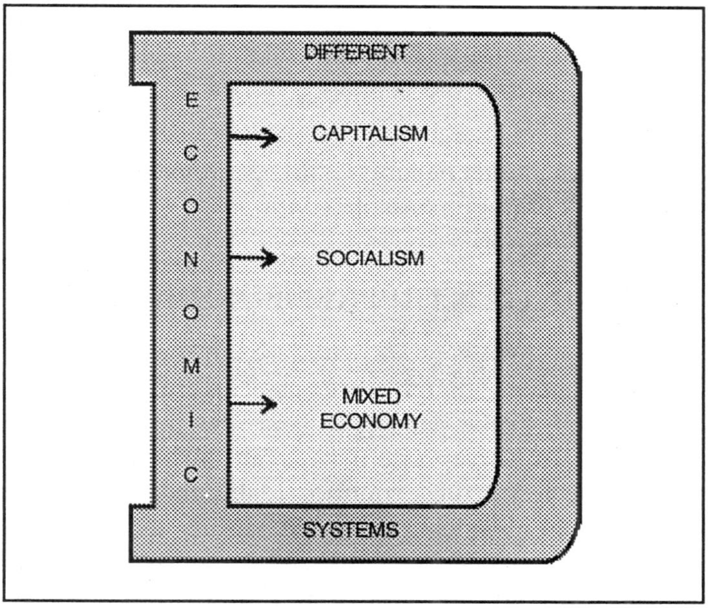


*Fig. 4.5: Different Economic Systems*

**Socialism:** Private, entrepreneurship is absent in a socialist economic system. Entrepreneurship is provided by a central authority consisting of economic and financial experts who perform the role of the entrepreneur not for profit but for social good. This central authority is appointed by the government to frame plans for the proper mobilization of resources and the allocation of resources into these industries of national importance. Thus, entrepreneurship plays a crucial role under socialism also, the only distinction is that the private entrepreneur has neither a role nor responsibility in this economic system.

**Mixed Economy:** Entrepreneurship has a vital role in the mixed economy. The mixed economy is characterized by the co-existence of both the private and public sectors in the same line of production. However, we find that in this economic system the government undertakes the production of capital goods while the production of consumer goods is left in the hands of private enterprises.

Like in a capitalist economy, basic problems are solved with the help of price mechanism. When the price mechanism is not able to solve basic problems the State intervenes in order to find a better solution to the various problems. Similarly, when the problem of production is not solved satisfactorily through private entrepreneurship, the State tries to increase the production of essential goods and discourage the production of non-essential goods.

In a mixed economy, restrictions are placed by the government to remove the evil of monopolistic capitalism. The mixed economy gives equal importance to both the public and private sectors and entrepreneurship is given due significance. In the private sector, profit motive acts as an incentive to the entrepreneur and the market mechanism plays its own role and this enhances the role of entrepreneurship in the mixed economy.

Thus, entrepreneurship has a great importance in all major economic systems. It has a special role under capitalism and mixed economy, where its responsibilities in production and distribution are recognized.

Therefore, its importance stands beyond challenge in every economic system where it appears in different forms. Yet entrepreneurship continues to exist in one form or the other in all economic systems.

## OBSTACLES INHIBITING ENTREPRENEURSHIP

Entrepreneurship development is greatly hindered in the less developed countries due to the presence of several obstacles. Though these obstacles are present in almost all countries they hardly have any strength in the developed countries. In the developed countries the environment is most ideal for entrepreneurship. Similarly, the presence of aggressive entrepreneurs has made the society in these countries realize their vital importance in economic advancement. Unfortunately, in most less developed nations, the role of entrepreneurship in the progress of the country has not been fully realized. The result is the presence of a number of obstacles which inhibit the development of entrepreneurship. These obstacles can be summarized as follows:

(1) An unwillingness to devote organizational abilities to business purposes.

(2) Restrictive effects of customs and traditions.

(3) Lack of adequate response to monetary incentives.

(4) Low status of businessmen in the eyes of the public.

(5) High risk involved in new enterprises.

(6) Lack of sufficient infrastructure and high cost of production.

(7) Market imperfections which deny potential entrepreneurs the resources they need for organizing new enterprises.

(8) Arbitrary changes in the administration of law by the Government which spread the element of uncertainty among entrepreneurs.

India provides us with a good example, where the environment has been highly hostile to promote entrepreneurship. The stimulation of entrepreneurial abilities is a complicated long run sociological problem. Social institutions like caste, joint family system, schools can actually motivate entrepreneurship. But in India they are not conducive to the development of entrepreneurship. The policy of the government had been more to promote 'imitative' entrepreneurs rather than the 'innovative' ones. The result is, the country is facing the problem of 'brain-drain'. All enterprising individuals finding the going tough in this country started migrating, no wonder this country has such a large number of Non-Resident Indians having immense financial power. The recent trend towards liberalization is aimed at removing the economic obstacles that are standing in the way of aggressive entrepreneurship. Non-Resident Indians are being accorded special status for investing their large financial resources in this country. The drastic changes in government's economic policy clearly shows the realization in this country that the future of this nation is in the hands of vigorous entrepreneurship and all efforts must be made to remove the obstacles which are hindering the full play of this vital factor of production.

## FACTORS AFFECTING ENTREPRENEURSHIP GROWTH

The countries of the world are experiencing an unprecedented burst of inventions. Even the least developed of nations is making conscious efforts in encouraging research and development. While the developed countries have the record of commercializing these inventions to their fullest advantage, the less developed ones find their inventions either lying idle or flowing out to the more prosperous nations. The proverbial 'brain-drain' that is affecting countries like India, is due to the absence of the necessary infrastructure to capitalize on the numerous inventions that are taking place. This essential is provided by the entrepreneur of the country. The secret of the success of most developed countries is the presence of a large number of dynamic entrepreneurs who provide the fillip for newer and better inventions. The less developed countries, on the other hand are confronted by a situation where the entrepreneurs just do not seem to come, those present tend to leave their countries in search of better opportunities. The economically backward nations are characterized by the scarcity of entrepreneurship. Several inimical factors are affecting the growth of this important factor of production.

Some societies, notably in the United States, South Korea and many South East Asian countries like Thailand and Singapore abound with entrepreneurs. Others like China and India have fewer entrepreneurs although these countries recently changed their laws to encourage entrepreneurship. Countries like England where many companies such as airlines and automobile manufactures have been operated by the government, have in recent times turned these firms onto the private sector encouraging entrepreneurship through new opportunities in private ownership. Other nations such as Japan, though are bound by strong traditions have in recent times started favouring entrepreneurship. Both economic and non-economic factors can affect the level of entrepreneurship within any society. A careful analysis of the factors that affect entrepreneurial growth will reveal that these factors can be classified under four major heads. They are economic factors, social factors, cultural factors, and personality factors. Economists agree that the lack of entrepreneurs is caused not by economic conditions alone, as was the earlier feeling. It is also due to the whole set of socio-cultural and institutional environments prevailing in the less developed countries.

The factors affecting growth of entrepreneurship are:

(1) Economic factors.

(2) Social factors.

(3) Cultural factors.

(4) Personality factors.

(5) Psychological and Sociological factors.

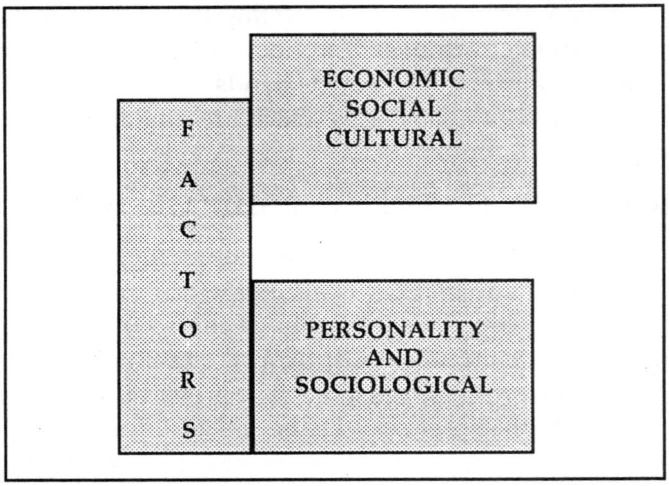


*Fig. 4.6: Factors Affecting an Entrepreneur*

## Economic Factors

The economic factors that are affecting the growth of entrepreneurship in the less developed countries are:

*(a)* Lack of adequate overhead facilities.

*(b)* Non-availability of capital.

*(c)* Great risks.

*(d)* Non-availability of sufficient labour and skills.

**(a) Lack of adequate overhead facilities:** Profitable innovations require certain basic facilities and services like transportation, communication, technical and economic information, supply of power, irrigation facilities, etc. They provide external economies and improve the efficiency of investments by entrepreneurs. They reduce the cost of production and increase output. This facilities are scarce in the less developed countries. Entrepreneurs have therefore to obtain them at their own expenses. They have either to provide these facilities themselves or obtain them at exorbitant costs. These greatly affect their profit margin and discourage the entrepreneur. One cannot expect an entrepreneur to construct his own railway network or set up his own power project and then indulge in innovational activity.

**(b) Non-availability of capital:** Reduction of cost and maximizing of output are the twin objectives of all inventions. Therefore, inventions have a tendency to be capital oriented. The requirements of capital for innovation are especially large in less developed countries where most capital equipment has to be imported. Imports involve large shipping and insurance expenses. Even the basic expertise has to be imported. Such imports also involve the use of considerable amount of foreign exchange, which would raise difficult problems especially if there are foreign exchange controls. The inadequacy of basic facilities makes initial expenses of investment extremely high. Very often the entrepreneur may have to obtain them at very high costs or provide for his own overhead facilities.

Another problem associated with this aspect is the necessity for the entrepreneur to store large stocks of inventories because a network to provide adequate industrial supplies is lacking in a less developed country. This raises the amount of working capital needed for the entrepreneur.

These capital requirements cannot be easily met. Due to the low rate of domestic savings and the deficiencies in the channelization of savings, capital does not flow into productive enterprises. Moreover, an entrepreneur is confronted by banking systems who charge very high interest rates for borrowed capital. Thus, the non-availability of capital hampers entrepreneurial growth in the poor nations.

**(c) Great risks:** Risks in business are greater in a less developed country than in a developed nation. Three reasons are given for this situation:

(1) There is the lack of reliable information on cost size of the market conditions of demand, overhead facilities, etc. An entrepreneur cannot make correct estimates under these circumstances.

(2) The market for goods and services is small. Ragnar Nurkse has pointed out that the lack of a strong domestic market inhibits new investments.

(3) Less developed countries are characterized by instability in both domestic and foreign economic policy. This discourages entrepreneurs. Several less developed nations are highly export oriented nations depending on a few primary products. These products are subject to violent swings of prosperity and depression that originate abroad.

The entrepreneurs are thus faced with situations where the capacity of their plant and the size of their investments are placed at the mercy of unforeseeable events. Moreover, the entrepreneurs face instability caused by seasonal fluctuations. In these circumstances of uncertainty and risks, entrepreneurs have a tendency to prefer short-term investments to long-term industrial ventures.

**(d) Non-availability of labour and skills:** Mostly less developed countries are labour rich nations owing to a dense and ever increasing population. But entrepreneurship in economic and emotional security inhibits labour's mobility. Entrepreneurs, therefore often find difficulty to secure sufficient labour. They are forced to make elaborate and costly arrangements to recruit the necessary labour.

Apart from the non-availability of labour, there is also general scarcity of skills at all levels.

This acts a strong deterrent, to entrepreneurship. Labour is not trained and lacks industrial skills. The traditional skills of the workmen are highly insufficient for modern industrial jobs. The lack of labour skills is the characteristic feature of the less developed nations, which are having primarily an agrarian character. There is also extreme scarcity of specialized skills. An entrepreneur finds difficulty to get in sufficient numbers skilled foremen, supervisory personnel, technicians, accountants, and industrial managers.

## Social Factors

Social factors can go a long way in encouraging entrepreneurship. In fact, it was a highly helpful society that made the industrial revolution a glorious success in Europe. It will not be wrong if one says that favourable social factors that prevailed in Europe during the 17th and 18th centuries following the 'Renaissance' led to the very emergence of the 'entrepreneur' as a factor of production.

A society that is rational in decision-making would be favourable to entrepreneurial growth. We call a society rational when decisions regarding resource uses are based on empirical facts and critical scientific standards. It would be non-rational if decisions regarding the use of capital, hiring of labour, designing of the products etc., are based on custom, tradition, and transcendental powers. While rational behaviour is the order of the day in the developed nations, most of the less developed nations are characterized by a non-rational society which is unsuitable to entrepreneurship.

When important production decisions are taken not on the basis of a critical assessment of facts and on the basis of custom and belief entrepreneurs are, discouraged. Society is also functionally, diffused. This means that the rights and duties of relationship of an individual are ill defined and limited. This also discourages individual initiative. For example, in a society where the joint family system is in vogue, those members of the joint family who gain wealth by their hard work are denied the opportunity to enjoy the fruits of their labour because they have to share their wealth with the other members of the family. In these circumstances, very few people would dare to be venturesome.

Several less developed countries are also characterized by the presence of a social set-up, which is generally hostile to entrepreneurship. Education, research and training are given very little importance. Appointments to responsible positions are guided by narrow parochial and caste considerations 'who a person is' is given more importance than 'what a person can do'. Therefore, there is very little vertical mobility of labour. The process of division of labour comes to be decided upon by the hereditary principle rather than by aptitudes, skills, and attainments of individuals.

## Cultural Factors

Motives impel men to action. Entrepreneurial growth requires proper motives like profit making, acquisition of prestige and attainment of social status. Ambitious and talented men would take risks and innovate if these motives are strong. The strength of these motives depends upon the culture of the society. If the culture is economical or monetarily oriented, entrepreneurship would be applauded and praised. Wealth accumulation as a way of life would be appreciated. In the less developed countries people are not economically motivated, monetary incentives have relatively less attraction. People have ample opportunities of attaining social distinction by non-economic pursuits, men with organizational abilities are therefore not dragged into business. They use their talents for non-economic ends. The absence of proper economic motives is a general characteristic of agrarian societies in which people do not attach great value to business talents, industrial leadership, etc.

## Personality Factors

According to Schumpeter, the social atmosphere in advanced capitalist societies is becoming inimical to entrepreneurship. In the less developed countries the entrepreneur is looked upon with suspicion. The result is the personality of the entrepreneur has got greatly affected. Public opinion in the less developed nations see the entrepreneur only as profit maker and an exploiter. Further, many of the less developed nations had the mortification of being exploited by foreigners for centuries.

The people and their leaders therefore tend to see in the entrepreneur a suspect personality. As one writer puts it, 'the figure of the entrepreneur has become odious'. If public opinion has become hostile to private entrepreneurship it has tended to favour direct state activity in the economy. It is argued that as the private entrepreneur has failed to promote economic development, the state must take steps in this direction. This has led to the emergence of planning, as means of achieving economic progress — in which the state shall play a pivotal role. It is difficult for an entrepreneur to work in a planned economy. Planning imposes controls and this goes against the very personality of the entrepreneur. In a planned economy, the entrepreneur should not only have initiative but also have the ability and willingness to adjust his attitudes and activities within the socio-economic framework set by the state. These qualities are contradictory and an entrepreneur cannot easily combine them.

## Psychological and Sociological Factors

Psychological and sociological factors are not always easy to distinguish. So in this analysis they are considered together.

**The Theory of Need Achievement:** This theory was put forward in the early 1960s by David McClelland and is regarded as the most important psychological theories of entrepreneurship.

According to McClelland 'need achievement' is a social motive to excel that tends to characterize successful entrepreneurs especially when reinforced by cultural factors. He found that certain kinds of people especially those who became entrepreneurs had this characteristics. Moreover, some societies tend to produce a larger percentage of people with high 'need achievement' than other societies. McClelland attributed this to sociological factors. Differences among societies and individuals accounted for 'need achievement' being greater in some societies and less in certain others. Analyzing this phenomenon Paul Wilken has said 'entrepreneurship becomes the link between need achievement and economic growth,' the latter being a specifically social factor.

The theory states that people with high need achievement are distinctive in several ways. They like to take risks and these risks stimulate them to greater effort. The theory identifies the factors that produce such people. Initially, McClelland attributed the role of parents specially the mother in mustering her son or daughter to be masterful and self-reliant. Later, he put less emphasis on the parent-child relationship and gave more importance to social and cultural factors. He concluded that the need achievement is conditioned more by social and cultural reinforcement, rather than by parental influence and such related factors.

**Psychosocial Theories:** There are several other researchers who have tried to understand the psychological and sociological roots of entrepreneurship. One such individual is Everett Hazen, who stresses the psychological consequences of social change. Hazen says at some point many social groups experience a radical loss of status. He gives the example of Catholic France where Protestants were tolerated in the 17th century, but were subjected to legal and social persecution. There are many ways of responding to such a loss of status. Hazen categorizes them into retreatism, situationalism, innovation, reformisms and rebellion.

Retreatism is most important in promoting entrepreneurship. At first, there is confusion in the ranks of those persons who have lost their status. But soon the women of such groups start holding high expectations about their sons. These sons would grow up with high need achievement. Since the law on social attitudes prevents them from seeking the usual forms of achievement like political office or owning land, they seek other outlets for their abilities. Business happens to be the only outlet available and consequently a group of highly motivated and achievement oriented individuals are created.

Other psychological theories of entrepreneurship stress, the motives on goals of the entrepreneur. Cole is of the opinion that besides wealth, entrepreneurs seek power, prestige, security and service to society. Stepanek points particularly to non-monetary aspects such as independence, personal self-esteem/power and regard of the society.

On the same subject Evens distinguishes by motive, three kinds of entrepreneurs, *viz.*

(a) Managing entrepreneurs whose chief motive is security.

(b) Innovating entrepreneurs who are interested only in excitement.

(c) Controlling entrepreneurs who above all other motives want power and authority.

Finally, Rostow has examined inter-generational changes in the families of entrepreneurs. He believes that the first generation, seeks wealth, the second prestige and the third art and beauty. Thomas Begley and David P. Boyd studied in detail the psychological roots of entrepreneurship in the mid-1980s. They came to the conclusion that entrepreneurial attitudes based on psychological considerations have five dimensions.

(1) First came 'need achievement' as described by McClelland. In all studies of successful entrepreneurs a high achievement orientation is invariably present.

(2) The second dimension is what Begley and Boyd call 'Locus of Control'. This means that the entrepreneur follows the idea that he can control his own life and is not influenced by factors like luck, fate and so on. Need achievement logically implies that people can control their own lives and are not influenced by external forces.

(3) The third dimension is the willingness to take risk. These two researchers have come to the conclusion that entrepreneurs who take moderate risk earn higher returns on their assets, than those who take no risk at all or who take extravagant risk.

(4) Tolerance is the next dimension of this study. Very few decisions are made with complete information. Hence, all business executives must have a certain amount of tolerance for ambiguity.

(5) Finally, here is what psychologists call 'Type A' behaviour. This is nothing but 'a chronic incessant struggle to achieve more and more in less and less.' Entrepreneurs are characterized by the presence of 'Type A' behaviour in all their endeavours.

*****

# 5

# Entrepreneurship Development

- *Personality Characteristics of Entrepreneurs*
- *Entrepreneurial Competencies*
- *Entrepreneurs in India*
- *Phases of Entrepreneurship Development*
- *Entrepreneurship Development in India*
- *Effectiveness of Entrepreneurship Development Programmes in India — Research Findings*
- *Environment for Entrepreneurship*
- *Barriers*
- *Position of Entrepreneurship in India*

The importance of entrepreneurial resource as a critical input in economic development has been well recognized, but a consensus about the definition of an entrepreneur is yet to emerge. However, personality characteristics of entrepreneur and entrepreneurial competencies are briefly indicated below:

## Personality Characteristics of Entrepreneurs

1. Need for achievement.
2. Average intelligence.
3. Sense of efficacy.
4. Moderate risk-taker.
5. Open to feedback and learns from experience.
6. Drive and energy.

7. Need for independence.
8. Hope of success.
9. Procreative.
10. Action oriented.
11. Need for influencing others.
12. Problem solving rather than problem avoiding attitude.
13. Initiative taking rather than confronting attitude.
14. Concern for society.
15. Money, an important measure.
16. Creative and innovative.
17. Take personal responsibility.
18. Opportunity seeker.
19. Time oriented.
20. Realistic.
21. Not too discouraged by failures.
22. Sensitive and perceptive.
23. Good communicator.
24. Assertive.
25. High tolerance of ambiguity.
26. Goal oriented.
27. Wants to make money.
28. Persistent.
29. Family and friends, second to business.
30. Good problem solver.
31. Resourceful makes good use of resources.
32. Knowledge of the business.

## Entrepreneurial Competencies

1. Initiative.
2. Sees and acts on opportunities.
3. Persistence.
4. Information seeking.
5. Concern for high quality of work.
6. Commitment to work contract.

7. Efficiency orientation.
8. Systematic planning.
9. Problem solving.
10. Self-confidence.
11. Assertiveness.
12. Persuasion.
13. Use of influence strategies.
14. Monitoring.
15. Concern for employees' welfare.

Larger the number of these attributes a person possesses, greater could be the chance of his or her entrepreneurial success.

## ENTREPRENEURS IN INDIA

It is generally believed that people coming from certain business, castes/communities and religious groups have been more enterprising than the rest. However, the findings of several research studies conducted in different parts of the country indicate contrary to such beliefs.

A study of manufacturing units in and around Chennai and Coimbatore cities in Tamil Nadu revealed that initial entry into industry was open to persons of diverse social standing and economic position (Berna, 1960). A study of small entrepreneurs in Andhra Pradesh revealed that all the entrepreneurs were persons having initiatives, drive and hard work, though a majority of them had neither technical knowledge nor strong economic base and political connections (Gaikwad & Tripathi, 1970). A study of small entrepreneurs in Gujarat revealed that entry into industry and success need not be the privilege of a few traditionally dominant groups (Patel, 1981).

Further study on small entrepreneurs in Uttar Pradesh revealed that the entrepreneurs coming from non-business families had higher degree of entrepreneurial orientation and commitment than the entrepreneurs coming from business families, business castes, and business regions (Sharma, 1975).

## PHASES OF ENTREPRENEURSHIP DEVELOPMENT

Broadly, entrepreneurship development consists of the three following phases:

(a) *Initial phase* — Creation of awareness about the entrepreneurial opportunities based on service and research.

(b) *Development phase* — Implementation of training programmes to develop motivation and management skills.

(c) *Support phase* — Infrastructural support of counselling, assisting to establish new enterprises and to develop existing units.

Entrepreneurship itself is a complex phenomenon, some thinking of it as job of innovators, some as managers of enterprise, some as bearers of risks and others as mobilizers and allocators of capital.

In the Indian context, however entrepreneurship may best be considered as creators of economic wealth for self and society at large, through commercial and productive activities. Hence, entrepreneurship development would mean all those activities aiming at development of individuals in such a way that an urge is ignited for becoming an entrepreneur. Phases could be three or more, all occurring one after another or simultaneously or concurrently.

## ENTREPRENEURSHIP DEVELOPMENT IN INDIA

It is true a person must have certain entrepreneurial attributes and need not necessarily belong to a particular caste, community or group to become an entrepreneur. But mere personality traits of an individual would not be sufficient condition for him/her becoming an entrepreneur. Other social, cultural, and economic factors as well as support system also influence to a considerable extent, promotion and development of entrepreneurship, however it has been found that the entrepreneurial attributes of an individual can be improved to a certain extent through stimulation and training, provided he or she has latent potential for entrepreneurship. The entrepreneurial potential of an individual thus developed can lead to the promotion of an enterprise with the help of counselling, infrastructural support, and financial assistance from institutional sources. In this way, the constraints in development of entrepreneurship due to unfavourable personality traits, social conditioning, cultural ethos and economic factors could be reduced to a great extent.

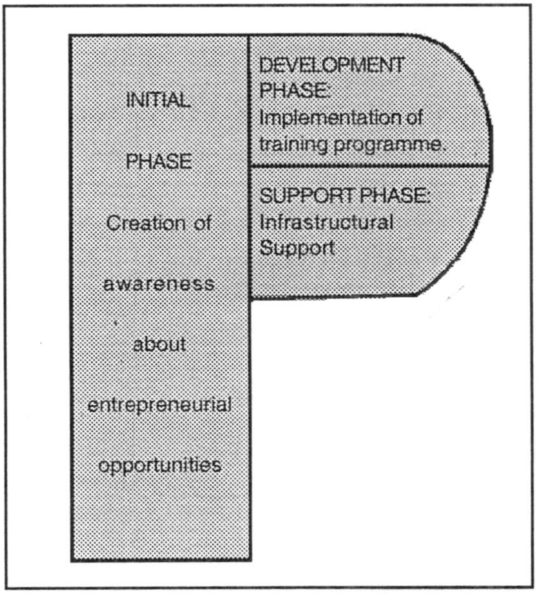


*Fig. 5.1: Phases of Entrepreneurship Development*

Though India has had a long tradition of institutional support for the promotion and development of industries, the first step towards developing entrepreneurs was taken in the early 1960s. The first programme on motivation training for developing entrepreneurship in India was organized by the National Institute of Small Industries Extension Training (NISIET), Hyderabad in 1964, under the leadership of David C. McClelland. In the first programme fifty-two persons were trained in four batches in Kakinada District of Andhra Pradesh. This was followed by another programme in which twenty-six persons from Vellore in Tamil Nadu were trained in two batches in 1965. Later on, NISIET evolved an integrated model for entrepreneurship, development based on its previous experience. This model was first of all tried in Assam and similar programmes were conducted later on in the states of Andhra Pradesh, Bihar and Jammu and Kashmir. During the period of April 1970 to September 1973, 1,240 potential entrepreneurs were trained at different centres in Gujarat through a series of Entrepreneurship Development Programmes (EDPs) sponsored by the state level financial institutions.

Following the success of these initial EDPs, entrepreneurship development through training came to be viewed as a useful instrument for widening and diversifying the entrepreneurial base of the country. Several national and state level institutions have been set up exclusively for entrepreneurship development. Also a variety of agencies in a large number have come forward to conduct EDPs, all over the country. In addition, a great deal of sophistication has also been achieved over the years in planning EDPs, selecting potential entrepreneurs, motivation, training, business opportunity, guidance and business management inputs.

## EFFECTIVENESS OF ENTREPRENEURSHIP DEVELOPMENT PROGRAMMES IN INDIA

Though a systematic documentation of entrepreneurship development and their effectiveness in India is yet to be done, some limited facts available provide an insight into the spread and effectiveness of EDPs. During the period of April 1970 to March 1980, 376 EDPs had been conducted in Gujarat and the effectiveness of these EDPs was reported to be about 63 per cent. In the state of Maharashtra and Goa, 88 potential entrepreneurs were trained during the year 1974, through several EDPs conducted in other five districts of Maharashtra during the years 1976 and 1977 was reported to be 31 per cent. The State Bank of India had conducted 10 EDPs in its 13 circles till 1985 and the effectiveness of these EDPs was reported to be about 28 per cent. In Pondicherry, the effectiveness of 32 EDPs conducted during the period 1985-87 ranged between 22 per cent in 1985 and 51 per cent in 1987.

From this limited information, it is obvious the EDPs have become popular throughout the country and their effectiveness has been varying from one region to another. With the growing awareness of the need for entrepreneurship development and increasing availability of trained manpower, the effectiveness of EDPs is bound to increase in future. However, it must be clear to all concerned that mere improvement in the quality of men and material for conducting EDPs would not make much difference. Equally or even more important are the quality and adequacy of institutional support provided by financial institutions and promotional agencies to the EDPs trained candidates for setting up and running of their enterprises.

Not much information is at present available on the reasons for not setting up of enterprises by a good proportion of the candidates trained through a variety of EDPs. Collection and analysis of such information would be very useful for identifying weakness in the process of entrepreneurship development and for evolving the strategy to overcome them in future. This becomes all the more important, keeping in view the rapid growth of population causing acute unemployment problem.

## RESEARCH FINDINGS

Apart from a broad review of the progress of Entrepreneurship Development in the country as presented above it may be appropriate to highlight some of the factors that have influenced the existing entrepreneurs to choose entrepreneurial careers. A study of small entrepreneurs conducted in Karnataka (Tewari Philip & Pandey, 1991), revealed that the better performing entrepreneurs were relatively young and the desire to be self-employed, was the greatest motivating factor for becoming an entrepreneur. Entrepreneurs were motivated by their own ambitions rather than the ambitions of their parents and other relatives. Also dissatisfaction with previous job or occupation was found to be the most compelling factor for motivating them to become entrepreneurs. While the greatest source of encouragement was entrepreneur's previous experience. Entrepreneurs developed greater confidence from their own abilities and skills rather than from financial and other material resources available to them.

Previous employment in industries or trade was found to be the most important consideration for the selection of products. Accommodation in an industrial estate and the availability of financial support from the institutional sources were the two greatest expectations of entrepreneurs. The entrepreneurs belonging to the sick group had received greater financial support in the initial stage than those belonging to the very successful group.

Manufacturing as a sole activity was more prominent in the successful group than in the sick group and smaller size of an enterprise in the initial stage was not a limiting factor for the growth and outstanding performance in future. Besides, utilization of capital was more efficient and the repayment behaviour of the entrepreneurs was better in the better performing groups. While ability and immediate environment of the entrepreneurs were considered to be the main factor responsible for outstanding performance, rather unsatisfactory performance of average group was attributed to their greater dependence on market situations than on their own entrepreneurial ability. Poor performance of the units belonging to the sick group was largely due to the unsatisfactory entrepreneurial efforts entailing a variety of problems.

## ENVIRONMENT FOR ENTREPRENEURSHIP

Entrepreneurs do not come into existence spontaneously on their own. While the other factors of production in principle can be hired, enterprise cannot be done so. Even, the educational system in most of the developing countries is designed in such a ways as to create more of job seekers. In many countries to sum up, entrepreneurs appear to have been motivated by a continuation and interaction of the following factors of environment:

1. Socio-economic environment.
2. Family background.
3. Standard of education and technical knowledge.
4. Financial stability.
5. Political stability and government's policy.
6. Caste and religious affiliation.
7. Availability of supporting facilities.
8. Achievement motivation.
9. Personality and personal skills.

The environmental factors may be summarized as follows:

1. Entrepreneurship is not influenced by a single factor but is the outcome of the interaction and continuation of various environmental factors.
2. By changing the environment, society can be recreated.
3. It is the 'desire to make money' that drives one to start an industry rather than the amount of money one owns.
4. Encouraging government policy and social recognition influence a person to become an entrepreneur.

## BARRIERS

Entry barriers are defined as those factors limiting access to identified business opportunities and capitalization on those opportunities. Survival barriers are defined as constraints on the conditions essential for the continuity of the small business entity. Exit barriers are defined as those constraints limiting the termination of those small industrial ventures that have outlived their business viability or the growth of such ventures to a different size category.

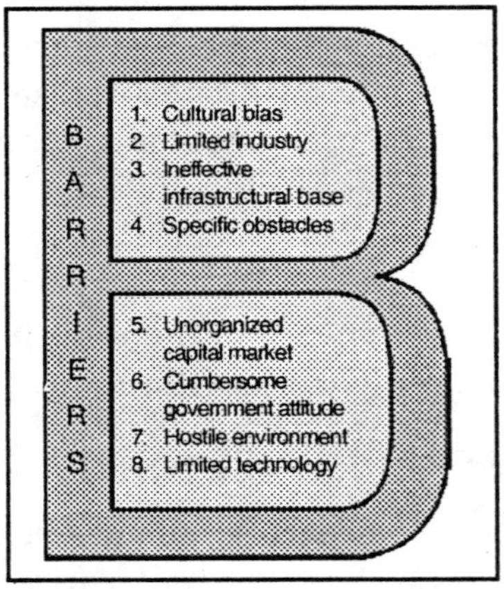


*Fig. 5.2: Entry Barriers*

The existing entry barriers are:

(1) A cultural bias in identifying and managing the entrepreneurial development process.

(2) Limited industry — by specific data and insufficient market information.

(3) Limited effectiveness of the infrastructural base.

(4) Existence of visible and invisible obstacles to entry of a specific societal group (*e.g.*, women) into business.

(5) Unorganized capital market and traditional feasibility assessment processes.

(6) Unsympathetic and cumbersome government attitude.

(7) Hostile environment.

(8) Limited access to technology.

Observed survival barriers include the following:

(1) A behavioural pattern that could impair basic managerial practices.

(2) Constraining practices within the capital market.

(3) The threatening shadow of changing technology.

(4) Limited learning.

(5) The cultural management of resources.

(6) Failure of guidance agencies to guide.

(7) Scarce information and limited dissemination of that information.

Identified exit barriers include:

(1) The emotional commitment of the entrepreneur to his venture.

(2) Specialized assets and sunk funds.

(3) The increasing demand for managerial skills.

(4) Fear of failure.

## POSITION OF ENTREPRENEURSHIP IN INDIA

India does not possess a very good record of entrepreneurship. However, its image is definitely improving, concerted efforts at liberalization has made the countries of the world sit back and look at India develop its own brand of entrepreneurship. In the recent past India's status, in the industrial world has grown. From humble surroundings, India is now the tenth largest industrialized nation of the world.

However, India has essentially been an 'adoptive' entrepreneur. It has now to prepare itself with an entrepreneurship of a different order, that of the innovative type. This will require harnessing of India's true potential through tremendous advances of science and technology.

It is essential that the government and the people must have a more mature and finer approach towards the concept of entrepreneurship. Then only would it be possible for this nation to match the level reached by advanced countries. A good beginning in this direction has been made and one hopes the adage 'Well begun is half done,' will hold good in case of India.

*****

# 6

# Entrepreneurship Development Programmes


- *Introduction*
- *Meaning*
- *Need*
- *Entrepreneurship Development*
- *Organizations for EDP*
- *National Institute for Entrepreneurship and Small Business Development*
- *Emerging Scene*
- *Entrepreneurship as a Field of Academic Enquiry*


## INTRODUCTION

Entrepreneurial talent exists in every society and in all sections of society. In developed countries a favourable socio-economic development helps in exploiting latent entrepreneurial talent. However, in less developed and developing countries particularly in certain backward areas, an unfavourable socio-economic environment hinders the emergence of entrepreneurial talent. In India, it is believed that tremendous latent entrepreneurial talent exists which if properly harnessed can help accelerate the pace of socio-economic development, balanced regional growth, exploitation of locally available resources and creation of gainful employment and self-employment. Such a realization, on the part of planners and policy formulators has resulted in the emergence of Entrepreneurship Development Programmes (EDPs), for various target groups of population in the country. EDPs are being offered by a large number of organizations with a view in bringing to the latent entrepreneurial ability in various target groups and motivating the programme participants to establish their own enterprises.

The movement has caught momentum in many other developing countries such as Sri Lanka, China, Thailand, Philippines, Indonesia, Bangladesh, Malaysia, and South African countries.

## MEANING

Entrepreneurship Development Programme means a programme designed to help a person in strengthening his entrepreneurial motives and in acquiring skills and capabilities necessary for playing his entrepreneurial role effectively. Towards this need, it is necessary to promote his understanding of motives, motivation pattern, their impact on behaviour and entrepreneurial value. A programme which seeks to do this can qualify to be called an EDP. Thus, an EDP aims at developing entrepreneurial motives, skills and helping to play his/her role as an entrepreneur effectively. There are a number of programmes which give information to the prospective entrepreneurs regarding a new business idea, how to set-up a new venture, how to prepare a project report, sources of finance, etc. These programmes should not be confused with EDP, they are all only a part of EDP. An EDP is primarily concerned with developing and motivating entrepreneurial talent and grooming him/her to be an effective entrepreneur.

## NEED

The economic progress of developed countries has shown that entrepreneurs play a vital role in economic development. The slow progress of developing countries indicates low level of entrepreneurship in those countries. Entrepreneurs make use of the factors of production to the fullest advantage of the society, create innovations, generate employment, improve the standard of living of people, develop backward areas, etc. All these ultimately lead to higher rate of economic growth. Hence, entrepreneurial development is very essential for the economic development of a country.

EDP has an important role to play in solving the unemployment problem. Unemployment, the state of being jobless is a burning problem that affects both developed as well as the developing countries. It has more serious effect on the developing countries than the developed ones. The problems of unemployment and underemployment in a developing country differ fundamentally from that of developed ones where it is more a social problem than an economic problem. Unemployment is demoralizing. Barbara Ward rightly said 'of all the evils — worklessness is the worst'. Unemployment is the major source of waste in our present economic system since 'idle hands are the symptoms of economic waste'.

India is facing a chronic unemployment problem. The most alarming form of unemployment today is educated unemployment. The educated unemployed represents the intellectual section of the society, the frustration and discontent of which pave the path of political instability as well as an atmosphere of pessimism and loss of confidence in the government. This type of unemployment consists of those young job seekers on whom the society has invested its most scarce resources. The unemployment among the educated is higher than among the uneducated. The rate of unemployment increases with the level of education.

## ENTREPRENEURIAL DEVELOPMENT PROGRAMME

The basic objectives of an entrepreneurial development programme can be summarized as follows:

*(i)* To develop and strengthen their entrepreneurial quality motivation.

*(ii)* To analyze environment relating to small industry and small business.

*(iii)* To select project product.

*(iv)* To formulate project.

*(v)* To understand the process and procedure of setting up of small enterprise.

*(vi)* To know and to influence the source of help support needed for launching enterprise.

*(vii)* To acquire the basic management skills.

*(viii)* To know the pros and cons of being an entrepreneur.

*(ix)* To acquaint and appreciate the needed social responsibility and entrepreneurial discipline.

An analysis of the development process that helps for emergence of people opting for entrepreneurial career in the society and succeeding in finally setting up an enterprise reveals that it follows a sequence of development in individual personality, ability, and capabilities.

*(a)* Entrepreneurial quality motivation.

*(b)* Capability for enterprise launching resourcing.

*(c)* Ability for enterprise management.

*(d)* Some of the responsibilities to the society that promote support them.

The cyclic process of developing an entrepreneur is given.

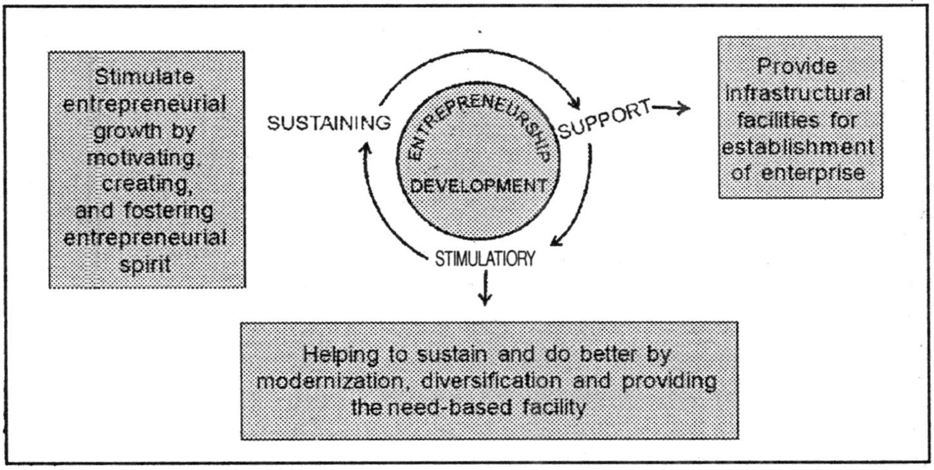


*Fig. 6.1: Cyclic Process of Developing an Entrepreneur*

The task of making entrepreneurs is by no means an easy job. Any programme striving to this end should be in tune with the existing government policies to encourage entrepreneurship. It is necessary that a favourable climate is built up and a friendly support system made available.

The task of developing entrepreneurship comprises of:

(*a*) Identifying and carefully selecting those who could be developed as entrepreneurs.

(*b*) Developing their entrepreneurial capabilities.

(*c*) Ensuring that they have a viable industrial project.

(*d*) Equipping them with basic administrative, financial and managerial capabilities, and

(*e*) Helping them to secure necessary financial and other infrastructural assistance.

The key to success lies in providing each of the above in an integrated manner since partial assistance either in the form of finance or training alone would not bring the desired results.

## ORGANIZATIONS FOR EDPs

Various state and national organizations are organizing Entrepreneurship Development Programmes. Of the various organizations, The National Institute for Entrepreneurship and Small Business Development is doing pioneering work. Entrepreneurship Development Institute also aims at providing entrepreneurial training and research.

## NATIONAL INSTITUTE FOR ENTREPRENEURSHIP AND SMALL BUSINESS DEVELOPMENT (NIESBUD)

The National Institute for Entrepreneurship and Small Business Development was established in 1983 by the Ministry of Industry, Government of India as an apex body for coordinating the activities of various institution and agencies engaged in Entrepreneurship Development, particularly in the areas of small industry and small business.

The activities of the Institute include evolving effective training strategies and methodology, standardizing model syllabi for training various target groups, formulating scientific selection procedure; developing training aids, manuals and tools, facilitating and supporting central, state and other agencies in executing Entrepreneurship Development Programmes, conducting such programmes for promoters, trainers and entrepreneurs which are commonly not undertaken by other agencies, maximizing the benefits and accelerating the process of entrepreneurship to development and above all, organizing all those activities that help develop entrepreneurial culture in the society. The Institute is also the secretariat for the National Entrepreneurship Development Board (NEDB), the apex body which determines policy for entrepreneurship development in the country. The Institute therefore performs the task of processing the recommendations made by the Board.

The Institute is actively involved in creating a climate conducive to the emergence of entrepreneurship and in developing favourable attitude among general public to support those who opt for entrepreneurial career.

Important organizations engaged in EDPs, are The National Science and Technology other Entrepreneurship Development Board (NSTEDB) of the Department of Science and Technology, Government of India, National Institute of Small Industry Extension Training, Government of India, Hyderabad and nationalized banks.

## EMERGING SCENE

With the opening up of the Indian economy by virtue of global changes and also globalization of markets, there is a need to have a fresh look at our strategies of gearing up our youth for an entrepreneurial career. The future entrepreneur has to face considerable challenges, severe competition not only from the national angle but also from the global angle. With the liberalization that is taking place the Indian entrepreneur has to face severe competition from the global players even in such areas like consumer products which till now had some protection. There are some glaring examples which the developers of future entrepreneurs have to keep in mind, *e.g.*, breakfast cereals (Kellogs), Kentucky Fried Chicken, readymade garments, etc.

The future entrepreneur has to be prepared through training, exposure for planning and when launching an enterprise keep in mind the following:

*(a)* Technology and scope for modernization.

*(b)* Quality including ISO 9000 requirements.

*(c)* Consumer satisfaction/customer service.

*(d)* Energy conservation.

*(e)* Pollution environmental aspects.

*(f)* Cost of production.

*(g)* Competition from both national and international angles.

The EDP models will therefore have to be developed taking those aspects into consideration. It is a matter of great satisfaction that in India today we have a vast talent of scientific and technical manpower. The school education system also now makes provision for vocational training. Unlike the past, today the openings are many to talented youth who can take certain amount of risk in planning entrepreneurship as a career either through manufacturing/processing industry or through servicing or business enterprises which support these activities. In this context it may be relevant to mention some new opportunities that have emerged in the last few years in our country.

*(a)* Floriculture/cut flowers (cut flowers are being exported from southern region of the country).

*(b)* Fruit juices and pulp (in aseptic packaging).

(*c*) Mushroom processing.

(*d*) Software exports.

(*e*) Sweetmeat exports (to Hong Kong).

Perhaps, some of these examples would have had no relevance a decade ago. With the emphasis now given to clean environment and clean technologies, there will be many more opportunities that will be emerging in future. The developers of entrepreneurs who have to meet the requirements of the next century will have to start visualizing the opportunities and gear up the prospective entrepreneurs. With the advent of new economic policies with liberalization, privatization, globalization as their major thrust the environment can create new vistas for entrepreneurship development. Promoting and encouraging competitive growth-oriented and quality conscious entrepreneurs is the need of the hour now. To make them think globally and operate efficiently is of utmost importance.

## ENTREPRENEURSHIP AS A FIELD OF ACADEMIC INQUIRY

### History of the Field

The initial era of entrepreneurship dates back to the concepts introduced by early economists, including Knight (1921) on risk and uncertainty, Schumpeter (1934) on new combinations and waves of creative destruction driven by entrepreneurs, and Penrose (1959) on entrepreneurial services and productive opportunities. The Austrian economists — Hayek, von Mises & Kirzner — were instrumental in recognizing the impact of the individual on the economy. Hayek (1945) introduced mutual learning and market participant awareness, and von Mises (1944) introduced human action and the entrepreneur. Later, Kirzner (1973, 1997), a student of von Mises, expanded the work of his mentor and Hayek to introduce 'entrepreneurial discovery'. According to Kirzner (1973), entrepreneurs are not economizing individuals, but rather they have alertness to opportunities that already exist in the market. The Austrian view, one of human action as creative and active, is in direct opposition with the more mainstream neoclassical view, which holds that human beings are passive, rational, and mechanical within ultimately efficient markets. While the Austrians argue disequilibrium as the prevailing state in an economy, Neoclassical economists theorize that economic forces alter equilibrium states but markets are assumed efficient at the equilibrium point.

Entrepreneurship as a field of study began to emerge in the 1970s. In 1974, Karl Vesper organized a special entrepreneurship interest group of the Academy of Management's Business policy division, which became a separate division in 1987. The finding of David Birch (1979, 1987) highlighted entrepreneurship as the engine of growth in the economy. Prior to Birch's work, general political and economic beliefs assumed that large corporations created most of society's jobs, yet Birch uncovered counterintuitive statistics regarding job creation. During the period studied, 1981-85, small firms (1-19 employees) created 88 per cent of all new jobs; firms with 20-99 employees created 27 per cent of new jobs; large corporations (5,000+employees) created 5 per cent of new jobs; and firms with 100 to 4,999 employees lost 20 per cent of the jobs created (Birch, 1987, 16). According to the *Global Entrepreneurship monitor,* since 1980,

*Fortune* 500 companies have lost more than five million jobs, but more than 34 million new jobs have been created (Reynolds, Hay, & Camp, 1999:7).

More recently, the OECD reported that 35 per cent of new jobs created in 1995 were generated by organizations with only one to four employees (Arzeni, 1998). The Birch studies and others (Kirchoff & Phillips, 1987, 1988; Reynolds, 1992; Reynolds, Hay, & Camp, 1999; Acs, 1999) revealed that the economic impact of entrepreneurship was not only attributed to business formation, but also to the growth of new businesses. Reynolds *et al.* (1999) reported that 15 per cent of the highest growth firms in 1996 created 94 per cent of new jobs. Because of the earlier findings relating entrepreneurship to firm growth, a movement began in the mid-1980s to separate entrepreneurship from small business management — the ultimate difference being the growth of the firm (Sexton and Smilor, 1997). Morris argues that, certainly in recent years, 'The entrepreneurial firm is defined as one that proactively seeks to grow and is not constrained by resources under its control' (1998). According to Sexton and Smilor, 'significant differences exist between the problems associated with starting a business and growing one' (1997) and they assert, 'Growth is the essence of entrepreneurship' (1997). Thus, managing growth is fundamental and the problems inherent in high-growth firms are well documented (*e.g.*, Penrose, 1959; Hambrick & Crozier, 1985; Kazanjian, 1988; Covin & Slevin, 1997; Welbourne, Meyer, & Neck, 1998), yet we believe more predictive studies are needed.

Entrepreneurship research, which began with the study of individual traits, has evolved into a comprehensive and complex phenomenon. Morris (1998) characterized the field as having seven perspectives that are quite representative of the evolution of the field while also emphasizing the apparent importance of 'creation' on the field. These perspectives are: the creation of wealth, the creation of enterprise, the creation of innovation, the creation of change, the creation of employment, the creation of value, and the creation of growth (1998).

Though the entrepreneurship field is still emerging, we believe the field is taking its natural course similar to other fields that have emerged in the organization sciences. Overall, the field has been subjected to criticism regarding the rigor of the research being produced as well as questions regarding the focus of entrepreneurship research. Today scholars of entrepreneurship are attempting to establish boundaries, definitions, domains, and discover theory. The following section discusses boundaries, definitions, domains, and discovered theory. The following section discusses these aspects as the field continues to struggle with its issues of legitimacy.

## Definition and Domain of Entrepreneurship Research

The 1999s was a decade of debate over the domain of entrepreneurship research, its legitimacy, and its contribution to management practice (Harrison & Leitch, 1996; Aldrich & Baker, 1997; Busenitz, *et al.* 2000). The establishment of entrepreneurship as a legitimate academic research domain has seen limited progress (Aldrich & Baker, 1997; Busenitz *et al.*, 2000) and without an entrepreneurship research paradigm, the progress of the field and its legitimacy will be limited (Venkataraman, 1997).

Entrepreneurship research has been criticized for lack of rigor (Schendel, 1990), multiple levels of analysis (Venkataraman, 1997), and an absence of a unifying framework to guide the field's research. The large public databases such as PIMS or COMPUSTAT uses in strategic management are not available for smaller, private, entrepreneurial firms. Consequently, data constraints, rather than research preference, may account partly for the nature of the work being done in entrepreneurship. But, even when databases for entrepreneurship research are available, sensitive financial information is not included (Phillips & Dennis, 1997), making it difficult to address performance queries. One could speculate that the lack of research progress in the field has resulted from our inability to define entrepreneurship using terms agreed upon by those in the field. Bygrave and Hofer (1991) contend that it is impossible to operationalize a concept that is not defined.

Entrepreneurship has multiple definitions (see table 6.1 for a selected review) of which no one definition has been accepted by the field. Morris (1998) found 77 different definitions in a review of journal articles and textbooks over a 5-year period. The lack of one definition leaves open multiple paths of inquiry and various perspectives of what entrepreneurship is. If not an agreed upon definition, then the field should atleast establish a dominant paradigm from which to build knowledge. Without such a framework, the field lacks boundaries, structure, and a legitimate course of scientific inquiry. Scholars have been and continue to address the domain-paradigm-definition issue in the entrepreneurship field.

Gartner (1988) believes that entrepreneurship is the creation of new organization while others argue that entrepreneurship encompasses organizational growth, strategic renewal, transformation and innovation (Schendel & Hofer, 1979; Schendel, 1990; Day, 1992; Barringer & Bluedorn, 1999; Sexton & Smilor, 1997, Van de Ven *et al.*, 1999; Hitt & Ireland, 2000). Entrepreneurship can take the form of a new venture or can occur inside an existing organization (Rumelt, 1987; Schendel, 1990; Guth & Ginsberg, 1990; Block & MacMillon, 1993; Morris & Sexton, 1996; Morris, 1998;

Sharma & Chrisman, 1999; Shane & Venkataraman, 2000).

We can study such topics as the individual entrepreneur (McClelland, 1961; Collins & Moore, 1970; Hornaday & Aboud, 1971; Hull, Bosley, & Udell, 1980), behaviours and actions (Gartner, 1988, Busenitz and Barney, 1997), opportunity recognition (Kirzner, 1973, 1979; Kaish & Gilad, 1991; Herron & Sapienza, 1992; Gaglio, 1997), population of foundings (Aldrich, 1990, 1999; Aldrich & Wiedenmeyer, 1993), entrepreneurship teams (Slevin & Covin, 1992; Cooper & Daily, 197; Ensley *et al.*, 1999), organizational growth (Churchill & Lewis, 1983; Eisenhardt & Schoonhoven, 1990; Covin & Slevin, 1997), firm performance (Cooper, 1993; Chandler & Hanks, 1994; McDougall *et al.*, 1994), and economic impact (Baumol, 1986; Birch, 1987; Kirchoff, 1991; Acs, 1999).

Without an overarching definition of entrepreneurship, however, each researcher's interpretation of entrepreneurship guides the research question, sample, and level of analysis. This limits the generalize ability of findings and leads to an inability to replicate studies. Additionally, without an accumulation of empirically driven and consistent findings, we are unable to apply our knowledge in good faith to the practicing field of entrepreneurs in the real world. But, Gartner even admits to having difficulty arriving at a definition and the research domain of entrepreneurship.

Table 6.1

Selected Definitions of Entrepreneurship

| Author | Deficition |
|---|---|
| Schumpeter (1934) | Entrepreneruship is seen as new combinations including the doing of new things or new things or the doing of things that are already being done in a new way.<br>Now combinations include: (1) introduction of new goods, (2) new method of production, (3) opening of a new market, (4) new some of supply, (5) new organizations. |
| Kirzner (1973) | Entrepreneurship is the ability to perceive new opportunities. This recognition and seizing of the opportunity will tend to 'correct' the market, and bring it back toward equilibrium. |
| Drucker (1985) | Entrepreneurship is an act of innovation that involves endowing existing resources with new wealth-producing capacity. |
| Stevenson, Roberts, & Grousbeck (1985) | Entrepreneurship is the pursuit of an opportunity without concern for current resources or capabilities. |
| Rumelf (1987) | Entrepreneurship is the creation of new business, new business meaning that they do not exactly duplicate existing businesses but have some element of novelty. |
| Low & MacMillan (1988) | Entrepreneurship is the creation of new enterprise. |
| Gartner (1988) | Entrepreneurship is the creation of organiztion, the process by which organizations come into existence. |
| Thommons (1987) | Entrepreneurship is a very of thinking, reasoning, and acting that is opportunity obsessed, holistic in approach, and leadership balanced. |
| Venkataraman (1987) | Entrepreneurship research seeks to understand how opportunities to bring into existance future goods and services are discovered, created, and exploited, by whom, and with what consequences. |
| Moris (1998) | Entrepreneurship is the process through which individuals and teams create value by bringing together unique packages of resource inputs to exploit opportunities in the environment. It can occur in any organizational context and results in a variety of possible outcomes, including new ventures, products, services, processes, markets, and technologies. |
| Sharma and Chrisman (1999) | Entrepreneurship encompasses acts of organizational creation, renewal or innovation that occur within or outside an existing organization. |

In commenting on the Domain Statement of the Entrepreneurship Division of the Academy of Management, he states: I am at a loss to ferret out the unique domain of entrepreneurship.... How is the study of 'maintaining an enterprise' and 'the creation and management of new businesses, small businesses and family businesses' different for entrepreneurship scholars than for [other] management scholars? He further goes on to say, 'I think the primary issue facing scholars interested in developing a domain statement for the field of entrepreneurship is the encroaching power of other academic disciplines (Gartner, 2000).

Scholars have significantly contributed to the literature in their attempt to define the domain of entrepreneurship research. For example, Bygrave and Hofer (1991) view entrepreneurship as a dynamic process that is an act of human volition analyzed at the firm level. The process is unique and dynamic with many antecedent variables, and these variables are sensitive to initial environmental conditions. Extending Bygrave's (1998) work on chaos theory, Bygrave and Hofer (1991) incorporated the notion of nonlinearity into to 'process' of entrepreneurship. Later, Bull and Willard (1993) noted that the field should cease its attempt to define and redefine entrepreneurship because Schumpeter (1934, 1942) gave the field its domain many years ago. Schumpeter's (1934) notion of new combinations (new organizations, new markets, new sources of supply, new methods of production, new products and services) that disrupt markets and shift or destroy demand and supply curves is a rigorous and broad enough view for entrepreneurship research (Bull & Willard, 1993).

Morris (1998) proposed an interesting input-output process model of entrepreneurship that incorporated much of the literature to date in the field. Inputs to the entrepreneurship process include opportunities, individuals, organizational context, unique business concepts, and resources, while the output of the process (or outcome) can be a going venture, value creation, new products or services, processes, technologies, profits and/or personal benefits, and growth (Morris, 1998).

The inputs of the entrepreneurship process are both necessary and constant whereas the outputs that determine 'entrepreneurial intensity' may vary. Accordingly, Morris proposes various dependent variables from which a researcher can choose depending on the research question of interest. Additionally, the definition of entrepreneurship proposed by Morris (see Table 6.1) is sufficiently broad to include multiple levels of analysis, and organizational size does not constrain entrepreneurial activity. Recently, Venkataraman (1997) and Shane and Venkataraman (2000) have been leading the challenge to establish a unique identity for the entrepreneurship field. Their view presumes a strong cognitive focus on opportunity identification, evaluation, and exploitation. Venkataraman defines the field of entrepreneurship as 'a scholarly field that seeks to understand how opportunities to bring into existence future goods and services are developed, created, and exploited by whom and with what circumstances' (1997). He is attempting to separate entrepreneurship from other disciplines, specifically strategic management, *vis-à-vis* a strong emphasis on the 'emergence' of new businesses. Venkataraman (1997) regards absolute economic value and social wealth as the relevant benchmarks for entrepreneurship research. Economic value, or entrepreneurial rents, is profit in excess of the cost of time, effort, resources, and uncertainty. Without taking these opportunity costs into consideration, any profit and economic contribution resulting from the entrepreneurial venture is incomplete and misleading. The second benchmark, social wealth, is byproduct of positive economic value. Through innovation, by way of self-interested opportunity exploitation and commercialization, entrepreneurs benefits society via new products, markets, and growth in demand and supply. Thus, entrepreneurial actions result in both personal and social wealth.

In 1999, Dale Meyer created the 'Task Force on Doctoral Education in Entrepreneurship' as part of the entrepreneurship Division of the Academy of Management. One of the primary challenges facing the Task Force is to develop a domain statement for research in entrepreneurship. The domain sub-committee comprised of Dale Meyer, S. Venkataraman, and William Gartner has been struggling to meet the challenge (Gartner, 2000). The most recent draft of the entrepreneurship research domain statement is reproduced in Figure 6.2. Meyer, Venkataraman, and Gartner (1999) focus on entrepreneurship as creation but broadly define creation to encompass multiple and multidisciplinary topics for examination.

Domain of Entrepreneurship Research
Task Force on Doctoral Education in Entrepreneurship

Entrepreneurship is about creation. Therefore, the research domain of the enterepreneurship field involves the:

- Creation of new ventures and organizations
- Creation of new combinations of goods and services, methods of production, markets, and supply chains
- Recognition and exploitation of new and existing opportunities
- Cognitive processes, behaviours and modes of action to exploit new and existing opportunities.

Entrepreneurship research examines these creation endeavours, the individuals and teams involved, the emergence of new ventures and organizations, and distinctive strategies utilized in the creation process; as well as the macroeconomic job and wealth creation impacts of Entrepreneurial endeavour.

Entrepreneurship research can vary in context examined, such as new firms and organizations, existing corporations, family business, franchises and new international Entrepreneurial activity.

*Fig. 6.2: Domain of Entrepreneurship Research (Meyer, Venkataraman, and Gartner, 1999)*

Scholars writing directly on the domain of entrepreneurship research are attempting to distinguish entrepreneurship from other disciplines — specifically strategic management. In summary, Gartner (1988) views entrepreneurship as the act of new venture creation where growth and survival are not topics of study. Bygrave Hofer (1991) take a strong process view but their work is very broad and leaves a considerable amount of room for interpretation. Bull Willard (1993) adhere to Schumpeter's view of new combinations as the impetus for creative destruction. Morris (1998) views entrepreneurship through an integrative input-output model where resource inputs are used to exploit opportunities that can result in various performance outcomes. Venkataraman (1997) and Shane Venkataraman (2000) focus on creation *vis-à-vis* opportunity identification, evaluation and exploitation. Finally, Meyer *et al.* (1999) view entrepreneurship as the examination of various creation endeavours.

All of these scholars have proposed domains to establish boundaries for entrepreneurship research, yet none have been fully accepted. The lack of agreement and ongoing conversation are evidence of the complexity of the entrepreneurship phenomenon as well as the youth of the field.

Perhaps, Baumol (1993) was correct when he implied (using the individual entrepreneur as opposed the process of entrepreneurship) that whatever boundaries are placed on the field, someone will claim them as too restrictive. Any attempt at rigid definition of the term *entrepreneur* will be avoided assiduously here, because whatever attributes are selected, they are sure to prove excessively restrictive, ruling out some feature, activity, or accomplishment of this inherently subtle and elusive character (Baumol, 1993).

However, entrepreneurship's documented importance to and impact on the global economy challenges researchers to continue seeking answers to important questions pertaining to the birth, growth, failure, renewal, and transformation of organizations. Because the resulting economic impact is wealth and job creation, organizational performance becomes a critical factor. Just as the individual can affect the firm, the firm can affect the economy. Because strategic management is most often concerned with decision and action that lead to improved firm performance, it is reasonable to suggest, as some scholars have, that the fields of entrepreneurship and strategic management have a sizeable intersection.

*****

7

# Emerging Areas of Entrepreneurship

- *Women Entrepreneurship*
- *Rural Entrepreneurship*
- *Social Entrepreneurship*
- *Sustainable Entrepreneurship*

This chapter is about the emerging areas of entrepreneurship and includes, women entrepreneurship, rural entrepreneurship, social entrepreneurship, and sustainable entrepreneurship.

## WOMEN ENTREPRENEURSHIP

The word 'Entrepreneur' does not discriminate between genders. Hence, all that is said and written about entrepreneur, entrepreneurship in preceding pages holds equally good for women entrepreneurs. Entrepreneur is a person who undertakes a business enterprise, for commercial purpose with both personal and financial risk.

Hence, in this definition the person can be 'he/she.' However, because of the economic restructuring and societal acceptance more and more women have started establishing enterprises. Being women for whom the social barriers are now breaking and acceptance coming, one should say that women entrepreneurship is in its nascent and transition period. Due to this fact, it has its own unique facets which need to be reckoned.

Women entrepreneurs may be defined as the women or a group of women who initiate, organize and operate a business enterprise. Women are expected to innovate, initiate or adopt an economic activity to be called 'women entrepreneurs'. The Government of India has defined woman entrepreneur as 'an enterprise owned and controlled by a woman having a maximum financial interest of 51 per cent of the capital and giving at least 51 per cent of the employment generated in the enterprise to women'. However, this definition has come in for severe criticism on the condition of employing more than 50 per cent women workers. The critics point out that this is discriminatory and any enterprise set up by women should qualify for the concessions offered to entrepreneurs.

## FUNCTIONS AND ROLE OF WOMEN ENTREPRENEURS

According to Frederick Harbison, like a male entrepreneur a woman entrepreneur has five functions:

(1) Explore the prospects of starting new enterprises.

(2) Undertaking of risks and handling of economic and non-economic uncertainties.

(3) Introduction of new innovations or imitation of successful ones in existence.

(4) Co-ordination, administration, and control.

(5) Supervision and providing leadership in all aspects of the business.

These functions are not always of equal importance. Risk taking and innovations are paramount for establishing or diversifying an enterprise. Co-ordination and supervision become increasingly important in improving the efficiency in the operation of the undertaking. Generally, it is found that the same lady performs all these functions. Modern writers have pointed out that women entrepreneurs are generally seen to undertake three types of industrial enterprise:

(1) Operate purely as a sub-contractor on raw materials provided by the customer.

(2) Manufacture items that are usually used by large-scale units.

(3) Manufacture of consumer products, which are directly sold in the market.

The first two types of enterprises are known as an ancillary industry. Women entrepreneurs, generally prefer the production of the goods which have a direct sale in the market, This is especially so in a country like India, where the women entrepreneurs in the small scale sector deal in the production of consumer durables and non-durables which are sold directly in the market.

## PROFILE OF A WOMEN ENTREPRENEUR

Who is this woman entrepreneur? What are her qualities?

The woman entrepreneur is the child of middle class parents, at least one of whom is independently employed. She has a close relationship with her father and after obtaining a graduate degree in some area of liberal arts gets married and has children. It is when the children are somewhat self-sufficient that she starts her first entrepreneurial venture in her late thirties or early forties. Her biggest problem is the lack of sufficient business training and this weakness is all the more glaring in the financial area.

The modern Indian woman especially in the cities is exposed to education and training. In fact, most cities-bred parents give the girl child education on par with their sons. This has helped the urban Indian woman to do all work which was once regarded as the prerogative of men.

Experience has shown that the jobs, which were hitherto the monopoly of men, women have excelled if not outshone the men in them. Over the years the educated women have become ambitious, acquired experience basic skills, competency, and self-assurance. Some of the outstanding qualities of women entrepreneurs are as follows:

(*a*) Accepts challenges.

(*b*) Ambitious.

(*c*) Adventurous.

(*d*) Conservative.

(*e*) Determined.

(*f*) Enthusiastic.

(*g*) Educated.

(*h*) Experienced.

(*i*) Full of drive.

(*j*) Hard-working.

(*k*) Industrious.

(*l*) Intelligent.

(*m*) Keen to learn and imbibe.

(*n*) Motivate.

(*o*) Optimistic.

(*p*) Patient.

(*q*) Perseverant.

(*r*) Skillful.

(*s*) Studious.

(*t*) Worldly wise.

## PROBLEMS OF WOMEN ENTREPRENEURS

The greatest deterrent to women entrepreneurs is that they are women. Male chauvinism is the order of the day. Therefore, women have a tendency to keep away from high flying economic activities which are regarded as the domain of men. Even the financial institutions are skeptical of their entrepreneurial abilities to risk their funds on them. Seemingly non-partisan even the bankers consider women loanees a higher risk than men loanees. They look for men behind the women applicants. They scare the women applicants with their greater and unwarranted inquisitiveness and put questions sometimes embarrassing and sometimes incomprehensible, often insisting on stiffer if not more unreasonable security considerations.

The social setting is still not conducive as the men folk are less understanding and less co-operative, if not antagonistic to such enterprises by women. Women in non-urban areas have to suffer still further. They have to face not only resistance from men but also of elderly women who are ingrained with this attitude of inequality. In rural India, joint families are still the order of the day. The overbearing presence of elders restrain even young men from venturing out, so one can imagine how much a young girl will have to put up with if she wishes to become economically independent.

The main problems faced by the women entrepreneurs can be summarized as follows:

**(1) Financial Constraints:** Like all small entrepreneurs, women entrepreneurs suffer from inadequate financial resources and working capital. They lack access to external funds due to their in ability to provide tangible security. Very few women have property in their names. However, male members think it a big risk financing the ventures run by women. Banks have also taken a negative attitude while providing finance for women entrepreneurs. They discourage women borrowers on the belief that they can at any time leave their business and become housewives again. The result is women entrepreneurs are forced to rely on their own savings and loans from family and friends. The quantum of such funds is often negligible leading to failure of enterprises.

**(2) Over-dependence or Intermediaries:** The enterprises run by women are characterized by inefficient arrangements for marketing and sale. The women entrepreneurs are most often dependent on intermediaries who eliminate the middlemen, but then it will necessitate a lot of running about which may be difficult for the women entrepreneurs. Further, women entrepreneurs find it difficult to capture the market and make their products popular.

**(3) Scarcity of Raw Materials:** Shortage of raw materials and other necessary inputs have sounded the death knell of many enterprise run by women. On the one hand, the prices of raw materials are very high and on the other hand they are able to get these raw materials at the minimum of discounts. A startling example is the failure of many women co-operatives in 1971, such as those engaged in basket-making. This was mainly due to the inadequate availability of forest-based raw materials.

**(4) Intense Competition:** Women entrepreneurs face stiff competition from organized industries and male entrepreneurs. Moreover, they do not have the organizational set-up to pump in a lot of money for advertisement. They also have the mortification of being questioned about the quality of their product since it has been produced by women. This is despite the fact that women entrepreneurs are more sincere in maintaining the quality and time schedule.

**(5) High cost of Production:** Like most productive enterprises high cost of production has restricted the development of women enterprises. Some states like Kerala have programmes to assist women entrepreneurs by providing them with the initial stage of setting up an enterprise. When it comes to expansion of productive capacity and installation of new machinery the help is negligible, dissuading many women entrepreneurs from venturing into new areas.

**(6) Low Mobility:** Women entrepreneurs are greatly handicapped by their inability to travel from one place to another, for business reasons. At the Government level, the licensing authorities, labour officers and sales tax officials make life miserable for women by often asking all sorts of humiliating questions. Many are the cases, where women have dropped out of business due to difficulties caused to them by the officialdom forcing them to run from pillar to post.

**(7) Family Ties:** In a country like India, family ties are very strong. Here looking after the children and other members of the family are looked upon as the duty of a woman. Married women entrepreneurs have to make a fine balance between business and home. Their success greatly depends on the support given by the family. One can see in India that behind the success of a female entrepreneur there is always the unstinted support of the family. Occupational background of families and education level of husbands have a direct bearing on the development of women entrepreneurship.

**(8) Social Attitudes:** This is regarded as the most important stumbling block in the path of women entrepreneurship. Despite constitutional equality, there is widespread discrimination against women. In a male dominated society, women do not get equal treatment. This is specially so in the rural areas of India. Rural women have the potential, but they lack adequate training. There is common belief that skill imparted to a girl is lost when she gets married. Therefore, girls continue to be helpers in agriculture and handicrafts and the rigid social attitude prevents them from becoming successful and independent entrepreneurs.

**(9) Adverse Effects of Risk Bearing:** Women in this country have led a protected life. This has reduced their ability to bear economic and other risk of business. Moreover, the impacts of losses are more severe on women since they lack sufficient social support. They live in a society where people wait to chastise the enterprising and the intensity will be greater in the case of women. Besides many women entrepreneurs lack the necessary initiative, suffer from inferiority complex and are easily disheartened by failure.

**(10) Lack of Education:** Surveys have found that literacy among women is very low in India. Due to the lack of education, many women are unaware of the latest technological developments and market trends. This creates further problems in setting up and running of business enterprises. Studies have revealed that uneducated women do not have the knowledge of measurement as well as basic accounting. They have their own system of accounting which may be sufficient for a petty business, but certainly not a business enterprise.

**(11) Low Need for Achievement:** The most important pre-requisites for success in entrepreneurship are, need for achievement, independence and autonomy. But in India, the common Indian woman is happy to bask in the glory of her parents, husband, children, etc. They have preconceived notions about their role in life and this inhibits achievement and independence. In the absence of the required urge to achieve, few women succeed as entrepreneurs.

## DEVELOPMENT OF WOMEN ENTREPRENEURS – CURRENT TRENDS

The modern chit fund organizations owe their beginning in the chits organized by army housewives in urban and semi-urban areas in the early 20th century. Their innate aptitude to match requirements with availability and instinct cultivated over decades of household management helped them cut costs and increase productivity. It is therefore true, that efforts are initiated to build on these few successes of women entrepreneurs and secure greater participating of women in economic development.

In this regard, the plan document has suggested the following:

(1) To treat women as specific target groups in all development programmes.

(2) To properly diversify vocational training facilities for women to suit their varied needs and skills.

(3) To encourage appropriate technologies, equipments and practice for reducing their drudgery and increasing their efficiency and productivity.

(4) To provide marketing assistance at the state level.

(5) To increase women's participation in decision-making.

The new Industrial Policy of the Government has stressed the need for conducting special entrepreneurship programmes for women with a view to develop women entrepreneurship. The policy has recommended that product and process-oriented courses may be conducted to enable women to start small-scale industries. The policy further adds that the objective of such courses should be to give representation to women in the field of small industry development with a view to uplift their status in the economic and social fields. The general consensus that is emerging in all discussions is that promotion of women entrepreneurs should form an integral part of all development efforts.

This is bound to offer a twin advantage:

(1) Economic growth

(2) Women's development.

Many are inclined to believe that the future of small-scale industry depends very much on the entry of women and their participation. Like men, lifestyle issues are a key factor, desire for more autonomy, control and flexibility to work around family schedules. An important trend that is being witnessed in the economy in recent times is where the major companies are paring down and re-engineering themselves for leaner times, the small business sector is witnessing unparalleled growth due to the proliferation of women entrepreneurs. The development of women entrepreneurship has created a situation in which the economy is being driven by smaller, more flexible and light footed units.

Promotion of women entrepreneurs requires a multi-pronged approach. Women should be motivated to come out of their traditional occupation for accepting more challenging and economic activities. Concurrently, an environment should be prepared to enable their participation. Principally this would necessitate motivating the funding agencies to be sympathetic towards aspirants to entrepreneurship. The other promotional and regulatory agencies should also be motivated to be considerate, understanding and helpful towards women entrepreneurs. In more explicit terms, banks and other financial institutions must provide credit to women entrepreneurs on both priority basis and concessional terms, the elaborate procedure of licensing and government sanction associated with the establishment of a new business enterprise should be dispensed with, in the case of application received from women entrepreneurs. An aid to such motivational efforts is the audio-visual media. Video cassettes of successful women entrepreneurs can go a long way in motivating new persons into this field.

The problems of women in the economic field have received the attention of international and national bodies in recent years. The United Nations declared the period 1975-85 as the 'Decade for Women'. The UNIDO preparatory meeting on the 'Role of Women in Industrialization in Developing Countries' held at Vienna, 1978, identified several constraints that stood in the way of the effective participation of women in the industrialization of developing countries. These included social, attitudinal and institutional barriers, insufficient employment opportunities, inadequate education and training and so on. Another landmark international conference on women was 'The World Conference of United Nations Decade for Women' held at Copenhagen, 1980. This conference adopted a programme aimed at promoting full and equal opportunities for women in employment, equal remuneration for work of equal value and promoting the access of women and girls to non-traditional skilled trades.

In India, several institutional arrangements have been made to protect and develop women entrepreneurship. The nationalized banks and State Financial Corporations advance loans to women entrepreneurs on preferential basis. State Industrial Development Corporations and District Industries Centers provide loans, subsidies, and grants to small-scale women entrepreneurs. State level agencies assist women entrepreneurs in preparing project reports, purchasing machinery, hiring of buildings and training the staff. Several voluntary agencies like FICCI Ladies Organization (FLO), National Alliance of Young Entrepreneurs (NAYE) and others assist women entrepreneurs. Case studies of successful women entrepreneurs have revealed that women possess a futuristic outlook and the capacity to nurture new enterprises. These case studies, relate to women who are not just self-employed, but have created jobs for others. The principal elements that these cases highlight are the struggle involved in the planning and execution of projects, the frustrations to which they are subjected to, the attitudinal and procedural problems they had to encounter and so on. They also give us an insight as to the steps these women entrepreneurs took to overcome the various obstacles inherent in the system and the road blocks they have to cross to succeed in their ventures to finally emerge as women entrepreneurs par excellence. These cases hopefully would have a multiplier effect on all those concerned and accelerate the growth of women entrepreneurs. There is no doubt that without the active participation of women entrepreneurs, industrial development in general and small-scale industry in particular would be in jeopardy.

## RURAL ENTREPRENEURSHIP.

As women forming about half of India's population make as case for developing women entrepreneurship in the country, so it is justified that developing rural entrepreneurship by about three-fourth of India's population is living in its vast rural areas. The rural urban dichotomy reveals wide disparities in various respects. The division of economic activities between rural and urban areas is one of them. Rural areas specialize more or less exclusively in agriculture, while industries are exclusively located in urban areas. Given the weak rural-urban or agriculture industry linkages, such a situation suffers from two serious shortcomings. *First,* as agriculture by itself has a tendency to develop at a slower pace than industry, the division of economic activities leads to uneven development. *Second,* since industry generally leads to higher level of output per worker than agriculture, the gap in income levels between those engaged in the two sectors tends to widen.

Further, the relationship between traditional agriculture and modern industry generally has a dependency structure which puts the rural sector at a greater disadvantage in appropriating the gains of development and, in turn, increases, the disparities between rural and urban income levels. As such, rural areas are ultimately marked by abject poverty and backwardness. In such situation, rural industrialization is viewed as an effective means of accelerating the process of rural development. Entrepreneurship precedes industrialization, hence, the need for understanding rural entrepreneurship.

Like entrepreneurship, rural entrepreneurship also conjures different meanings to different people. Without going into semantics, rural entrepreneurship can simply be defined as entrepreneurship emerging in rural areas is rural entrepreneurship. In other words, establishing industrial units in the rural areas refers to rural entrepreneurship. Or say, rural entrepreneurship implies rural industrialization. Let us know, for the sake of our knowledge, the meaning of rural industry. Rural industries are generally associated with agriculture. According to the Khadi and Village Industries Commission (KVIC), 'village industry or rural industry means any industry located in rural area, population of which does not exceed 10,000 or such other figure which produces any goods or renders any services with or without use of power and in which the fixed capital investment per head of an artisan or a worker does not exceed a thousand rupees'.

The definition of village industry has been modified by the government so as to enlarge its scope. Accordingly, any industry located in rural area, village or town with a population of 20,000 and below and an investment of ₹ 3 crores in plant and machinery is classified as a village industry. As a result of widening of the scope of village industries, 41 new village industries have been added making a total of 101 as against 70 industries earlier.

All the village industries have been grouped into seven major categories as follows:

*(i)* Mineral-based industry.

*(ii)* Forest-based industry.

*(iii)* Agro-based industry.

(iv) Polymer and chemical-based industry.

(v) Engineering and non-conventional industry.

(vi) Textile industry (including khadi)

(vii) Service industry.

Having understood the meaning of rural entrepreneurship and rural industry, let us move on to appreciate the need for and significance of entrepreneurship in India.

## NEED FOR RURAL ENTREPRENEURSHIP

The need for rural entrepreneurship for developing industries in the rural areas imbued with multiplicity of justifications as listed below:

1. Rural industries being labour intensive have high potential in employment generation. Thus, they serve as an antidote to the widespread problems of disguised unemployment or underemployment stalking the rural territory.
2. By providing employment, these industries have also high potential for income generation in the rural areas. These, thus, help in reducing disparities in income between rural and urban areas.
3. These industries encourage dispersal of economic activities in the rural areas and, thus, promote balanced regional development.
4. Development of industries in the rural areas also helps build village republics.
5. Rural industries also help protect and promote the art and creativity, *i.e.*, the age-old rich heritage of the country.
6. Rural industrialization fosters economic development in rural areas. This curbs rural-urban migration, on the one hand, and also lessens the disproportionate growth in the cities, reduces growth of slums, social tensions, and atmospheric pollution, on the other.
7. Last but not the least, rural industries being environment friendly lead to development without destruction.

## PROBLEMS OF RURAL ENTREPRENEURSHIP

Developing entrepreneurship especially rural entrepreneurship is important, but is not so easy. It is constrained with several problems. The general bottleneck in the development of village industries are financial constraints, lack of technical know-how, lack of training and extension services, management problems, lack of quality control, high cost of production due to high input cost, lack of communication and market information, poor quality of raw materials, lack of storage and warehousing facilities, obsolete and primitive technology, and lack of promotional strategy.

According to the Ninth Plan, the major problems faced in developing entrepreneurship in rural areas are:

1. Inadequate flow of credit.

2. Use of obsolete technology, machinery, and equipment.
3. Poor quality standards
4. Inadequate infrastructural facilities.

One of the major problems faced in developing entrepreneurship in rural areas is lack of awareness and knowledge about the importance of developing industries in rural areas. Added to this is disinterest shown by rural people towards assuming the career as an entrepreneur for one reason or the other. Rural/village people generally want to take up salaried employment because of assured income, lesser hours of work, lesser degree of responsibility etc. This is supported by the societies higher degree of status accorded to the salaried people than to self-employed ones, or say, entrepreneurs. Further, the rural people are generally not aware about the entrepreneurial opportunities available and also about support organizations and other information required to take the first step in their entrepreneurial career. Even those who are aware about the facilities and support system for starting entrepreneurial career find organizational climate to be not so helpful. Thus, the environment in the family, society and the support system is generally not conducive to encourage the rural people to consider self-employment and entrepreneurial career as an option to salaried employment. Besides, developing rural entrepreneurship has all those problems that are faced in the development of small-scale industries in the country.

## HOW TO DEVELOP RURAL ENTREPRENEURSHIP?

Establishing an industry and, thereby developing entrepreneurship is not one-man activity. In fact, it involves multi-pronged activities. Though the answer to the question how to develop entrepreneurship lies in the solutions of the problems faced in this regard, yet the following measures are yet suggested for developing entrepreneurship in the rural areas in the country.

1. Raw material is a must for any industry, however, the non-availability of raw materials accompanied by their prohibitive cost have weakened the viability of these industries. Past experience bears evidence that rural industries with employment potential cannot be sustained for long unless a strong raw material base is created in rural areas itself. Therefore, an urgent policy is called for to strengthen the raw material base in rural areas.

2. Finance is considered as a lubricant for setting up and running an industry, funds therefore, need to be made available on time at soft terms and conditions to those who really need it.

3. In order to solve the problem of marketing for rural industries, common production-cum-marketing centres need to be set up and developed with modern infrastructural facilities, particularly, in the areas having good production and growth potential. This would help in promoting export business, on the one hand, and bringing the buyers and sellers in close interaction avoiding middlemen in between them, on the other. Legislative measures have to be taken to make the government purchases compulsory from rural industries.

4. One peculiarity of rural entrepreneurs is that most of them chose entrepreneurial career not by choice but by chance. Lack of aptitude and competency on the part of such entrepreneurs

makes the units sick. Hence, there is a need to develop entrepreneurial attitude and competencies among the prospective entrepreneurs through the training interventions like Entrepreneurship Development Programmes (EDP), Women Entrepreneurship Development Programmes and TRYSEM.

5. One effective way to inculcate the entrepreneurial acumen and attitude may be imparting entrepreneurial education in the schools, colleges, and universities. That younger minds are more susceptive to be molded is well evidenced by the popularly known 'Kakinada Experiments' in Andhra Pradesh.

6. Sometimes the real problem in setting up industries is not the non-availability of facilities, but non-awareness of facilities whatever they are available. The need is, therefore, to disseminate information about all what is available to provide to the entrepreneurs to facilitate them in setting up industries.

7. Proper provisions need to be made to impart the institutional training to orient the entrepreneurs in specific products and trades so that the local resources can be harnessed properly.

8. Accumulated experience bears ample evidence to the fact that the non-governmental organizations, popularly known as NGOs, can prove instrumental in developing rural entrepreneurship in the country.

Rural industrialization provides the best solution to tackle with the twin problems of unemployment and poverty stalking the rural areas in the country. That is why the Government of India has been assigning increasing importance to the development of rural industrialization or entrepreneurship in her subsequent Five-Year Plans. However, the development of rural industrialization is plagued by some major problems like inadequate flow of credit; use of obsolete technology, machinery and equipment, and inadequate infrastructural facilities. Solving these problems is necessary for developing rural industries/ entrepreneurship. Of late, NGOs have proved as an effective agent in developing rural areas of the country.

## SOCIAL ENTREPRENEURSHIP

Social entrepreneurship is the art and science of bringing entrepreneurial zest to social sector with zeal. But the biggest task lies in rescuing social entrepreneurship from the dark corners of business, academia and bringing it to the spotlight of scholarly attention. Now that the social entrepreneurship is brought to the curricula of the best B-Schools, the concept has gathered sufficient momentum. 'The idea of social entrepreneurship has struck a responsive chord, it's a phrase well suited to our times. It combines the passion of a social mission with an image of business like discipline, innovation, and determination commonly associated with, for instance, the high-tech pioneers'. The intention is not to recreate the social sector in the image of business. Instead by focusing and dealing with it correctly and at appropriate level of education processes, one can hope that a systematic search can begin for better ways to serve the common good by breaking the boundaries between the social, private and public sectors, and of course, academia. The social sector has for long had powerful entrepreneurial leaders, but the opportunity to promote cross-sector learning is relatively new. Recent trends in the social sector have lead to blurring of distinctions between business, non-profit and government organizations.

As non-profits begin to adopt the language and tools of business — and some even begin to explore the option for profit operations — academics will act as stewards of change. Whether it's homeless shelters training their residents on how to earn a livelihood, or environment organizations working with corporates to develop sustainable programmes, or art groups using marketing to generate revenues, encouragement to all is a must. In the world of social entrepreneurship, everyone profits.

## GENESIS OF SOCIAL ENTREPRENEURSHIP

The term social entrepreneurship means the act of finding new, better, and more effective ways of serving social needs. The central idea is about innovation. Social entrepreneurship's roots are in the theory of entrepreneurship, which says that entrepreneurs, when they work well, shift resources to more productive uses.

There is a school of thought that defines entrepreneurship very simply as starting a business — and then defines social entrepreneurship as the starting a business for a social purpose, or starting a business that is owned by a non-profit organization and generates funding for a social purpose even though the business itself may not serve any direct social purpose. So the core idea is to bring entrepreneurial traits — like innovation — to bear on the social sector.

The way entrepreneurship is defined is that it is the pursuit of opportunity without regard to resources currently at hand. That pursuit of opportunity often involves finding innovative or new ways of doing things. Thus, it is a natural extension to think of social entrepreneurs as people who see an opportunity to improve society, and bring about change in the way things are done. They often do it without having all the resources they need in their hands. So, social entrepreneurs are also very skilled at mobilizing resources as well as being innovative.

While the idea of social entrepreneurship has been around for more than 20 years, the concept has only recently gained momentum. What has changed in the last few years is the increased acceptance of this concept in the decade of the 1990s, in most of the countries and places around the world, this seems to be correlated with a perception that there has been a triumph of capitalism over communism. Markets and businesses are being more openly embraced as an important part of the pathway to prosperity, and as an important part of solving any long-term social problem, and generating resources or wealth for society. This was crucial for opening the doors on this concept in a couple of different ways. On the non-profit side, people had been very frustrated and challenged about mobilizing the resources they needed to do their work. They felt the need for new approaches and many leaders in the non-profit sector were willing though cautiously, to experiment with business-like approaches. On the flipside, business schools and business leaders started to see an opportunity to bring some of their skills into the arena of social problems.

Today, the thinking is that, a convergence between government, private and social sectors is a good way of addressing social issues. But in the early days, it had been hard to convince people to cross boundaries in the Name of social entrepreneurship. In the early nineties, there wasn't real openness. But by 1994-95, social entrepreneurship was coming into limelight. The momentum was building. Since there was a sense of frustration with the methods and strategies used by non-profit organizations and the government at one point of time in the eighties, there was disillusionment. Many of the programmes that were thought to be major as a breakthrough for tackling issues like poverty, drug abuse, improving schools, or providing access to health-care, weren't working. Many major housing projects were disaster areas and were being torn down. And even a number of environmental groups recognized that they needed to find new tactics to create sustainable ways — economically and environmentally — to protect the environment. People started realizing that there was a need to cut across sector boundaries. Terms like social entrepreneurship signaled that: don't focus just on non-profit or for-profit or the government. The need was to look for innovative solutions that cut across sector boundaries. Old techniques and methods had missing elements of learning, that certain approaches don't create sustainable improvement. They don't tackle a problem in a systemic way. They simply put a Band-Aid on the issue or provide a temporary solution that doesn't lead to long-term outcomes. People began looking for more systemic and sustainable solutions to social problems because the methods that they thought would work and were smart, simply weren't working towards long-term social outcomes.

## CHARACTERISTICS OF A SOCIAL ENTREPRENEUR

- Intuitive mindset.
- Viewing self not as a helper or saviour.
- Encourages self-help.
- Teaching skills.
- Creativity.

Social entrepreneur is thus someone who teaches a needy person to fish, rather than giving him a fish. Social entrepreneurs need to switch to that kind of mindset. It does not mean there is not a need to provide charitable relief to people in desperate need. That needs to done too; otherwise they may starve before they ever learn how to fish. The difference now is that people are being creative. They are trying to move out of traditional models of sheltered workshops for disadvantaged folks to business that are really much more viable in the market-place, and which pay good wages. There is a push and moment in that direction. Social entrepreneurship has been around for a very long time in some non-profits. But social entrepreneurship is not just about teaching a man to fish — it's teaching him how to sell the fish after catching it. That part was difficult for many non-profits because it smacked of commercialization. One valuable aspect of the language of social entrepreneurship is that it breaks people out of traditional ways of thinking.

The AWAKE and SEWA movement in India is another example as it has opened the possibility of more social entrepreneurs getting into the business of running organizations especially by women or members of lower income group. AWAKE or SEWA member organizations are businesses in India supported and financed by the same per unit funds that traditional businesses receive. Unlike traditional organizations or businesses however, they are held accountable for achieving entrepreneurial results. In return, they receive waivers that exempt them from many restrictions and bureaucratic rules that shape traditional ways of starting and running the organizations and businesses. The AWAKE and SEWA movement brings together for the first time in social entrepreneurship four powerful ideas: choice among prospective entrepreneurs and entrepreneurial opportunities for improved achievement, as measured by standardized tests and other measures and carefully designed competition in various types or classes of propositions. Some of those organizations are being very innovative in the methods of conducting businesses or launching a product and the way they are implementing policies and the way they are managing the units. This reflects the changing environment and the role of government in an era of social entrepreneurship.

In this case, the government is allowing private providers to bring in innovative approaches as long as they meet the standards. Members can take different approaches to achieving them in ways that just were not happening much in earlier times. There are many examples of this kind of opportunity. Thus, the movement towards social entrepreneurship also implies that a non-profit approach does not quite cut it. Moreover, philanthropy needs to be 'profitable' in terms of goals achieved. In terms of goals achieved there is more sense if one looks for a social return on investment. The need is to start thinking about the way philanthropic money is invested. Instead of focusing on 'need' the focus will have to be on 'impact' results — results for the rupee. So if one is putting a million rupees into X programme and a million rupees into Y programme, they should be capable of evaluation based on the kind of results they yield.

Where should we do our work? 'In the areas of greatest need'. In many cases people did not have a good new theory for how they were going to intervene and have effective social impact and many programmes didn't have very good social impact. These people were just noble, they would sacrifice and work on very thin budgets and give up much higher salaries they could earn in business. They toiled with the poorest of the poor but didn't make a lasting difference. Moreover, aim of social entrepreneurship is to try to break that vicious cycle. Hence, encouraging people to tackle the most difficult neediest problems is not as important or vital as the need to have some viable plan for creating an impact and to make sure that it is the best way to use resources. However, there is the danger that people will go for low-hanging fruit. If people want to demonstrate results quickly they may go for the easy cases. So instead of providing job-training for the hardest-to-employ, for example, they may provide job-training to those who are just on the margin of needing help and show more results. Social entrepreneurs need to guard against this by constantly keeping this issue at the top of their minds.

What is needed in social entrepreneurship is a degree-of-difficulty measure — as in Olympic diving — so that people are rewarded for taking on challenges. The degree of difficulty should be taken into account when assessing results. A suburban school can't be measured by the same standards as a sanitation project working with a much more difficult population.

A weighted measure for success makes sense nationally, but it is tough to come up with measures of social return that everyone can agree on. There are different priorities and preferences — some find the environment the most important issue, some focus on family planning, others look at education and access to health-care. Getting all to agree on how to weigh things is extremely difficult. But the intuition behind the concept is right on target. In the for-profit enterprise, risk is taken into account and one looks at risk-adjusted returns instead of simply going for the highest expected returns. In social entrepreneurship too, a similar factor is needed.

Since there are no thumb rules on how social entrepreneurs should measure success, there are wide variations across different sub-sectors. Each one has to go through the process of figuring out an appropriate measure, given the mission of the organization and the kind of impact it hopes to achieve. Too many or too little measures would be unworkable and any social enterprise/entrepreneur will have to boil it down to bring focus to their guidelines. Generally, three categories of guidelines would be sufficient to evaluate any social enterprise. They should include:

Mission-related performance to measure direct impact capacity and activity measures to measure the capacity of the organization (are we building the ability to function in the future?)

- Activity measures (are we doing the things we claimed we will be doing?)
- Bottom line (is there right impact of the mission?).

Social entrepreneurship is not a vehicle for seeking management best practices into a sector that didn't have them but its seeking of some principles. There is a problem with best practices because what's best varies from condition to condition. But there exists some principles, from which the social sector can learn about in terms of how to approach situations and look for creative solutions. It's not enough to simply create social entrepreneurs and make them more broadly available so that other folks who can benefit from these programmes have access to them. The history of the non-profit sector illustrates that this is often a very slow and difficult process. Business can grow very rapidly; they've got concepts that seem to take off. Look at Reliance or Infosys — all these were developed in the 1980s and now are all over the world. If you look on the non-profit side you will find very few examples of that kind of scaling. There is also the fear that if we are not careful, we will spread ineffective programmes. The other point is that there is research which shows that while non-profits grow more slowly than business, they also shrink more slowly. This means that market forces in social entrepreneurship are much more imperfect and weak and this is a great issue: how can one find mechanisms that will serve as surrogates for market discipline so that organizations that should go out of business do go out of business. On the other hand, organizations, which are successful, and having impact actually get the resources and grow. Mechanisms need to be developed, that direct resources to those that are most effective. Right now that does not exist and it is imperfect. It's getting better, but the market discipline will never ever be quite as right as in business.

## SUSTAINABLE ENTREPRENEURSHIP

Sustainable entrepreneurship is a spin-off concept from sustainable development that can be defined as the continuing commitment by business to behave ethically and contribute to economic development while improving the quality of life of the workforce, their families, local communities, the society and the world at large as well as future generations. Sustainable entrepreneurship is an approach that is applied mostly by large, often industrial companies. In their wake, a whole range of sustainability certificates came about. Because of the proliferation of complex and costly procedures to obtain them, SMEs have almost unanimously ignored and repudiated the idea of sustainable entrepreneurship. Since the gains can be substantial in terms of risk control, business relationships with large companies and positive reputation, the question is raised whether SMEs can actually afford it to do business in a sustainable manner.

Currently, there is business hype in sustainable entrepreneurship. Every self-respecting company tries to brand itself as a sustainable entrepreneur. Business schools and employers' organizations devote whole conferences to the topic. Many terms are used like corporate social responsibility, ethical funds, and eco-efficiency and so on. Although these words reflect different concepts, they all point at various aspects of sustainable development. There is also a booming business in (expensive) sustainable entrepreneurship certificates. Yearly sustainability reports are published almost exclusively by big companies. This raises the question whether SMEs that constitute up to 90 per cent of all businesses, actually can afford to be sustainable entrepreneurs?

In 1987, the World Commission on Environment and Development of the United Nations (the often cited Brundtland Commission) first described and defined sustainable development as a process in which the exploitation of natural resources, the allocation of investments and the process of technological development and organizational change are in harmony with each other for both current and future generations. Sustainability is a concept that is oriented towards the long-term and future generations as much as the present. Therefore, sustainability is at conflict with our fast consuming society and short-term and short-sighted policies. Sustainability fits nicely in the altering view on the prime responsibilities of companies and organizations and their stakeholders that go beyond the classical view in which a company's sole aim was profit maximization in the interest of the shareholders.

Thus, sustainable entrepreneurship can be interpreted as a spin-off concept from sustainable development. Sustainable entrepreneurs are those companies that contribute to sustainable development by doing business in a sustainable way. As Kofi Annan pointed out (United Nations Global Compact Network): '... let's choose to unite the powers of markets with the authority of universal ideals. Let us choose to reconcile the creative force of private entrepreneurship with the needs of the disadvantaged and the requirements of the future generations ...'

Sustainable entrepreneurship can be defined as the continuing commitment by businesses to behave ethically and contribute to economic development while improving the quality of life of the workforce, their families, the local and global community as well as future generations

(World Business Council for Sustainable Development). From a sustainable entrepreneurship perspective, a company is a nexus of responsibilities towards the shareholders, but also towards nature, society and future generations. When the interests of these stakeholders are part of the decision-making process in a company, we can genuinely speak about a whole new type of a company with a new type of operational management. A company does not operate on a deserted island, but is embedded in an economic, social, cultural and ecological environment. This offers possibilities and poses threats and obligations.

And the theory and concepts of sustainable entrepreneurship try to find the right balance.

## ESSENCE OF SUSTAINABLE ENTREPRENEURSHIP

Following a well-known marketing principle, sustainable development is said to deal with the 3'P's, which stand for People, Planet, and Profit. All three aspects (including the last) have to be satisfied before an entrepreneurial activity can be labeled as sustainable. The first aspect 'people' is about the behaviour of companies in social and ethical issues. How does a company treat their employees (or human resources) and does it promote social cohesion? The issues that need to be adequately dealt with are the protection of human rights, the non-indulgence towards fraud and corruption, the use of child labour, the gender relationships and discrimination on the work floor, labour participation in management and profits, behavioural codes and so on. While many labour regulations were imposed in the beginning of the 20th century by labour and socialist movements as well as in the golden sixties, voluntary, self-imposed systems in this area are most recent, for example internal audits, quality audits, accreditations.

Secondly, sustainable entrepreneurship takes care of the natural environment. 'We did not inherit the earth from our ancestors, the earth is on loan from our children', says the Indian adage that clearly summarizes individual and corporate responsibility towards the natural environment. The second aspect 'planet' raises the question of the effect and remedy of the impact of a company on natural resources and the landscape. Environmental care, chain management, eco-efficiency, clean products, sustainable technology development, sustainable industry fields and eco-design are concrete examples of these issues. The consequence for business behaviour is that either environmental integrity becomes a business goal next to profit seeking or that environmental protection becomes a real constraint on profit maximization (the mathematical calculus in business optimization model leads in both instances to same outcome). The integration of environmental concerns into business practices is driven by both regulation (environmental legislation) and self-regulation (ISO 14000 and so on).

Finally, the third aspect 'profit' does not — as one might expect — relate solely to the purely financial results of an enterprise. Profit is also about the use and allocation of value added for employment, investments in machines and infrastructure and sponsoring and about the distribution (*e.g.* labour participation). The definition of sustainable entrepreneurship is not a static one since the world and the ideas that emerge are by nature dynamic. But, while the former two aspects of sustainable entrepreneurship (which relate to the material and immaterial contributions of dynamic corporate behaviour to nature and to global and local communities which shape our natural and social environment (Bos, 2002)) are subject to changing views on people and planet, the last aspect is the very essence of a business enterprise.

Janssen (2001) provided a list of ten ground rules for becoming a sustainable entrepreneur:

1. The corporation should start reducing the environmental damage, respecting human rights and treating its employees with great care.
2. Sustainable entrepreneurship has to be a self-initiated process and should not simply be a response to external pressure.
3. If a corporation wants to practice sustainable entrepreneurship, it should identify clear aims and targets.
4. The aims should be closely related to the corporation's practice and should match the corporate values and its primary activities.
5. The aims have to be closely related to the consumers' needs.
6. The corporation has to be capable of explaining the relationship between sustainability and its activities and production process.
7. The corporation should adhere to these aims on a long-term basis.
8. Consumers and pressure groups should have a transparent overview of investments made by the corporation related to sustainable entrepreneurship.
9. Sustainable entrepreneurship practiced by the corporation should not be shifted to the consumers via a price increase
10. A corporation should not attempt to overemphasize its efforts.

Bos (2002) added an additional rule to the list:

11. A corporation should make sure that its practices are shared by the corporation as a whole, and that they are not solely efforts of the management.

## SUSTAINABLE ENTREPRENEURSHIP AND SMES

Sustainable entrepreneurship is a business approach that seems almost exclusively reserved for large industrial companies. They certainly took the lead in this development after Shell decided in 1995 to dump the Brent Spar Oil Platform in the Atlantic Ocean. The pressure from Greenpeace and other environmental organizations as well as the heated protests by consumers and ecological activists alike forced the Shell Oil Company to reconsider and change its plan. Although initially unintended, it is fair to say that the decision about the final destination of the Brent Spar was made in consultation with Shell's stakeholders, in particular public opinion and environmental interest groups. The affair had some further consequences: it changed Shell's global style of doing business. Sustainable entrepreneurship became their business approach and, from previously irresponsible polluter, Shell is now clearly one of the (self-declared) market leaders in sustainability. The old policy of Shell, summarized as 'Decide Act Defend' was transformed into a business model 'Dialogue Decide Act' that determines the process of important decisions. Many (big) companies followed suit: Nike, Levis, Philips, Unilever, and so on. More large companies are engaging in sustainable entrepreneurship policies, more specifically the ones that focus on product- and chain-directed environmental care.

Sustainable entrepreneurship presupposes that companies are fully aware of the impact of their behaviour on the material and immaterial situation of their direct and indirect environment. It involves not only the scanning of opportunities and threats in the market, but also of the environment. The fact that sustainable entrepreneurship is up till now largely a large companies' playground is partially due to the more limited resources of SMEs. However, it is impossible for them to ignore this new economic reality.

## GAINS OF SUSTAINABLE ENTREPRENEURSHIP

Bos (2002) states there are two main reasons for corporate organizations to take into account the socio and eco-ethical aspects of their behaviour. The first consequence for not doing so is bad publicity. When a corporate enterprise is perceived by the general public as unethical, this will damage its corporate reputation, which, in turn, may result in a loss of income, profits and share value from a conscious consumers' boycott or unconscious bypass of its products. Secondly, Bos emphasizes that idealism drives more and more organizations to consider they to be more than solely profit-making ventures. If not led by idealism, however, corporate enterprises can still enhance their public reputation by showing respect for people and planet instead of only for profit.

A general gain of adapting sustainable entrepreneurship in SMEs is the internal dynamics that sustainable approaches introduce in the production process and human resource management. It is likely to lead to a more bold investment policy in both technology and personnel that will yield results in the long run. A direct and obvious gain accrues to those SMEs that supply their products to large companies which themselves are sustainable entrepreneurs and require from their supplier to be so as well in order to be in business. Such large companies may have a direct interest in product and chain directed environmental care as well as labour conditions. SMEs that do not anticipate these developments and requirements, seriously risk loosing business to small- and medium-sized competitors those do or did invest in sustainable production methods. Another argument for adopting sustainable entrepreneurship lies in the concentration trend of big, global companies. SMEs obviously cannot compete with these international players. SMEs should therefore focus on their surroundings, an essential part of the definition of sustainability. Being involved in the local community may prove a sustainability technique for SMEs those global companies will find hard to copy which, for that reason, turn to locally well embedded SMEs. The other benefits of sustainable entrepreneurship can be summarized as follows:

- A positive image and reputation.
- Lesser dependency on depleted resources.
- Higher motivation of employees and attractiveness for new employees.
- Efficient production due to superior technologies and better skilled staff.
- Superior insight in market preferences and opportunities.

- Risk control (environmental accidents, scandals, bad publicity, etc.).
- Lower burden from changes in (environmental and social) legislation.
- Corporate social responsibility.
- Internal business dynamics.
- Business partnerships with other sustainable entrepreneurs.
- Business partnerships with global players.

Sustainable entrepreneurship requires an ongoing dialogue between shareholders and stakeholders. Since a healthy financial basis remains essential, not only will shareholders have to live up to their social and environmental responsibility, but — especially in the case of SMEs — stakeholders have to understand that sound financial results are essential for the survival of the company. If not, there is no company, let alone a sustainable one. While there has been a large increase in the number of initiatives aimed at SMEs, the measures of support have not always been correctly tailored to the needs of SMEs. Support systems are often found to be too abstract and impractical, too general (insufficiently apt for specific industries), too passive, superficial or lacking in quality, too expensive, time-consuming or inflexible or poorly targeted or promoted.

Sustainable entrepreneurship can be defined as the continuing commitment by business to behave ethically and contribute to economic development while improving the quality of life of the workforce, their families, local communities, the society and the world at large as well as future generations. Though there are certain preconditions for the implementation of sustainable business practices by SMEs, it is important to understand that less financial resources is not necessarily a constraint. When SMEs choose to become sustainable entrepreneurs, what they need to do is that, they should be willing to devote time and effort, select a simple, pragmatic and effective setup that is tailored to their needs and compatible with their style. Furthermore, they should look at the return and the opportunity costs of a sustainability strategy rather than the financial costs.

*****

# PART II : ROLE OF GOVERNMENT

8. Introduction
9. Role of Central and State Government
10. Government Procedures for Starting a Venture
11. Forms of Organizations
12. Relevant Acts of Entrepreneurs
13. Government Policies — Small-Scale Industries
14. Role of Agencies in Enterpreneurship Development
15. Problems of Small-Scale Industries
16. Causes of Sickness in Small-Scale Industries

# 8

# Introduction

There is a growing recognition worldwide that Small and Medium Enterprises (SMEs), earlier known as small industry have an important role to play in the present context given their greater resource-use efficiency, capacity for employment generation, technological innovation, promoting inter-sectorial linkages, raising exports, and developing entrepreneurial skills. Their locational flexibility is an important advantage in reducing regional imbalances. The future of SMEs is of major policy concern given their strategic importance in any discussion of reshaping the industrial sector. This is more so in the case of India, which has one of the longest histories of government support to the small-scale industrial sector since independence compared to most developing countries.

In the Indian context, we have not so far defined medium enterprises clearly. What is neither small nor large is being loosely defined as medium. Further, enterprise encompasses businesses, services and industries. In the broadband of 'small', the discussion extends to medium as well. Another possible connotation for the SMEs is the small manufacturing enterprises.

Small and medium enterprises, both in size and shape, are not uniform across the globe. This asymmetry comes in the way of any effort of their integration. The way they are defined depends on the stage of economic development and the broad policy purposes for which the definition is used. According to a World Bank study, there are said to be more than 60 definitions of small and medium industries used in 75 countries surveyed (cited in Kim Seung Jin and Suh Jang-Won, 1992, 9). The most commonly used definitions relate to either size of employment and/or quantum of capital investment/fixed assets. As the process of economic development leads to changes in industrial sector shares in GDP and the contribution of sub-sectors within industry, the definition is extended to include not only manufacturing industries but all enterprises which fall within or below the defined cut-off point. In the ASEAN countries in general, the definition is restricted to SMIs in the manufacturing sector only, whereas in the OECD group, the definition is broadened to include all Small and Medium Enterprises.

In India, Small-Scale Industries (SSIs) were given due importance in the process of industrialization as far back as 1951 when post-independence economic planning was initiated. The Industries Development and Regulation Act legislated by the Centre in that year, became the framework for the small-scale industrial sector's development. The Act determined licensing policies for the sector and the reservation of products, among several other important provisions. The definition of small-scale industries is mainly in terms of investment ceilings which have changed over the years to keep pace with economic development. Though employment and turnover are also used to define small industries, these indicators being implicit in the requirement for registration under the Factories Act, the core definition of SSIs in India remains based on investment limits of 'historical costs of plant and machinery'. Therefore, the contribution of SME sector to the GDP in different countries is not on comparable parameters. Still, in both developed and developing economies, they were accorded special status, specific dispensations and particular attention. Although the broad canvas of 'enterprise' suggests that we look at the contribution of both industry and trade, more particularly exports, in the growth of GDP, lack of separate data on SME's contribution in the developed economies like the US, Canada, Japan, and Germany restricted the scope of this paper to having a look at some policy interventions in ASEAN and OECD economies.

## THE SMALL-SCALE INDUSTRIES (SSI) SECTOR IN INDIA

The promotion of the small-scale sector in India has been an important thrust of industrial policy since independence though the focus of concern changed with the priorities of each five - year plan. The six Industrial Policy Resolutions which have been framed since 1948 have set out the guidelines for the country's industrial development with different degrees of emphasis on the main objectives. The Industries Development and Regulation Act of 1951, as mentioned earlier, provided the basic framework for the post-independence industrialization strategy. Since the model for industrialization in the 1950s was based on capital-intensive heavy industries, the priority of employment generation required the development of widely dispersed, mass consumption-good producing, labour-intensive, small-scale industries. As the process of economic development led to changing priorities, the policy focus shifted to Regional Imbalances (1977), Ancillarization (1980), Exports and Dispersal in Rural Areas (1990), and then to Small, Tiny and Village Industries (1991).

The organizational structure for SSIs was set up in the 1950s with the establishment of a Small Scale Industries Board in 1954. Other important institutions at the national level were the Department of Small-Scale Industries and Agricultural and Rural Industries and the Small Industries Development Organization (SIDO) which was under the Development Commissioner, Small-Scale Industries. At the State level, the Commissioner/Directorate of Industries were the main institutional authority for SSIs. This structure has remained, though several other institutions have come into being in the 1970s and 1980s, particularly at the State level.

During the last 40 years, several Committees have been constituted by the Government of India to examine the functioning of SSIs with a view to promoting their growth and efficiency within the context of the main objectives of the national economic plans. The Karve Committee Report (1955) was one of the earliest of these exercises which recommended a protective environment for the growth of small industries in India. Since then, policies targeted for the SSI sector have aimed at fostering its growth through positive policy interventions in the areas of finance, technology, infrastructure and extension services, among several other requirements of the sector. Supportive policies through the 1960s, 70s, and 80s took the form of reservation of products exclusively for the SSI sector (836 products are reserved exclusively for SSIs at present) grant of fiscal concessions and government procurement of supplies from the sector. At present 836 products are reserved exclusively for SSIs. For increased credit flow to the SSI sector, a policy of priority sector lending through nationalised banks has been followed, though this has not been adequate for the growth requirements of the sector.

Since the 1980s and, more particularly, in the 1990s, there have been marked changes in the policy climate across the globe towards free markets and reduced government intervention. The global economy is characterised by greater integration, a more liberalized international trade regime following the set up of the World Trade Organization (WTO), a rapid pace of technological change, especially in some high-growth areas such as information and knowledge-based industries, and intensified international competition. India's economic policies are in the process of being restructured, through the second generation reforms, to adjust to the emerging challenges. The main emphasis of future policy will be to promote the growth of this dynamic sector through focussed, sustained and wide-ranging interventions, as the SSI sector has so far been insulated to a large extent from pressures of competition both domestically and internationally.

What are the problems and prospects for the development of the SSI sector over the medium-term? Before turning to the issues involved, the economic profile of the SSI sector is useful as an indicator of the success or failure of past policies.

The SSI sector is non-homogenous in structure and includes diverse types of production units ranging from traditional crafts to high-tech industries. The total number of SSI working units in the country is estimated to be around 3 million. In terms of ownership, the vast majority of SSI units are proprietary concerns (80.5 per cent) with only 16.8 per cent functioning as partnerships and private limited companies. The first census of SSIs in the country was undertaken in 1972 and the second in 1987-88. Tamil Nadu occupied the first rank in both years in terms of number of units and employment, followed by Maharashtra. Andhra Pradesh was placed at No. 6 and 7 respectively. By 1993, Punjab emerged at the top. (AIMA, 1997) One important factor to be noted in the statistics on small industries is the mortality rate. While the industries may get registered at the entry point, there is no record of their exit. There are at least 3 lakh units declared as sick and out of production, accounting for 10 per cent of the recorded units.

The potential of SSIs to generate employment has remained the strongest argument in their favour. The sector now employs 17 million persons and is the second largest employer of

India's workforce after agriculture. The role of SSIs in the economy can be seen from the fact that it now accounts for 95 per cent of all industrial units in the country and 40 per cent of total output. About 7,500 products are manufactured in the small-scale sector. The export share is 35 per cent. The composition of exports shows the largest shares of SSIs are in the industry groups: hosiery and garments (29.0 per cent), food products (21.4 per cent) and, leather products (18 per cent). The industry groups which have recorded high growth rates and a large share in total production of SSIs are: textile products, wood, furniture, paper and printing, and metal products, etc.

The future policy focus for SSIs will be on the development of industrial clusters which have been found in several studies to be efficient in terms of resource use and in promoting inter-industry and inter-sectorial linkages. A cluster is defined as a geographically bound concentration of similar, related or complementary businesses. A UNIDO study defines clusters as 100 registered small-scale units (MukeshGulati, 1998). There are estimated to be 350 SME clusters in India which contribute directly and indirectly to 60 per cent of India's exports. However, the spatial concentration in clusters wills earns a slower dispersion of industrial activity to backward areas. The location-wise distribution of clusters shows 65 per cent concentrated in cities and metros and only 13 per cent in small towns and rural areas. There is scope for encouraging the development of clusters in rural areas and rural-based artisan centres.

## IMPACT OF WTO

The emerging challenges to the small-scale sector are to come from the impact of the Agreements under WTO to which India is a signatory along with 134 member countries. The setting up of the WTO in 1995 has altered the framework of international trade towards non-distortive, market-oriented policies. This is in keeping with the policy shift that occurred worldwide since the early 1980s in favour of free market forces and a tilt away from State regulation/intervention in economic activity. This is expected to lead to an expansion in the volume of international trade and changes in the pattern of commodity flows. The main outcomes of WTO-stipulated requirements will be brought about through reduction in export subsidies, greater market access, removal of non-tariff barriers and reduction in tariffs.

There will also be tighter patent laws through regulation of intellectual property rights under the TRIPS Agreement which lays down what is to be patented (both products and processes), for what duration (20 years instead of the present 7 years under India's 1970 Patent Law), and on what terms.

The responses by trading countries and the reframing of domestic economic policies which will result from the impact of WTO and the repercussions on the global economy of all these changes are highly uncertain as they involve several unforeseeable factors. However, there are certain indications of the shape of future trade patterns.

Increased market access to imports (of around 3 per cent of domestic production to be raised to 5 per cent) will mean opening up the domestic market to large flows of imports. The removal of Quantitative Restrictions (QRs) on imports has been speeded up to 2001. At present

714 items are in the restricted category but imports of these items will soon be freed from all restrictions as announced in the recent EXIM policy.

Increased market access under WTO requirements will also mean that our industries can compete for export markets in both developed and developing countries. But the expected surge in our exports can come about only if the SSI sector is restructured to meet the demands of global competitiveness which is the key to the future of small industries in the present context.

*****

# 9

# Role of Central and State Government

- *Role of Central and State Government in Promoting Entrepreneurship*
- *Various Incentives, Subsidies, and Grants*
- *Export Oriented Units*
- *Fiscal and Tax Concessions Available*
- *Other Measures to Induce Investment Growth*

## ROLE OF GOVERNMENT IN PROMOTING ENTREPRENEURSHIP

Pandit Jawaharlal Nehru laid the foundation of modern India. His vision and determination have left a lasting impression on every facet of national endeavour since Independence. It is due to his initiative, that India now has a strong and diversified industrial base and is a major industrial nation of the world. The goals and objectives set up for the nation by Pandit Nehru on the eve of Independence,namely, the rapid agricultural and industrial development of our country, rapid expansion of opportunities for gainful employment, progressive reduction of social and economic disparities, removal of poverty and attainment of self-reliance remain as valid today as at the time Pandit Nehru first set them out before the nation. Any industrial policy must contribute to the realization of these goals and objectives at an accelerated pace. The present statement of industrial policy is inspired by these very concerns,and represents a renewed initiative towards consolidating the gains of national reconstruction at this crucial stage.

In 1948, immediately after Independence, Government introduced the Industrial Policy Resolution. This outlined the approach to industrial growth and development. It emphasized the importance to the economy of securing a continuous increase in production and ensuring its equitable distribution. After the adoption of the Constitution and the socio-economic goals, the Industrial.

Policy was comprehensively revised and adopted in 1956. To meet new challenges, from time, it was modified through statements in 1973, 1977, and 1980.

The Industrial Policy Resolution of 1948 was followed by the Industrial Policy Resolution of 1956 which had as its objective the acceleration of the rate of economic growth and the speeding up of industrialization as a means of achieving a socialist pattern of society. In 1956, capital was scarce and the base of entrepreneurship was not strong enough. Hence, the 1956 Industrial Policy Resolution gave primacy to the role of the State to assume a predominant and direct responsibility for industrial development.

The Industrial Policy Statement of 1973, *inter alia*, identified high priority industries where investment from large industrial houses and foreign companies would be permitted.

The Industrial Policy Statement of 1977 laid emphasis on decentralization and on the role of small-scale, tiny and cottage industries.

The Industrial Policy Statement of 1980 focused attention on the need for promoting competition in the domestic market, technological up gradation and modernization. The policy laid the foundation for an increasingly competitive export base and for encouraging foreign investment in high technology areas. This found expression in the Sixth Five-Year Plan which bore the distinct stamp of Smt. Indira Gandhi. It was Mrs. Indira Gandhi who emphasized the need for productivity to be the central concern in all economic and production activities.

These policies created a climate for rapid industrial growth in the country. Thus, on the eve of the Seventh Five-Year Plan, a broad-based infrastructure had been built up. Basic industries had been established. A high degree of self-reliance in a large number of items — raw materials, intermediates, and finished goods had been achieved. New growth centers of industrial activity had emerged, as had a new generation of entrepreneurs. A large number of engineers, technicians and skilled workers had also been trained.

The Seventh Plan recognized the need to consolidate on these strengths and to take initiatives to prepare Indian industry to respond effectively to the emerging challenges. A number of policy and procedural changes were introduced in 1985 and 1986 under the leadership of Mr. Rajiv Gandhi aimed at increasing productivity, reducing costs and improving quality. The accent was on opening the domestic market to increased competition and readying our industry to stand on its own in the face of international competition. The public sector was freed from a number of constraints and given a larger measure of autonomy. The technological and managerial modernization of industry was pursued as the key instrument for increasing productivity and improving our competitiveness in the world. The net result of all these changes was that Indian industry grew by an impressive average annual growth rate of 8.5 per cent in the Seventh Plan Period.

Government is pledged to launching a reinvigorated struggle for social and economic justice,to end poverty and unemployment and to build a modern, democratic, socialist, prosperous, and forward-looking India. Such a society can be built if India grows as part of the world economy and not in isolation. While Government will continue to follow the policy of self-reliance, there would be greater emphasis placed on building up our ability to pay for imports through our own foreign exchange earnings. Government is also committed to development and utilization of indigenous capabilities in technology and manufacturing, as well as its upgradation to world standards.

Government will continue to pursue a sound policy framework encompassing encouragement of entrepreneurship, development of indigenous technology through investment in research and development, bringing in new technology, dismantling of the regulatory system, development of the capital markets and increasing competitiveness for the benefit of the common man. The spread of industrialization to backward areas of the country will be actively promoted through appropriate incentives, institutions, and infrastructure investments.

Government will provide enhanced support to the small-scale sector so that it flourishes in an environment of economic efficiency and continuous technological upgradation.Foreign investment and technology collaboration will be welcomed to obtain higher technology,to increase exports and to expand the production base.

Government will endeavour to abolish the monopoly of any sector or any individual enterprise in any field of manufacture, except on strategic or military considerations and open all manufacturing activities to competition.

The Government will ensure that the public sector plays its rightful role in the evolving socio-economic scenario of the country. Government will ensure that the public sector is run on businesslines as envisaged in the Industrial Policy Resolution of 1956 and would continue to innovate and lead in strategic areas of national importance. In the 1950s and 1960s the principal instrument for controlling the commanding heights of the economy was investment in the capital of key industries.

Today, the State has other instruments of intervention, particularly fiscal and monetary instruments. The State also commands the bulk of the nation's savings. Banks and financial institutions are under State Control. Where State intervention is necessary, these instruments will prove more effective and decisive. Government will fully protect the interests of labour, enhance their welfare and equip them in all respects to deal with the inevitability of technological change. Government believes that no small section of society can corner the gains of growth, leaving workers to bear its pains. Labour will be made an equal partner in progress and prosperity. Workers' participation in management will be promoted. Workers' co-operatives will be encouraged to participate in packages designed to turnaround sick companies. Intensive training, skill development and upgradation programmes will be launched. Government will continue to visualize new horizons. The major objectives of the new industrial policy package will be to build in the gains already made, correct the distortions or weaknesses that may have crept in, maintain a sustained growth in productivity and gainful employment and attain international competitiveness. The pursuit of these objectives will be tempered by the need topreserve the environment and ensure the efficient use of available resources. All sectors of industry whether small, medium or large, belonging to the public, private or co-operative sector will been couraged to grow and improve on their past performance. Government's policy will be continuity with change.

In pursuit of the above objectives, Government has decided to take a series of initiatives inrespect of the policies relating to the following areas:

*(A)* Industrial Licensing.

*(B)* Foreign Investment.

*(C)* Foreign Technology Agreements.

*(D)* Public Sector Policy.

*(E)* MRTP Act.

**(1) Industrial Licensing Policy:** Industrial Licensing is governed by the Industries (Development and Regulation) Act, 1951. The Industrial Policy Resolution of 1956 identified the following three categories of industries: those that would be reserved for development in the public sector, those that would be permitted for development through private enterprise with or without State participation, and those in which investment initiatives would ordinarily emanate from private entrepreneurs. Over the years, keeping in view the changing industrial scene in the country, the policy has undergone modifications. Industrial licensing policy and procedures have also been liberalized from time-to-time. A full realization of the industrial potential of the country calls for a continuation of this process of change.

In order to achieve the objectives of the strategy for the industrial sector and beyond it is necessary to make a number of changes in the system of industrial approvals. Major policy initiates and procedural reforms are called for in order to actively encourage and assist Indian entrepreneurs to exploit and meet the emerging domestic and global opportunities and challenges. The bedrock of any such package of measures must be to let the entrepreneur's make investment decisions onthe basis of their own commercial judgment. The attainment of technological dynamism and international competitiveness requires that enterprises must be enabled to swiftly respond to fastchanging external conditions that have become characteristic of today's industrial world. Government policy and procedures must be geared to assisting entrepreneurs in their efforts. This can be done only if the role played by the Government were to be changed from that of only exercising control to one of providing help and guidance by making essential procedures fully transparent and by eliminating delays.

The winds of change have been with us for some time. The industrial licensing system has been gradually moving away from the concept of capacity licensing. The system of reservations for public sector undertakings has been evolving towards an ethos of greater flexibility and private sector enterprise has been gradually allowed to enter into many of these areas on a case by case basis. Further, impetus must be provided to these changes which alone can push this country towards the attainment of its entrepreneurial and industrial potential. This calls for bold and imaginative decisions designed to remove restraints on capacity creation, while at the same time,ensuring that over-riding national interests are not jeopardized.

In the above context, industrial licensing will henceforth be abolished for all industries, except those specified, irrespective of levels of investment. These specified industries (Annexure — II), will continue to be subject to compulsory licensing for reasons related to security and strategic concerns, social reasons, problems related to safety and over-riding environmental issues, manufacture of products of hazardous nature and articles of elitist consumption. The exemption from licensing will be particularly helpful to the many dynamic small and medium entrepreneurs who have been unnecessarily hampered by the licensing system. As a whole, the Indian economy will benefit by becoming more competitive, more efficient and modern and will take its rightful place in the world of industrial progress.

**(2) Foreign Investment:** While freeing Indian industry from official controls, opportunities for promoting foreign investment in India should also be fully exploited. In view of the significant development of India's industrial economy in the last 40 years, the general resilience, size and level of sophistication achieved, and the significant changes that have also taken place in the world industrial economy, the relationship between domestic and foreign industry needs to be much more dynamic than it has been in terms of both technology and investment. Foreign investment would bring attendant advantages of technology transfer, marketing expertise, introduction of modern managerial techniques and new possibilities for promotion of exports. This is particularly necessary in the changing global scenario of industrial and economic co-operation marked by mobility of capital. The Government will, therefore, welcome foreign investment which is in the interest of the country's industrial development.

In order to invite foreign investment in high priority industries, requiring large investments and advanced technology, it has been decided to provide approval for direct foreign investment upto 51 per cent foreign equity in such industries. There shall be no bottlenecks of any kind in this process.

This group of industries has generally been known as the 'Appendix — I Industries' and is the areas in which FERA companies have already been allowed to invest on a discretionary basis. This change will go a long way in making Indian policy on foreign investment transparent. Such framework willmake it attractive for companies abroad to invest in India.

Promotion of exports of Indian products calls for a systematic exploration of world markets possible only through intensive and highly professional marketing activities. Expertise of this nature is not well developed so far in India. Government will encourage foreign trading companies to assist us in our export activities. Attraction of substantial investment and access to high technology often closely held, and to world markets, involves interaction with some of the world's largest international manufacturing and marketing firms. The Government will appoint a special board to negotiate with such firms so that we can engage in for purposive negotiation with such large firms, and provide the avenues for large investments in the development of industries and technology in the national interest.

**(3) Foreign Technology Agreements:** There is a great need for promoting an industrial environment where the acquisition of technological capability receives priority. In the fast changing world of technology the relationship between the suppliers and users of technology must be a continuous one. Such a relationship becomes difficult to achieve when the approval process includes unnecessary governmental interference on a case to case basis involving endemic delays and fostering uncertainty. The Indian entrepreneur has now come of age, so that he no longer needs such bureaucratic clearance of his commercial technology relationships with foreign technology suppliers. Indian industry can scarcely be competitive with the rest of the world if it is to operate within such a regulatory environment.

With a view to injecting the desired level of technological dynamism in Indian industry, Government will provide automatic approval for technology agreements related to high priority industries within specified parameters. Similar facilities will be available for other industries as well, if such agreements do not require the expenditure of free foreign exchange. Indian companies will be free to negotiate the terms of technology transfer with their foreign counter parts according to their own commercial judgment. The predictability and independence of action that this measure is providing to Indian industry will induce them to develop indigenous competence for the efficient absorption of foreign technology. Greater competitive pressure will also induce our industry to invest much more in research and development then they have been doing in the past. In order to help this process, the hiring of foreign technicians and foreign testing of indigenously developed technologies, will also not require prior clearance as prescribed so far, individually or as part of industrial or investment approvals.

**(4) Monopolies and Restrictive Trade Practices Act (MRTP Act):** The principal objectives sought to be achieved through the MRTP Act are as follows:

1. Prevention of concentration of economic power to the common detriment, and control of monopolies.
2. Prohibition of monopolies and restrictive and unfair trade practices.

The MRTP Act became effective in June 1970. With the emphasis placed on productivity in the Sixth Plan, major amendments to the MRTP Act were carried out in 1982 and 1984 in order to remove impediments to industrial growth and expansion. This process of change was given a new momentum in 1985 by an increase of the threshold limit of assets.With the growing complexity of industrial structure and the need for achieving economies of scale for ensuring higher productivity and competitive advantage in the international market, the interference of the Government through the MRTP Act in investment decision of large companies has become deleterious in its effects on Indian industrial growth. The pre-entry scrutiny of investment decisions by so called MRTP companies will no longer be required. Instead, emphasis will be on controlling and regulating monopolistic, restrictive and unfair trade practices rather than making the expansion, establishment of new undertakings, merger, amalgamation and takeover and appointment of certain directors. The thrust of policy will be more on controlling unfair or restrictive business practices. The MRTP Act will be restructured by eliminating the legal requirement for prior governmental approval for expansions relating to merger, amalgamation, and takeover will also be repealed, the provisions regarding restrictions on acquisition of and transfer of shares will be appropriately incorporated in the Companies Act. Simultaneously, provisions of the MRTP Act will be strengthened in order to enable the MRTP Commission to take appropriate action in respect of the monopolistic, restrictive and unfair tradepractices. The newly empowered MRTP Commission will be encouraged to require investigation *suomoto* or on complaints received from individual consumers or classes of consumers.

**(5) Decisions of Government:** In view of the consideration outlined above Government has decided to take a series of measures to unshackle the Indian industrial economy from the cobwebs of unnecessary bureaucratic control. These measures complement the other series of measures being taken by Government in the areas of trade policy, exchange rate management, fiscal policy, financial sector reform and overall macroeconomic management.

*(A) Industrial Licensing Policy*

*(i)* Industrial Licensing will be abolished for all projects except for a short list of industries related to security and strategic concerns, social reasons, hazardous chemicals and over-riding environmental reasons, and items of elitist consumption (list attached as Annexure II). Industries reserved for the small-scale sector will continue to be so reserved.

*(ii)* Areas where security and strategic concerns predominate will continue to be reserved for the public sector. (List attached as Annexure I.)

*(iii)* In projects where imported capital goods are required, automatic clearance will be given, in case where foreign exchange availability is ensured through foreign equity.In other cases, imports of capital goods will require clearance from the Secretariat of Industrial Approvals (SIA) in the Department of Industrial Development according to availability of foreign exchange resources.

*(iv)* In locations other than cities of more than 1 million populations, there will be no requirement of obtaining industrial license from the Central Government except for industries subject to compulsory licensing. In respect of cities with population greater than 1 million,industries other than those of a non-polluting nature such as electronics, computer software and printing will be located outside 25 kilometers of the periphery, except in prior designated industrial areas.A flexible location policy would be adopted in respect of such cities (with population greater than 1 million) which require industrial re-generation. Zoning and Land Use Regulation and Environmental legislation will continue to regulate industrial locations. Appropriate incentives and the design of investments in infrastructure development will be used to promote the dispersal of industry particularly to rural and backward areas and to reduce congestion in cities.

*(v)* The system of phased manufacturing programmes run on an administrative case by case basis will not be applicable to new projects. Existing projects with such programmes will continue to be governed by them.

*(vi)* Existing units will be provided a new broadbanding facility to enable them to produce any article without additional investment.

*(vii)* The exemption from licensing will apply to all substantial expansions of existing units.

*(viii)* The mandatory convertibility clause will no longer be applicable for term loans from the financial institutions for new projects and substantial expansions.

## PROCEDURAL CONSEQUENCES

All existing registration schemes (De-licensed Registration, Exempted Industries Registration, DGTD Registration) will be abolished. Entrepreneurs will henceforth only be required to file an information memorandum on newprojects and substantial expansions.

The lists at Annexures II and III will be notified in the Indian Trade Classification (Harmonized System).

## VARIOUS INCENTIVES, SUBSIDIES AND GRANTS

India has embraced economic reforms partly through well-defined strategies and partly through the forced readjustments required in a rapidly globalizing world. India's economic reform process is often described as a top down approach going from broad economic reforms in the macro sectors towards the individual sectors. This is in stark contrast to the economic reforms in transition economics such as China where the now famous household responsibility systems began with agricultural sector. In that process, agriculture sector has been treated variously over the years and the budget allocations depending on how different sub-sectors within agriculture needed reforms.

While the Indian approach to reforms and liberalization aims at robust economic growth that would eventually trickle down to several aspects of economic reforms, it is imminent to ask several questions about how such reforms have affected the structure, conduct and performance of Indian agriculture, industry and external sectors.

**Section I:** The significance of the participation of grants in aid in creating productive capacity in any counting are:

*(i)* Foreign grants and aid has helped to raise the level of investment.

*(ii)* Grants and aids used to stabilized food prices and import raw materials.

*(iii)* Aid used for the enlargement of irrigation and power potential.

*(iv)* Aid used to enlarge technical resources internal assistance also has helped to enlarge technical resources through the provision of expert services, training of Indian personal and helping the establishment of new or the development of existing educational research training.

**Section II:** Subsidies are necessary in the Indian Economy for three reasons: they are mitigate the effects of extreme inequalities of income and wealth of the country of TSC employment andprotecting infant industrial country. The National Institute of Public Finance and Policy (NIPFP) classifiedsubsidies into two types:

1. Subsidies on merit goods/services.
2. Subsidies on non-merit goods/services.

The estimation of subsidies is based on a standard classification relating to subsidies into three categories.

*(i)* public goods, *(ii)* merit goods, and *(iii)* non-merit goods.

**Public goods:** Examples: Police, National defense, general administration characterized by Non-rivalry.

**Merit goods:** Environmental protection and minimum level of education-provide-externality, beneficial to the society as a whole, road, bridges, flood control and research, pertaining to age, space, atomic energy, etc.

**Non-merit goods:** Accrues to the individual consumers the cost of providing the goods/ services to society is higher than the price fixed for providing it to the consumer:

*(i)* Cash subsidies.

*(ii)* Interest or credit subsidies (*i.e.*, small-scale industries).

*(iii)* Tax subsidies: exemption of medical expenses, postponing collection of tax arrears.

*(iv)* In kind subsidies — free medical services through government dispensaries, provision of equipment to physically handicapped persons.

*(v)* Procurement subsidies — purchase of food grains at an assured price which is higher than the prevailing market price.

*(vi)* Regulatory subsidies — fixation of prices of goods produced by the public sector, at less than the cost with a view to providing inputs to industry or helping consumers.

*Examples:* making steel, coal, providing electricity to farmers at a rate much lower than the cost and cooking gas.

## SUBSIDIES IN INDIA

Non-merit subsidies were 10.71 per cent of GDP and merit goods subsidies were 3.69 per cent of GDP. Subsidies on all services were 14.40 per cent of GDP. Subsidies can be made to break up into social services and economic services. Economic services accounts nearly 93 per cent of total subsidies provided by the center of social services merely amount 7 per cent. The major beneficiaries of the center subsidies are industries (10,874 crores) agriculture (8,214 crores), and power (3,929 crores).

At the State level — social services account for about 39 per cent and EOC services 61 per cent, since education, health, water supply and sanitation are primarily the responsibility of the states, the level of subsidies is much higher in social sector.

**Food subsidy:** Food subsidy in India comprises of three components: *(i)* subsidies to farmers through prices, *(ii)* subsidies to consumers through public distribution system, and *(iii)* subsidies to the Food Corporation of India (FCI) in its purchase and maintenance of buffer stocks.

**Fertilizer subsidy:** It is also provided by the Government. And it is difference between the retention price of fertilizers and the price at which fertilizers are made available to consumers. The difference is paid to industry as subsidy.

**Petroleum subsidy:** Two major components of petroleum subsidies are: *(a)* subsidy for kerosene for domestic use and *(b)* LPG subsidy due to the difference between international price and the priceat which it is supplied to consumers.

**Section III:** A developing country such as India generally finds it difficult to expand its exports, at the same time; it does not like to reduce its imports as foreign assistance comes in three forms*(a)* loans, *(b)* grants and *(c)* PL 480/665 assistance. In recent years, India's dependence of foreign aid in absolute term has increased. In principle, foreign aid is meant to do three things, they are:

*(i)* To supplement domestic savings.

*(ii)* Make available additional supplies of foreign exchange

*(iii)* Facilitate transfer of technology.

The extent to which the grants and aid can contribute to the development of the country depends on the judicious use of grants and aids, the effort and the total disposable resources of the recipient country. Besides, foreign aid creates growth potential far beyond the point where it is applied.

Central Government gives assistance to state Government for infrastructural development in one or two growth centers in each non-industry districts. A growth center scheme is being implemented, where basic infrastructural facilities like power, water, telecommunication, banking etc., will be made available in selected growth centers. Financial Institutions like IDBI, ICICI, IFCI, etc., grants loans on concessional terms to units located in backward areas. The concession includes lower interest rates, lower underwriting concession on shares, etc.

## INCENTIVES FOR AGRICULTURE

*(i)* The Government makes efforts to improve the terms of trade for agriculture with manufacturing sector, *(ii)* removal of quantitative restriction on inputs as per WTO agreement on agriculture, in order to protect the interest of farmers, continuous monitoring of international prices will be undertaken and appropriate tariff protection, and *(iii)* the structure of taxes on food grains, other commercial crops and excise duty on farm machinery and implements, fertilizers, etc.

### Industry

*(i)* SSI units obtaining ISO 9000 certification will get reimbursement of 75 per cent expenses in obtaining ISO 9000 certification, subject to ceiling of ₹ 75,000.

*(ii)* SSI is exempt from Central excise duty upto a turnover of ₹ 50 lakhs.

*(iii)* Advances to SSI are considered as priority sector advances by banks, small advances are given at concessional rate of interest.

(iv) Special Act has been passed for automatic payment of interest if payment to a small-scale industry is delayed by the buyer.

(v) De-licensing of many industries.

(vi) Central Government gives income-tax exemption to industries which are in backward areas. In backward hill areas, government. grants transport subsidy. Income-tax benefits are available for industries in backward regions. Central Government gives assistance to State Governments for infrastructural development in one or two growth centers in each no industry districts. Four growth center schemes are being implemented, where basic infrastructural facilities, like power, water, telecommunication, banking etc., will be made available in selected growth centers.

(vii) Financial Institutions like IDBI, ICICI, IFCI, etc., grant loans on concessional terms to units located in backward areas. The concessions include lower interest rates, lower underwriting concession on shares etc.

(viii) Industrial parks — A scheme to encourage private investment in setting up industrialparks/model towns has been devised. The scheme aims at setting up industrial model towns/industrial parks for development of industrial infrastructure facilities for integrated manufacturing activities, including common facilities such as roads, power, water, drainage and telecommunications and R & D.

*Foreign Trade*

(a) Indigenous inputs without payment of excise duty or rebate if duty paid.

(b) No excise charged on final product or rebate if duty paid.

(c) Imported inputs without payment of customs duty or rebate if duty paid.

(d) No export duty on export of final product.

(e) Bank finance on priority basis and at concessional rate interest.

(f) Import of capital goods at concessional rate under EPCG scheme.

(g) Exemptions/relaxation from income tax.

(h) Exemption from sale tax on final product.

(i) Duty free import under EPCG (Export Promotion of Capital Goods).

## EXPORT ORIENTED UNIT

**1.** The EOU scheme was introduced in the year 1980 *vide* Ministry of Commerce resolution dated 31st December 1980. The purpose of the scheme was basically to boost exports by creating additional production capacity. This was introduced as a complementary scheme for the Free Trade Zones/Export Processing Zone (EPZ) Scheme, in the sixties, since it had not attracted many units due to locational restrictions. The exporters showed willingness to set up units with long-term commitment to exports under Customs Bond Operations, provided they had the freedom to locate them in places of their choice and given most of the benefits as provided to units set up in these Zones.

2. Over the years, the scheme has undergone various changes and its scope also expanded substantially as compared to the initial scheme, which was basically for manufacturing sector with certain minimum value addition in terms of export earnings. Under this scheme, the units undertaking to export their entire production of goods are allowed to be set up. These units may be engaged in the manufacture, services, development of software, trading, repair, remaking, reconditioning, reengineering including making of gold/silver/platinum jewellery and articles thereof, agriculture including agro-processing, aquaculture, animal husbandry, biotechnology, floriculture, horticulture, viticulture, poultry, sericulture, and granites. The EOUs can export all products except prohibited items of exports in ITC (HS).

3. Under the EOU scheme, the units are allowed to import or procure locally without payment of duty all types of goods including capital goods, raw materials, components, packing materials,consumables, spares and various other specified categories of equipment's including material handling equipment's, required for export production or in connection therewith.

4. The Customs exemption notifications for import and related Central Excise exemption notification when the goods are procured from local manufacturing units, prescribe several conditions to be fulfilled by the beneficiaries keeping in view the objective of the scheme and to prevent abuse. Working in Customs Bond is one of the essential prerequisite — there being few exceptions. They also provide various flexibilities in the matter of taking out the materials for job work, inter-unittransfer.

5. The EOUs are licensed to manufacture goods within the bonded premises for the purpose of export. As per the policy, the period of bonding is initially for five years, which is extendable to another five years by the Development Commissioner. On completion of the bonding period, it is for the unit to decide whether to continue under, or to opt out of the scheme. The imported capital goods are allowed to be warehoused for a period of 5 years. For other goods, the warehousing period is one year, which can be extended further by the Commissioner/Chief Commissioner of Customs.

6. The EOUs basically function under the administrative control of the Development Commissioner of the Export Processing Zones, whose jurisdiction has been notified by the Ministry of Commerce. In all, there are seven Development Commissioners at Mumbai, Gandhidham, Chennai, Cochin, Vizag, Noida, and Kolkata, who supervise the functioning of the EOUs and eight Export Processing Zones/Special Economic Zones in the country. The Development Commissioners of the EPZs/SEZs are the Licensing Authorities in respect of units under the EOU Scheme, as per specified territorial jurisdiction as indicated in the Export and Import Policy.

7. The provisions of the Customs and Central Excise law in respect of the EOUs are administered by the Commissioners of Customs and Central Excise, who work under the control of Central Board of Excise and Customs. The work relating to EOUs is handled by the staff of jurisdictional Commissioner of Central Excise.

8. For setting up of an EOU, three copies of the application in the prescribed form are required to be submitted to the Development Commissioner. In certain cases, approval of the

Board of Approval (BOA) is required. Applications for setting up of Electronic Hardware Technology Park/Software Technology Park units are submitted to the officer designated by the Ministry of Information Technology for this purpose. After approval of the application and issuance of Letter of Permission, the applicant is required to execute a legal undertaking with the Development Commissioner or Designated Officer concerned within the prescribed time period. On execution of legal undertaking, a green card is issued to the unit.

**9.** On the policy front, all decisions relating to the EOUs are taken by the Board of Approvals (BOA), set up under the Ministry of Commerce. The BOA is chaired by the Secretary, Ministry of Commerce and includes the Chairman, C.B.E.C. or his nominee as a member. In the case of units engaged in manufacture of electronic hardware and software, the policy decisions are taken by the Inter Ministerial Standing Committee (IMSC) set up under the Ministry of Information Technology and the same are implemented through its Designated Officers. Chairman, C.B.E.C. or his nomineeis a member of the IMSC. The availability of any benefit under Customs or Central Excise Acts or the notifications issued there under has, however, to be determined by the Commissioner of Customs or Central Excise having jurisdiction-guided by CBEC in areas of doubt. Appropriate inter-Ministerial liaison is maintained for ensuring uniformity as far as possible in the Exim Policy provisions and theprovisions built in the relevant Customs and Central Excise notifications.

**10.** The premises of EOU are approved as a Customs bonded warehouse under the warehousing provisions of the Customs Act. The manufacturing and other operations are carried out under customs bond and the unit bearing appropriate charges for officers on cost recovery basis. In case of units in Aquaculture, Horticulture, Floriculture, Granite quarrying etc., exemption from bonding is given for administrative reasons with certain other safeguards being put in place to check that duty free benefits where availed are not abused. The EOUs are required to execute a multi-purpose bond with surety/security with jurisdictional Customs/ Central Excise officers.

## Setting Up 100 per cent EOUs

The Government amended in November 1983 a concession scheme to facilitate the setting up of Export-Oriented Units (EOUs) in order to enable them to meet requirements of foreign demand interms of pricing, quality, precision, etc. EOUs can be set up anywhere in the country and may be engaged in the manufacture and production of software, floriculture, horticulture, agriculture, aquaculture, animal husbandry, pisiculture, poultry and sericulture or other similar activities.

A 100 per cent export-oriented unit is an industrial unit offering for export its entire production, excluding the permitted levels of domestic tariff area sales. EOUs may be set up with a foreign equity participation of upto 100 per cent. For setting up a 100 per cent, EOUs the following conditions are applicable:

*(i)* The entire production and operation of 100 per cent EOUs must be in a customs bonded factory, unless specifically exempt from physical bonding. Goods will be imported into the customs bonded factory.

*(ii)* The unit shall undertake to manufacture in the bonded area and to export its entire production for a period of 10 years ordinarily and 5 years in case of products liable to rapid technological change

Regarding the export obligations of 100 per cent EOUs, the following conditions apply:

- EOUs need not export their manufactured goods themselves but may use an export house/trading house/star trading house or other EOUs subject to certain conditions.
- EOUs may execute export orders also through third parties given that the goods will be directly transferred from the customs bonded factory to the port of shipment and all export benefits will be to EOUs only.

*(iii)* An approved EOU will execute a bond/legal undertaking with the Development Commissioner concerned. Failure to fulfill the obligations stipulated in the letter of approval or intent will render the unit liable to penalty.

*(vi)* EOUs have to adhere to the minimum value addition conditions incorporated in the letter of permission/letter of intent/industrial license issued to them. In general, such minimum value addition will be 35 per cent for automatic approvals and 20 per cent for other cases.

*(v)* EOUs have to maintain a proper account of the imports, consumption and utilization of all imported materials and exports made by the unit. These accounts will be submitted periodically to the Development Commissioner. Wherever an existing industrial unit is operating both as a domestic unit as well as an approved 100 per cent EOU, it should have two distinct identities with separate accounts.

*(vi)* EOUs are permitted to sell part of the production in the domestic tariff area subject tocertain limits.

*(vii)* The f.o.b. value of exports of an EOU can be clubbed with the f.o.b. value of exports of its parent company in the domestic tariff area to attain export house, trading house, or startrading house status for the parent company.

*(viii)* Supplies produced in the domestic tariff area under global tender conditions, against payment in foreign exchange, against advance licenses and other import licenses, and to other EOUs with the permission of the Development Commissioner, will be counted towards the fulfillment of export obligations.

## Benefits Offered to 100 per cent EOUs

The main advantages in setting up a unit as a 100 per cent export oriented unit are:

- Full duty exemption on all imports.
- Tax holiday for any 5 consecutive years within 8 years from the commencement of production.
- Full exemption from sales tax and excise duty on all local purchases.
- Permission to convert all foreign exchange earnings at market determined rate
- Permission to have upto 100 per cent foreign equity.

- EOUs/EPZ units can raise foreign currency loans, subject to certain conditions;
- Industrial plots and standard design factories are available to EOUs/EPZ units atconcessional rates. For plots the concession will be 75 per cent for the first year, 50 per cent for the second year, and 25 per cent for the third year, if and only if production had commenced in the first year or the second year not otherwise. For SDF buildings shed the concession will be 50 per cent for the first year and 40 per cent for the second year if production had commenced inthe first year. The concession will be 25 per cent for the third year. These concessions are also only if production had commenced by the end of the first year, not otherwise.

## Additional Benefits

100 per cent export oriented units are permitted to sell a certain specified percentage of theirproduction in the domestic market. Units having an indigenous input content of 30 per cent are allowed tosell upto 25 per cent of their production in the local market, if indigenous input content is less than 30 per cent thedomestic sales can be upto 15 per cent of the total production.

## Fiscal and Tax Concession Available

Investment subsidy to all new tiny and small scale industries to be established in areas other than developed areas. The quantum of subsidy ranges from 10 to 25 per cent of the value of fixed assets. This subsidy is also available to all existing tiny and SSIs undertaking expansion, diversification, or modernization.

- Additional subsidy to an extent of 5 per cent of the value of fixed assets subject to a ceiling of ₹ 1 lakh to entrepreneurs belonging to SC and ST and Women Categories.
- Entry Tax Exemption to all new industries including large- and medium-scale industries for a period of 3 - 8 years depending on the location of the project and subject to certain conditions.
- Special concessions for Export Oriented Units and 100 per cent export-oriented units by way of exemption from payment of ST and ET on purchase of raw materials, components, packing materials, etc.

Incentives pertaining to Special Economic Zone (SEZ) Government of India, in order to boost exports from the country formulated a new scheme, *viz.*, Special Economic Zone (SEZ) during 2001.

Accordingly, the State Governments have formulated a State Policy for Special Economic Zone (SEZ). As per this policy, following incentives are offered to the investors:

1. Exemption from all state local taxes and levies.
2. Exemption of stamp duty and registration fees.

In addition, following initiatives have also been spelt out in the policy:

- Delegation of Labour Commissioner's power to the designated Development Commissioner.

- SHLCC to consider special package of incentives and concessions to Anchor and downstream projects.

Further, Lok Sabha has passed the Special Economic Zone Bill 2005, in May. The Bill provides a Single Window Clearance and approval mechanism for establishment of SEZs as well as production units inside the Zones. The Bill contains income tax concessions for SEZ units, as well as SEZ developers, who will be eligible for 100 per cent tax exemption for five years, 50 per cent for the next 5 years and 50 per cent of the ploughed back export profits for the next five years. SEZ developers continue to get 100 per cent income tax exemption for 10 years in a block period of 15 years.

In addition to Income Tax related concessions, developer and the entrepreneur of SEZ are and entitled to exemption of Services Tax under the Chapter V of the Finance Act, 1994 and fiscal concessions under Customs Act, 1962, Central Excise Act, 1944 and Central Sales Tax Act, 1956 as envisaged in the Bill. Currently, units in SEZs are allowed 100 per cent deduction of export profits for 5 years, 50 per cent of the export profits for the next 2 years and 50 per cent of the export profits ploughed back for the next 3 years. To be eligible for this tax concession under Section 10A of the Income Tax Act, an SEZ unit should have started manufacturing or developing computer software.

## Tax Incentives for Foreign Investors in India

There are a variety of tax concessions. The most important are the partial tax holiday for newly established small scale industrial undertakings, full 5 year tax holiday for entrepreneurs building infrastructure facilities and the full tax holiday for industrial units established in Free Trade Zones (FTZs) and for 100 per cent export-oriented units. Also, all profits derived from export of computer software are deductible in computing taxable income.

Exporters of goods or merchandise are also allowed 100 per cent deduction in respect of profits derived from export trade in computing the taxable income. These benefits can be passed on to the manufacturers whose goods are exported through the trading or export houses.

Special tax treatment has been provided to foreign institutional investor in respect of income from securities and capital gains. Dividends and interest on investments made by foreign institutional investors are taxed at a concessional rate of 20 per cent and long-term gains at a rate of 10 per cent. Short-term capital gains on sale of securities are subject to tax at the rate of 30 per cent. Indian companies are required to pay 30 per cent tax on long-term capital gains. However, foreign companies and non-resident non-corporate tax payers are charged a concessional rate of 20 per cent on long-term capital gains. The existing tax incentives can be divided into two groups:

- Measures specifically aimed at attracting foreign capital and augmenting exchange earnings.
- Other measures including investment growth.

## OTHER MEASURES TO INDUCE INVESTMENT GROWTH

**1. Tax Holiday:** Section 801A of the Income Tax Act, 1961 allows a certain percentage of taxable income derived from the small-scale new industrial unit, as deduction. The deduction rateis 30 per cent of profits derived from the new industrial undertaking, etc. in the case of companies for a period of 10 years and 25 per cent of such profits for a like period in the case of other business entities. For co-operative societies, the benefit period is 12 years. In addition to this general, partial tax holiday, enterprises engaged in specific investment projects are entitled to other full tax holidays as well. These are described below.

**2. Tax Holiday for New Industrial Undertakings in Underdeveloped Areas:** With a viewto encouraging new investment in industrially underdeveloped states and Union Territories, the government offers a full 5 year tax holiday commencing in the year of production begins for new industrial undertakings located in the North-Eastern States of Jammu and Kashmir, Himachal Pradesh, Sikkim, Goa and the Union Territories of the Andaman and Nicobar islands and Dadra and Nagar Haveli, Daman and Diu, Lakshdweep and Pondicherry. A similar deduction is offered tonew industrial undertakings in certain backward areas of other states.

After the fifth year, the industrial undertaking is entitled, for the balance of the applicable period (*i.e.*, seven additional years for co-operative societies and five for other entities), to the profits deduction provided under Section 801A (a 30 per cent deduction of the profits of such undertakings in the case of companies and a 25 per cent deduction in the case of other entities).

**3. Tax Holiday for Infrastructure Building:** To promote the expansion of equality infrastructure, a full 5 year tax holiday is allowed to any enterprise that builds, maintains, and operates any infrastructure facility, such as roads, highways or expressways, new bridges, airports, ports, or rapidrail transport systems on a BOT (Build, Operate, Transfer), BOOT (Build, Own, Operate, Transfer), or similar basis. The enterprise must have entered into an agreement with the Central or State Government, local authority, or any other statutory authority for this purpose. The period within which the infrastructure facility has to be transferred, needs to be stipulated in the agreement between the undertaking and the government concerned.

The tax holiday is allowed in respect of income derived from the use of the infrastructure facilities developed by the tax-payer. The five-year tax holiday is available to an entrepreneur that has begun or will begin to operate infrastructure facilities on or after 1 April, 1995. When the tax holiday expires, the entrepreneur will be allowed to deduct 30 per cent of its profits, if it is a company and 25 per cent if it is a non-corporate entity. The incentive is available to co-operative societies for the first 12 years and to other for the first 10 years of operation.

An entrepreneur is allowed to choose the initial year from which he wants to avail of the 5 year tax holiday. The tax holiday has to be availed of within the means that an entrepreneur (in case of co-operative societies) who chooses the fourth year of operation as the initial year gets a full tax holiday for 5 years from the fourth to the eighth year and the 30 per cent deduction from its remaining 4 years, that is from the ninth year to the twelfth year. As an incentive for financial institutions to provide long-term financing for the development of infrastructure facilities, the budget also proposes to allow a deduction of 40 per cent which is allowed to such institutions of the taxable income derived from financing investments in infrastructure facilities, provided this amount is credited to a special reserve.

**4. Deduction of Expenditures for Scientific Research:** Section 35 of the Income Tax Act allows a deduction for contributions to approved scientific research associations, universities, colleges, or other institutions that are to be used for scientific research. To encourage industry to make use offacilities offered by national laboratories and research institutes, this section also allows a weighted deduction of 125 per cent of contributions to approved national laboratories and institutions carrying out research and development in natural and applied sciences. A 'National Laboratory' is defined as a scientific laboratory functioning at the national level under the aegis of the Indian Council of Agricultural Research, the Indian Council of Medical Research and the Council of Scientific and Industrial Research, Department of Electronics, the Defence Research and Development Organization, the Department of Biotechnology and the Department of Atomic Energy and which is approved by the prescribed authority for this purpose.

**5. Exemption of Venture Capital Income:** To encourage venture capital financing, clause (23F) to Section 10 of the Income Tax Act provides an income tax exemption for all dividends and long-term capital gains of a venture capital fund or a venture capital company from investments made by way of equity shares in venture capital undertakings. To obtain this exemption, the venture capital fund or company must obtain approval from the prescribed authority and satisfy the prescribed conditions. The approval by the prescribed authority will have effect for the immediate assessment year of upto three assessment years, as may be specified in the order of approval. If the equity shares are transferred by the venture capital fund or company at any time within 3 years from the date of their acquisition (other than in the event of shares are listed on a recognized stock exchange of India), the aggregate amount of dividend income on such equityshares that has not been included in income in years preceding that in which the transfer has taken place shall be deemed to be income of the venture capital fund or company for the years in which the transfer took place. The exemption also will not be allowed in respect of long-term capital gains, if any, arising on the transfer of shares.

**6. Adjustment for Business Losses:** In India, there are five broad heads of income under which a taxpayer's different sources of income may be grouped. Except for speculation losses, long-term capital losses, losses from some specified sources like horse races, gambling, etc., loss from any other source is eligible for set-off against the profits from any other source under the same head of income. The net loss under any head is further eligible for set-off against the income from other heads but is allowed to be carried forward to be set-off against capital gains in the subsequent years.

*****

# 10 Government Procedures for Starting a Venture

- *Naming and Registering Business*
- *Procedure for Registration of a Private Limited Company*
- *Procedure for Registration of a Public Limited Company*
- *Regulatory Requirements*
- *Industrial Licensing Policy*
- *Taxation*

A business enterprise is an economic institution engaged in the production and/or distribution of goods and services in order to earn profits and acquire wealth. The scope of a business is very wide. It includes a large number of activities which may be classified into two broad categories, *i.e.*,Industry and Commerce. Production of goods is the domain of 'Industry' and distribution comes under 'Commerce.' Once a plan is prepared, the entrepreneur faces various challenges while implementing the plan.

- Naming and Registering a Business.
- Regulatory Requirements.

The Commissioner or Directorates of Industries are the nodal agencies in different states which assist and guide new entrepreneurs in starting up an industrial unit in the concerned State. They provide an interface between industry and other agencies for industry inputs and enable the entrepreneur to get different industrial approvals and clearances from various departments at a Single Point-Single Window. They sanction incentives to eligible industrial undertakings and create a transparent and automatic system of allotment of scarce raw materials to industrial units. Hence, a new entrepreneur must approach the concerned commissioner while setting up a business firm.

## NAMING AND REGISTERING BUSINESS

Incorporation of a company in India is governed by the Companies Act 1956. The Companies Act is administered by the Central Government through Department of Company Affair. The new companies are registered with the Registrar of Companies (ROC). For registration and incorporation of a company, an application has to be filed with Registrar of Companies. Application for registration of a company accompanied by the selected names, Memorandum of Association and Articles of Association and other necessary documents is to be filed with the Registrar of Companies of the State in which the company is proposed to be incorporated.

Under the Companies, Act 1956, a company could be a Private Limited Company or a Public Limited Company.

## PROCEDURE FOR REGISTRATION OF A PRIVATE LIMITED COMPANY

- Select, in order of preference, a few suitable names, not less than four, indicative of the main objects of the company. Ensure that the name does not resemble the name of any other company already registered and also does not violate the provisions of Emblems and Names (Prevention of Improper Use) Act, 1950.
- Apply to the concerned ROC to ascertain the availability of name in e-Form 1 A of General Rules and Forms along with a fee of ₹ 500. If proposed name is not available apply for a fresh name on the same application, the digital signature of the applicant proposing the company has to be attached in the form.
- After the name approval, the applicant can apply for registration of the new company by filing the required forms (e-Forms 1, 18, 32) within 6 months of name approval.
- Drafting of the Memorandum and Articles of Association by the solicitors, vetting of the same by ROC and printing of the same.
- Stamping of the Memorandum and Articles with the appropriate stamp duty.
- Obtain Certificate of Incorporation from ROC. If the Registrar is satisfied that all the requirements have been complied with by the Companies Act, it will register the company and issue a Certificate of Incorporation of the company. The date mentioned in the certificate is the date of incorporation of the company.

Under Section 149(7) of the Companies Act, a private company can commence business right from the date of its incorporation.

## PROCEDURE FOR REGISTRATION OF A PUBLIC LIMITED COMPANY

A Public Limited Company, in addition to the steps followed by a Private Limited Company has to obtain a Certificate of Commencement of Business before they can commence the business.

To obtain Commencement of Business Certificate after incorporation of the company, the public company has to:

- File a declaration of compliance with the provisions of Section 149(2)(b) of the Act in e-Form 20 and attach the statement in lieu of the prospectus (Schedule III) OR
- File a declaration of compliance with the provisions of Section 149 (1) (a), (b), (c) of the Act in e-Form 19 and attach the prospectus (Schedule II) to it.

## REGULATORY REQUIREMENTS

Once an entrepreneur has taken all the important decisions relating to starting a business, he/she has to take into account the basic regulatory requirements which are to be followed for setting up the organization. The most important regulation is the Companies Act, 1956, which regulates all the affairs of a company. It contains provisions relating to: formation of a company, powers and responsibilities of the directors and managers, raising of capital, holding company meetings, maintenance and audit of company accounts, powers of inspection and investigation of company affairs, reconstruction and amalgamation of a company and even winding up of a company.

The next important regulation relates to environment. The Environmental regulatory requirements envisage a wide legislative framework covering every aspect of environment protection. Broadly, it includes the set emission standards for air, noise, water, etc. Separate set of laws for emission of hazardous wastes have also been enacted. Effluent standards for 37 categories of industries and Emission Standards for 31 categories of industries have been evolved and notified. Besides, standards for ambient air quality, ambient noise, automobile and fuels quality specifications for petrol and diesel are in place. Environmental Impact Assessment (EIA) division has been set up to ensure sustainable development. Besides, certain categories of industries are subjected to mandatory environmental clearances. Hence, every industry has to abide by these guidelines and parameters for environmental protection because only this will ensure its sustainable progress and growth.

## INDUSTRIAL LICENSING POLICY

*(i)* Industrial licensing will be abolished for all projects except for a short list of industries related to security and strategic concerns, social reasons, hazardous chemicals and overriding environmental reasons, and items of elitist consumption (list attached as Annexure II). Industries reserved for the small scale sector will continue to be so reserved.

*(ii)* Areas where security and strategic concerns predominate will continue to be reserved for the public sector (list attached as Annexure I).

*(iii)* In projects where imported capital goods are required, automatic clearance will be given:

*(a)* In cases where foreign exchange availability is ensured through foreign equity or

*(b)* If the CIF value of imported capital goods required is less than 25 per cent of total value (net of taxes) of plant and equipment, upto a maximum value of ₹ 2 crore.

## TAXATION

India has a well-developed tax structure with a three-tier federal structure, comprising the Union Government, the State Governments and the Urban/Rural Local Bodies. The power to levy taxes and duties is distributed among the three tiers of Governments, in accordance with the provisions of the Indian Constitution. The main taxes/duties that the Union Government is empowered to levy are Income tax (except tax on agricultural income, which the State Governments can levy), Customs duties, Central Excise and Sales Tax, and Service Tax. The principal taxes levied by the State Governments are Sales Tax (tax on intra-State sale of goods), Stamp Duty (duty on transfer of property), State Excise (duty on manufacture of alcohol), Land Revenue (levy on land used for agricultural/non-agricultural purposes), Duty on Entertainment and Tax on Professions and Callings.

The local bodies are empowered to levy tax on properties (buildings, etc.), Octroi (tax on entry of goods for use/consumption within areas of the Local Bodies), Tax on Markets and Tax/User Chargesfor utilities like water supply, drainage, etc. Since 1991 tax system in India has underg one a radical change, in line with liberal economic policy and WTO commitments of the country. Some of the changes are:

- Reduction in customs and excise duties.
- Lowering corporate tax.
- Widening of the tax base and toning up the tax administration.

For domestic companies, this is levied at 35 per cent plus surcharge of 5 per cent, whereas for a foreigncompany (including branch/project offices), it is at 40 per cent plus surcharge of 5 per cent. An Indian registered company, which is a subsidiary of a foreign company, is also considered an Indian company for this purpose.

*****

# 11 Forms of Organizations

- *Sole Proprietorship Business*
- *Partnership*
- *Joint Stock Company Form of Enterprise*

Economic activity is daily increasing in complexity. Governmental legislation, awakening social conscience, economic necessities – each plays a role in the creation and existence of enterprises. Entrepreneurship has several dimensions and an entrepreneur is expected to know them thoroughly to be successful. One such dimension is a legal dimension. An entrepreneur is concerned with law from the very beginning. From the point of view of ownership, there are in the private sector, three forms of organization to run a business unit. They are:

*(a)* Sole Proprietorship.

*(b)* Partnership Firm.

*(c)* Joint Stock Company.

Hindu Undivided or Joint Family (HUF) Firm can be considered as the fourth form of organization although, this is fast losing ground as a form of business organization.Thus, conforming to legal requirements will be the first thing for starting an enterprise. Then of course any enterprise has to be run within the legal framework, *i.e.*, doing business according to mercantile law, labour laws, tax laws, etc. The Chart below shows the forms of legal ownership.

| *Forms of Legal Ownership* | *Enterprise Commercial/Industrial* | |
|---|---|---|
| | *Private Sector* | *Public Sector* |
| Individual Ownership | Group Ownership | |
| Sole Proprietorship | (i) Partnership | (i) Government Department |
| | (ii) Company | (ii) Public Corporation |
| | (iii) Co-operative | (iii) Company |
| | (iv) Hindu Joint Family Firm | (iv) Societies |

***Source:*** *'A Complete Guide To Entrepreneurship'*, Pandey.

## SOLE PROPRIETORSHIP BUSINESS

This is the oldest form of business ownership. It is also the simplest and the most natural form.

**Characteristics:**

(1) One-man Ownership.

(2) Personal Control.

(3) Total or Undivided task.

(4) Liability is Unlimited.

**Suitability:**

(1) When enterprise is small in size.

(2) When little capital is required.

(3) Where risk involved is not heavy.

(4) When control by one man is sufficient.

(5) Where personal attention to customers' needs and tastes is important.

**Advantages:**

(1) Ease of formation.

(2) Complete degree of control.

(3) Promptness in decision making.

(4) Maintenance of survey.

(5) Flexibility in operation.

(6) Catering to individual tastes.

(7) Minimum governmental regulation.

**Disadvantages:**

(1) Limited amount of capital.

(2) Limited managerial ability.

(3) Liability is unlimited.

(4) Risk is individually heavy.

(5) Uncertainty of continuity.

## PARTNERSHIP

The law of partnership is contained in the Indian Partnership Act, 1932. The Act defines partnership as 'the relation between persons who have agreed to share the profits of a business carried on by all or any of them acting for all'.

The essential characteristics of partnership are:

(1) Association of two or more persons.

(2) Agreement.

(3) Business.

(4) Sharing of profits.

(5) Mutual agency.

A partnership is based on an agreement. The partnership agreement may be made orally or in writing or may be implied from the course of dealing among partners. However, all the essential elements of a valid contract must be present.

Legal Implications of Partnership:

(1) Legal position – not a legal entity.

(2) Liability – unlimited joint and individual.

(3) Utmost good faith.

(4) Implied authority – each partner is an agent and hence has an implied authority to bin dall the partners.

(5) Unanimity of consent is a must.

(6) Non-transferability of share or interest without the consent of other partners.

(7) Dissolution, unless there is an agreement to the contrary. Death or insolvency of a partner dissolves the firm.

### Registration of a Partnership Firm

The Partnership Act does not provide for the compulsory registration of firms. But indirectly by creating disabilities from which an unregistered firm suffers, it makes registration advantageous.

### Partnership Deed

Though a partnership is continued by agreement between the parties, it need not necessarily be in writing. It may be of the most informal character even oral, though the business of partnership may involve millions of rupees or on the other hand, it may be an elaborate written document called the 'deed of partnership' or 'articles of partnership' and drafted by a lawyer. Where the partners have decided to enter into a deed of partnership, it should be stamped according to the provisions of the Stamp Act. A properly drawn up deed of partnership should ordinarily cover the following points:

(1) Name of the firm together with the names of the partners composing it.

(2) The nature of business and the duration of partnership.

(3) The amount of capital each partner undertakes to contribute and the manner of its contribution.

(4) The ratio for sharing profit and loss.

(5) Salaries, commissions, etc., if any payable to partners and also any drawings which may be allowed.

(6) Valuation of goodwill.

(7) Matters relating to retirement, death and admission of partners.

(8) Settlement of account at the dissolution of the firm.

(9) Arbitration clause.

(10) Any other clause or clauses found necessary.

## JOINT STOCK COMPANY FORM OF ENTERPRISE

For enterprises which require huge capital base, individual properties or partnership may not be able to supply the required capital. Therefore, it becomes necessary to have another form of organization, through which large sums of money could be arranged from a large number of people who are either not capable of running business enterprises or have no time to do so. They will however be willing to invest their savings in a business provided they are assured that their money is safe and they will not be called upon to pay anything more than what they undertake to invest.

The form suitable to serve these purposes is found to be in a limited company. This firm enables the entrepreneurs to get the necessary capital from friends, relatives, general public etc., retaining at the same time the control and management in their own hands. Joint Stock Company is in fact much better than partnership form of business.In Joint Stock Companies, the capital is contributed by a large group of people known as shareholders and the organization has a separate entity. It is a person in the 'eye of law' hence, it is rightly said 'Members may come, Members may go, but the Company goes on forever'.

*****

# 12

# Relevant Acts for Entrepreneurs

- *Introduction*
- *The Factories Act, 1948*
- *The Industrial Disputes Act, 1947*
- *The Indian Trade Unions Act, 1926*
- *The Payment of Wages Act, 1936*
- *Employees State Insurance Act, 1948*
- *Workmen's Compensation Act, 1923*

## INTRODUCTION

Regulations refer to the statutes which come into force by the government. Statutes, regulations or Acts whatever be the nomenclature, mean they are rules which are enforceable by law. In case of non-compliance with these, anybody would be punishable and held guilty. In a society, regulations are required to ensure that everything occurs with the plan and the policy adopted. Regulations operate on everything, people, objects and actions. Thus, a regulation is a process to ensure that the laid objectives are achieved.

Example:

*(i)* The worker gets his minimum wages.

*(ii)* The entrepreneurs get their raw materials.

*(iii)* The environment is saved from pollution.

The regulations governing small-scale industries are of two types, namely, protective and promotional. A small-scale entrepreneur has to be well-versed and right from the beginning of establishing a small-scale industry, there are regulations to adhere to. A point worth mentioning is, the entrepreneur should seek necessary professional assistance for ensuring that statutory defaults do not take place.

Salient features of the important statutes with respect to entrepreneurs/small-scale industries are summarized in the preceding pages. Discussing all these statutes would be beyond the scope of this book. However, the most relevant are:

(1) The Factories Act, 1948.

(2) The Industrial Disputes Act, 1947.

(3) The Indian Trade Unions Act, 1926.

(4) The Payment of Wages Act, 1926.

(5) Employee's State Insurance Act, 1952.

(6) Workmen's Compensation Act, 1923.

## THE FACTORIES ACT, 1948

**(i) Definition of a Factory:** Section 2(m) defines a factory as any place where in, ten or more persons are working and in which manufacturing process is carried on with the aid of motive power supplied by steam, oil or electricity. Premises in which power is not used come under the term of a factory if twenty or more persons are working in it. This definition brings a greater number of places under the purview of this Act than was the case under the Act of 1934.

**(ii) Employment of Children:** The Act fixes the minimum age of persons who can enter a factory for work at 14 years. It prohibits the employment of children upto the age of 13. The Act further lays down that a qualified surgeon must certify that a person has completed the age of 14. Such certificates must be obtained by a factory manager and must be available for inspection by a factory inspector.

**(iii) Hours of work for Children:** The Act reduces the hours of work for children between the ages of 14-17 from 5 hours a day to 4½ hours a day. It also prohibits work at night for such persons.

**(iv) Hours of work for Adult Female and Male workers:** The Act prohibits employment of women in factories between 6 pm to 7 am. It reduces the hours of work for adult men and women workers from 54 to 48 hours, per week and from 9 hours to 8 hours a day. The Act also lays down that the 8 hours of work will be spread over a period of not more than ten and half hours. Further it provides that no worker shall work for more than five hours before he has had an interval or rest of at least half an hour. Lastly, the Act lays down that those workers who are made to work for more than 8 hours a day or 48 hours a week shall be paid for the extra hours at the rate of twice their ordinary rate of wages.

**(v) Cleanliness:** The Act lays down that every factory shall be kept clean and free from effluvia arising from any drain, privy or other nuisance. Accumulation of dirt and refuge shall be removed daily from the floor, the benches of workrooms, from staircases and passages and shall be disposed of in a suitable manner.The floor of every workroom in a factory shall be cleaned once a week. All inside walls, ceilings, and partitions shall be white washed atleast once in 14 months; and if they are painted or varnished they shall be repainted or re-varnished once in five years. Effective arrangements shall be made in every factory for the disposal of wastes arising out of the manufacturing processes carried on therein.

**(vi) Ventilation and Temperature:** Effective and suitable provision shall be made in every factory for securing and maintaining in every workroom adequate ventilation by the circulation of fresh air and the maintenance of such temperature as will secure therein reasonable conditions of comfort for those working there. Where excessively high temperatures are necessary for technical reasons, adequate measures shall be taken by the management to protect the workers from such temperatures.

The state government may prescribe a standard of adequate ventilation and reasonable temperature for any factory or, class of factories and can suggest ways and means for reducing excessively high temperatures. In any factory where dust or fumes injurious to the health of workers arise in any manufacturing process effective measures shall be taken to prevent their inhalation or accumulation in any workroom.

**(vii) Artificial Humidification:** In factories where humidity is artificially increased, the state government may make rules:

*(a)* Prescribing standards of humidification.

*(b)* Regulating methods used for humidification.

*(c)* Directing prescribed tests for determining humidity and directing that such tests are carried out and their results recorded.

*(d)* Prescribing methods to be adopted for securing adequate ventilation and cooling of the air in those rooms where artificial humidity is introduced.Water used for the purpose of humidification shall be such as has been certified by the municipal authorities as fit for drinking.

**(viii) Overcrowding:** To prevent overcrowding in a factory, the Act lays down that in factories built before the passing of this Act, there shall be a space of atleast three hundred and fifty cubic feet per worker and in factories built after the Act came into force it shall not be taken into consideration. In accordance with this rule, the Chief Inspector of factories will communicate each factory manager the maximum number of workers that may be employed on any premises. He has however the power to exempt any factory or workroom from this rule if he is satisfied that observance of this rule is not necessary in the interest of the workers employed therein.

**(ix) Lighting:** It is the duty of the management of a factory to maintain sufficient suitable lighting, natural or artificial or both in a factory and in all the workrooms. All glazed windows and sky-lights shall be kept clean on both the inner and outer surfaces and effective measures shall be taken for the prevention of glare and formation of any shadows which may cause eye-strain or create risk of accidents. The state government may make rules as to what is sufficient and suitable lighting for a factory or a class of factories.

**(x) Drinking Water:** In every factory effective arrangements shall be made to provide at suitable points conveniently situated for all workers employed wherein sufficient supply of wholesome drinking water. In every factory where more than 253 workers are ordinarily employed, provision shall be made for cool drinking water during the hot weather.

**(xi) Latrines and Urinals:** In every factory sufficient latrine and urinal facilities of the prescribed types shall be provided at places which are conveniently situated and are easily accessible to workers at all times while they are at the factory. The state government may prescribe the number of latrines and urinals to be provided in any factory in proportion to the number of male and female workers ordinarily employed therein.

**(xii) Provision of Spittoons:** In every factory there shall be sufficient numbers of spittoons in convenient places and they shall be maintained in a clean and hygienic condition.

**(xiii) Safety Provisions:** According to the Act of 1934, a factory manager could afford to wait till an inspector of factories gave instructions as to what ought to be done to ensure the safety of workers. However, the Act of 1948, has placed the responsibility for safety matters on the shoulders of the occupier or the manager of a factory. He must comply with all the safety provisions without waiting for the inspector's instructions. Secondly, the Act places legal responsibility on the management for the maintenance and use of safety guards. It is its duty to supervise the use of these guards by the workers.The specific provisions for safety are as follows: In every factory all dangerous parts of all machines such as the moving parts of prime movers, flywheels, electric generators, motors' rotary converters, etc., shall be securely fenced by safety guards of substantial construction which shall be kept in position while the parts of machines they fence are in motion.

**(xiv) Dangerous Fumes:** Adequate provision shall be made in a factory where dangerous fumes are present in any chamber, tank, pipe, etc., for such fumes.

**(xv) Explosive Gases, Dust, Fumes:** If in any factory the manufacturing process raises dust, gas, fume, or vapour which is likely to explode on ignition, all measures shall be taken to prevent any such explosion by:

*(a)* Providing an effective enclosure of the plant as machinery used in the process.

*(b)* The removal or prevention of accumulation of such dust, gas, or fumes.

**(xvi) Safety of Factory Buildings and Machinery:** If it appears to the inspector that any building, part of the factory is in such a condition that it is dangerous to human life or safety, he may serve on the manager of the factory an order in writing specifying the measures that should be adopted and the specific date by which they should be carried out to ensure the safety of the building or factory. He may also serve an order on the manager prohibiting its use until proper repairs or alterations have been carried out.

**(xvii) Welfare Provisions:**

(a) *Facilities for Washing:* In every factory adequate and suitable facilities for washing shall be provided and maintained for the workers separately. Such facilities shall be conveniently accessible and shall be kept clean.

(b) *Storing and Drying Clothes:* The state government may require any factory or class of factories to make provision, therein of suitable places for keeping clothes not worn during working hours and for drying wet clothes.

(c) *Facilities for Sitting:* In every factory suitable arrangement for sitting shall be provided and maintained for all workers obliged to work in a standing positions, in order that they may take advantage of any opportunity for rest which may occur in the course of their work.

(d) *First Aid Appliances:* First aid boxes equipped with the prescribed contents which will be readily accessible during all working hours shall be provided and maintained in every factory. The number of such boxes shall not be less than one for every 150 workers.

**(xviii) Penalties for Breach of Provisions of The Act:** For any contravention of the Act, the occupier and the manager of a factory shall each be held guilty of an offence and shall be punishable with imprisonment for a term not exceeding 3 months or with a fine upto rupees 500 or with both. If any person who has been convicted of any offence punishable under the provisions of this Act is again found to be guilty of an offence involving of conviction, then he is punishable with imprisonment upto 6 months or with a fine upto 1000 rupees or with both. This Act for the time provides that if any worker contravenes any provision of this Act or any rules or orders such as the use of safety grounds, spitting only in spittoons provided for the purpose, he shall be punishable with fine upto 20 rupees.

India's ratification of International Labour Convention No. 90 prohibiting the employment of young persons in factories at night necessitated an amendment of the relevant sections of the Factories Act, 1948. This was achieved by passing an Amendment Act in April, 1954. This Act added a new chapter on 'Annual Leave with Wages to the Factories Act, 1948'. It lays down a period of two hundred and forty days as the minimum attendance necessary during a calendar year to qualify for leave with wages. It also prohibits employment of young persons on cleaning, lubricating or adjusting any prime mover or transmission machinery while in motion if such work exposes them to a risk of injury.

## THE INDUSTRIAL DISPUTES ACT, 1947

Industrial disputes, strikes and lockouts were not very common occurrences in India till 1914-18. After that the strike came to be regarded as an ordinary weapon of industrial warfare. During the war while the cost of living went on rising the wages did not keep pace with it. This gave rise to serious discontent among industrial workers and led to a series of strikes, notably in the textile industry in Mumbai in the post-war period. In addition to low wages there were many other causes which were partly responsible for the outbreak of strikes during this period. The more important of these were long hours of work, bad conditions, housing conditions, absence of any provision till 1925 of the right to form a trade union, ill treatment of workmen by foremen or other mill officials etc.

The important provisions of the Industrial Disputes Act of 1947 are:

*(i)* If any industrial dispute exists or is apprehensible the appropriate government may by order in writing, refer the dispute to a Board for promoting a settlement thereof,

*(a)* Refer any matter appearing to be connected with or relevant to the dispute to a court of inquiry or refer the dispute to a tribunal arbitration.

*(ii)* If either of the parties to a dispute or both of them apply to the government to refer a dispute to a Board, court of tribunal the appropriate government if satisfied that the person applying represents majority of each party shall make the reference accordingly.

*(iii)* If a dispute has been referred to a Board or a tribunal the government may prohibit the continuance of any strike or lock-out in connection with such a dispute.

*(iv)* A settlement arrived at, in the course of conciliation under the Act or an award which is declared by the government is binding on all the parties to the dispute for atleast six months.

*(v)* An award declared by a government shall come into operation on such date as may be specified by the government and shall remain in operation if so fixed by the government.

*(vi)* Workers employed in public utility industries shall not go on a strike and the employers in such industries shall not resort to lock-outs: *(a)* Without giving a fourteen days'notice and before the period of notice expiry or *(b)* During the pendency of conciliation proceedings.

*(vii)* Workers employed in any industrial establishment shall not go on strike: *(a)* during the pendency of conciliation proceeding, *(b)* during the pendency of proceeding before a labour court, tribunal or national tribunal, *(c)* during a period in which a settlement or award is in operation.

A strike or a lockout in contravention of any of these provisions shall be illegal. No person shall knowingly expend or apply any money in direct furtherance of support or any illegal strike or lock-out.

**Penalties:** Any worker, who commences, continues or acts in furtherance of an illegal strike shall be punishable with imprisonment upto 1 month or with fine upto 50 rupees or both.

## THE INDIAN TRADE UNIONS ACT, 1926

The experience of the working of the system of free enterprise in the industrial field revealed that though theoretically both the employers and workers were free to enter into a contract and to agree upon the wages to be paid and received, in point of fact for various reasons this freedom did not benefit the workers in anyway. *Firstly,* the commodity that a worker has to sell is highly perishable in the sense that if he refuses to work on a particular day because the wages offered are low he cannot store up his labour of that day to be used the next day. This compels him to accept work even if the wages offered are unsatisfactory. *Secondly,* as his income is very low he is not able to accumulate any savings on which he can fall back if and when he refuses to work. The only alternative for refusal to work because of low wages is starvation. These two factors compel a worker to accept low wages and so the theoretical freedom of contract is not of much use to him. *Lastly,* the fact that a worker is a small-scale seller and the employer is a large-scale buyer reduces his bargaining power to a very great extent. It is possible for the employer to refuse the wage which a worker demands because it is possible for him to engage somebody else who is willing to work on lower wage. It is however relatively difficult for a worker to find an alternative employer who would pay him the wage he demands. His weak bargaining power thus compels him to accept whatever wages are offered to him.

## Rules of Trade Union

The rules of a trade union contain the following provisions:

*(a)* The name.

*(b)* The objects for which it has been established.

*(c)* The purpose for which its general funds will be applicable.

*(d)* Maintenance of the list of members for the inspection by officers and members of the union.

*(e)* The admission of ordinary members who shall be persons engaged in the industry with which the union is connected and also the admission of honorary members to form the executive of the union.

*(f)* The conditions under which fines or forfeiture may be imposed on them.

*(g)* The manner in which any rule shall be amended, altered, or deleted.

*(h)* The manner in which the members of the executive and other officers of the union shall be appointed and removed.

*(i)* The safe custody of the funds of the union, the audit of accounts and inspection of the account books by the officers and members.

*(j)* The manner in which the union will be dissolved.

## Rights of Registered Trade Unions

A registered trade union has a right:

*(a)* To collect membership fees on the premises of the factory without interference from the management.

*(b)* To put up notices of the meetings of the union and of the other activities of the union on the premises of the factory.

(*c*) To use the general funds for specific purposes.

(*d*) To raise funds for political purposes at the option of the members.

(*e*) To conduct a strike by peaceful methods.

(*f*) To be exempted from the provisions of Section 120B sub-section 2, of the Indian Penal Code if the members, conduct a peaceful strike.

(*g*) To appoint outsiders in a number which is not more than one half of the total number of office bearers to the executive of the union.

(*h*) To send the Registrar, every year an audited statement of receipts and expenditure.

## THE PAYMENT OF WAGES ACT, 1936

The payment of wages to factory workers in a particular form and at regular intervals without any unauthorized deductions is the objective of this Act.

**Scope of the Act:** The provisions of the Act are applicable to workers engaged in factories as defined by the Factories Act of 1948, and to persons employed on any railway by contractor or subcontractor. The state government may after giving 3 months' notice of its intension of doing so by a notification in the *Official Gazette* extend the provisions of this Act to any class of persons employed in any industrial establishment. The provisions of this Act are applicable to those persons whose wages do not exceed 400 rupees per month.

**The Date of Payment of Wages:** The wages of every person employed in a factory, industrial establishment or a railway where less than 1000 persons are employed shall be paid before the expiry of the seventh day after the completion of wage period, generally a month; the wages for a month for example, shall be paid before the seventh day of the next month. In the factories, in which more than a thousand persons are employed the wages shall be paid before the expiry of the tenth day of the next month. The wages of a person whose services have, been terminated shall be paid on the next working day after such termination. The payment of wages shall be made on a working day.

**Authorized Deductions:** The Act authorizes the employer to make deductions from wages for the following purpose only:

(*a*) Fines.

(*b*) Absence from duty.

(*c*) Damage to or loss of goods or money where such damage or loss is due to the negligence or default on the part of the employee.

(*d*) Housing accommodation supplied by the employer.

(*e*) Such amenities and services supplied by the employer as the state government may authorize.

Further to it:

*(i)* Fines shall be imposed for those acts of commission and omission which the employer with the approval of the state government may have specified by notice, to his employees.

*(ii)* Fines shall not be imposed on any employee unless he has been given an opportunity to show cause why the fine should not be imposed.

*(iii)* No fines shall be imposed on persons below the age of 15.

*(iv)* The fine so imposed shall be recovered in installments or after the expiry of 60 days from the day on which it was imposed.

*(v)* The fine and the actual amount recovered shall be recorded in a separate register in the prescribed form and all amounts of fines realized shall be utilized only for such purposes as are beneficial to the employees and as are approved by the prescribed authority. Applications for the recovery of fines or of deduction not authorized under the Act for delay in payment of wages shall be presented within 6 months of the date on which such fines were imposed or deductions were made or wages were due.

## THE EMPLOYEES STATE INSURANCE ACT, 1948

Experience in the working of the Workmen's Compensation Act of 1923, revealed that the benefits conferred by it upon the factory workers in many cases did not reach them. This was due to various reasons, *viz., Firstly,* a claim for compensation for injury had to be filed in an ordinary court of law and the lack of finance often made it impossible for a worker to file such a suit and fight it out. *Secondly,* armed with expert legal advice, it was often possible for an employer to prove that the accident either did not arise out of and in the course of employment, or that it was due to the worker concerned being under the influence of drink or drugs at the time of the accident or that it was due to his negligence or his disobedience of safety rules. In such conditions, workers were generaly unwilling to go to court of law and preferred to accept whatever compensation employers chose to pay out of a sense of pity or charity. The Employees State Insurance Act of 1948 was framed to prevent such victimization of the worker by the employer.

**Contributions:** Every person, who is employed for wages in or in connection with the work of a factory or establishment to which this Act applies, shall be insured. All the insured workers except those who earn wage of less than one rupee per day shall pay their contributions to the Employees State Insurance Corporation at the rates specified in the first schedule to the Act. The employers shall pay their contributions at the rates specified in the above schedule.

**Distribution of Benefits under the Act:** The insured persons or as the case may be, their dependents shall be entitled to the following benefits, namely:

*(a)* ***Sickness Benefits:*** Periodical payments to any insured person in case of his sickness being certified by a duly appointed medical practitioner.

(b) *Maternity Benefits:* Periodical payments in case of confinement to an insured woman certified to be eligible for such payments by an authority specified in this behalf by the regulations.

(c) *Disablement Benefits:* Periodical payment to an insured person suffering from disablement as a result of an injury sustained in the course of his employment.

(d) *Dependents' Benefits:* Periodical payment to such dependents of an insured person who dies as a result of an injury sustained in the course of his employment.

(e) *Medical Benefits:* Medical treatment for and attendance on an insured person.

The Corporation may at the request of the Government of India extend medical benefits to the family of the insured person. Accordingly, these benefits have been so extended from 1 January 1962.

A person who is in receipt of sickness or disablement benefits must observe the following conditions:

(a) He shall remain under medical treatment at dispensary, hospital, clinic or other institution provided under this Act and shall carry out the instructions of the medical officer or medical attendant in charge thereof.

(b) He shall not, while under treatment, do anything which might retard or prejudice his chances of recovery.

(c) He shall not leave the area in which medical treatment provided under this Act is being given without the permission of the medical officer or such other authority as may be specified in this behalf under the rules framed for this purposes; and

(d) He shall allow himself to be examined by any duly appointed medical officer or any other person authorized by Corporation in this behalf.

**Penalties:** If a person makes a false statement for the purpose of causing any payment or benefit to be made where no payment or benefit is authorized or for the purpose of avoiding any payment to be made by himself, he shall be punishable with imprisonment for a term up to three months or with fine up to 500 rupees or with both.

If any person fails to pay any contribution which he is liable to pay or deducts from the wages of an employee the whole or any part of the employee's contribution or reduces the wages or any privileges or benefits admissible to an employee, dismisses, discharges, reduces or otherwise punishes an employee in contravention of Section 73 or fails or refuses to submit any return required by the regulations or makes a false return or obstructs any inspector or other official of the Corporation in the discharge of his duties or is guilty of contravention of and non-compliance with any of the requirements of this Act, he shall be punishable with imprisonment upto a period of 3 months or with fine upto 500 rupees or with both.

## THE WORKMEN'S COMPENSATION ACT, 1923

With the installation of machinery operated by motive power the number of accidents in factories have increased considerably. Many a times, workers have lost their fingers, sometimes their hands and feet and in some cases even their lives, while working on machines in the factories. This meant the loss of earnings for those who were involved in the accident and in cases where a worker died his dependents were left to starve. From a purely humanitarian point of view, it would be natural to expect that employers should give some compensation to such workers or their dependents. Further, even on economic grounds it could be argued that the amount of compensation is a legitimate element of the cost of production under the factory system and therefore neither society nor employers should grudge to pay it, whenever workers were involved in accidents. Some enlightened employers did pay compensation to their employees when they suffered accidents, but a large majority was not willing to accept this responsibility. The workers however could not claim compensation as a matter of right; and even when compensation was paid there was bound to be an honest difference of opinion between an employer and an employee as regards the fairness of the amount paid. In order, to provide some basis for a statutory claim for compensation to be paid to the disabled factory worker, Workmen's Compensation Act, have been passed in almost all the countries.The following are the provisions of the Indian Workmen's Compensation Act:

**Employer's Liability for Compensation:** If a personal injury is caused to a worker by an accident arising out of and in the course of his employment, his employer shall be liable to pay any compensation in accordance with the provisions of this Act.

**When Employer is not Liable:** The employer, however, shall not be liable if:

*(a)* The injury results in a partial or total disablement of the worker for less than 3 days.

*(b)* If the injury can be directly attributed to the worker having been under the influence of drink or drugs.

*(c)* If the injury can be directly attributed to the willful disobedience by the worker of an order expressly given.

*(d)* To the willful removal or disregard by the worker of any safety guard or other device which he knew to have been provided for the purpose of his safety.

**Occupational Diseases:** If a worker engaged in any employment which involves the handling of wool, hair, bristles, or animal carcasses or loading or unloading of such merchandise or in processes carried on in compressed air or in processes which involve the use of lead or tetraethyl or in processes involving exposure to nitrous fumes contracts diseases like, anthrax, compressed airillness, lead poisoning or poisoning by nitrous fumes, respectively, or when engaged continuously for not less than 6 months in any employment specified in Part B of Schedule III, contracts any disease specified in this Schedule as an occupational disease, the contracting of such a disease shall be regarded as an injury by accident and shall be deemed to have arisen out of and in the course of employment. The State Government in the case of employments specified in Part C of the Schedule may make additions to the list of employments in Schedule III and specify the corresponding diseases after giving 3 months' notice in the *Official Gazette*.

**Types of Injuries:** Injuries for the purposes of this Act have been classified into the following categories:

(1) Death.

(2) Permanent total disablement.

(3) Permanent partial disablement.

(4) Temporary disablement Partial or total.

**Amount of Compensation:** The Act provides for compensation for these categories of injuries in Schedule I-IV.

**Medical Examination:** A worker who has given notice of an accident shall submit himself to a medical practitioner free of charge. Similarly, a worker who is in receipt of half monthly payments under this Act shall submit himself to such medical examination from time to time. If a worker refuses to submit himself to such an examination without sufficient cause, his right to compensation shall be suspended.

## CONCLUSION

In short, it is pertinent for an entrepreneur/small-scale industry to be aware of all the statuteswhich would affect its existence. It is said ignorance of law is no excuse and hence, an entrepreneur/SSI is no exception. Moreover, being updated with respect to legislations and laws enforced time to time form an important part of business environment and strategic planning for even small enterprises.

*****

# 13

# Government Policies – Small-Scale Industries

- *Introduction*
- *Objectives*
- *Tracing Small-Scale Industry Policy Since Independence, Industrial Policy Resolution, 1948*
- *Industrial Policy Resolution, 1956*
- *Industrial Policy, 1977*
- *Industrial Policy Resolution, 1980*
- *1991 Policy Measure*
- *Other Important Aspects of Government Policy*
- *Tiny Sector*
- *Handloom Sector*
- *Village Industries*
- *Rural Industries*
- *Khadi and Village Industries*
- *Industrial Estates*
- *Ancillary Industries*

## INTRODUCTION

Policies constitute the framework or guidelines for appropriate decisions at varied levels. They generally consist of statements that affect the working of a sector of the economy. The working of small-scale industries, too, is molded by a number of policies which are the base for effective plan development. The living standards of the people in the world vary considerably

Generally speaking, industrialized countries are known as developed countries in which industrial development is based on modern technology and research. The countries in which agriculture predominates are referred to as underdeveloped/developing countries. Underdeveloped countries are those where even agriculture is quite traditional. Developing countries have accepted mechanization as a way of life all along and have concentrated on developing large industries.

For a developing country like India, the growth of small-scale industries is of great significance. Apart from increased production, the growth of small-scale industries helps to serve as an important milestone in the country's march towards industrial democracy. This movement has to be fostered by all-round efforts, so that a new class of talented entrepreneurs, endowed with initiative andenterprise, come to the forefront, in this country.

## OBJECTIVES

The basic objectives of these industries are to create immediate and permanent employment on a large scale at a relatively small cost to meet a substantial part of the increased demand for consumer goods, and simple producer's goods, to facilitate the mobilization of resources of capital and skills, which might otherwise remain inadequately utilized, and to bring about an integration of the development of these industries with the rural economy on the one hand and large scale industry on the other. Further, these industries are said to offer a method of ensuring a more equitable distribution of the national income and of avoiding some of the problems that unplanned urbanization tends to create.

Basically, small industries are important for national development programmes because they can make a definite contribution to the realization of the central purpose of such a problem, *i.e.*, to bring about an efficient utilization of natural, human, and capital resources of the country and for the achievement of predetermined ends.

## TRACING THE SMALL-SCALE INDUSTRIAL POLICY SINCE INDEPENDENCE

The need for the development of small-scale, village and cottage industries has been the objective of the government since independence. Before we discuss the New Industrial Policy Resolution, it would be proper to recapitulate the important features of the earlier Industrial Policy Resolutions, since 1948.

## INDUSTRIAL POLICY RESOLUTION, 1948

The importance of small-scale industries was specifically defined in the Industrial Policy Resolution dated 6 April 1948. It was stated: 'Cottage and Small Industries have a very important role in the national economy, offering as they do scope for individual, village or co-operative enterprises and means for rehabilitation of displaced persons. These industries are particularly suited for the better utilization of local resources and for the achievement of local self-sufficiency in respect of certain types of essential consumer goods.

The Resolution added:

'The healthy expansion of cottage and small-scale industries depends on a number of factors, such as the provision of raw materials, cheap power, technical advice, organized marketing of their products and, where necessary, safeguards against intensive competition by large scale manufacturers; it also depends on the education of the workers in the use of the best available techniques'.

## INDUSTRIAL POLICY RESOLUTION, 1956

The Second Industrial Policy Resolution, enunciated in 1956, reiterated the desirable features of small industry. In this resolution, an attempt was made to rephrase industrial policy in the light of the changes that had taken place in the intermediate period of 8 years. The objective of economic policy now was to establish a socialistic pattern of society.

The role of village and small-scale industries in the development of the national economy was stressed once again. 'The State has been following a policy of supporting cottage as well as village and small-scale industries by restricting the volume of production in the large-scale sector by differential taxation, or by direct subsidies. While such measures will continue to be taken whenever necessary, the aim of State Policy will be to ensure that the decentralized sector acquires sufficient vitality to be self-supporting, for its development is integrated with that of large-scale industry. The State will, therefore, concentrate on measures designed to improve the competitive strength of small-scale producer. For this purpose, it is essential that the techniques of production should be constantly improved and modernized and the pace of transformation should be so regulated as to avoid, as far as possible, technological unemployment. Lack of technical and financial assistance, of suitable working accommodation and inadequacy of facilities for repair and maintenance are among the serious handicaps of small-scale producers. A start has been made with the establishment of industrial estates and rural community workshops to make good these deficiencies. The extension of rural electrification and the availability of power at prices which the workers can afford will alsobe of considerable help. Many of the activities relating to small-scale production will be helped bythe organization of industrial co-operatives'.

'The basic objectives of all these measures were to ensure that the decentralizedsector acquires sufficient vitality to be self-supporting and its development is integrated with that of large-scale industries'. This programme of industrial development will make large demands on the country's resources,of technical and managerial personnel. To meet these rapidly growing needs for the expansion of the public sector and for the development of village and small scale industries, proper managerial and technical cadres in the public services are being established, steps are also being taken to meet shortages of supervisory levels, to organize apprenticeship schemes of training on a large-scale both in public and in private enterprises and to extend, training facilities in business management in universities and other institutions'.

The Resolution recognized the importance of locational factors like the availability of raw materials, cheap water supply, transport facilities, etc. It reiterates very clearly that these facilities will be provided in those regions where they are not available at present, so that the unbalanced growth in the various regions may be corrected and the country as a whole may achieve higher standards of living.

## INDUSTRIAL POLICY, 1977

Industrial Policy presented to Parliament on 23 December, 1977 was primarily directed towards removing the distortions of the past, so that the goals of faster economic development can be achieved within a time-bound programme.

The essence of the Industrial Policy, 1977, was that the prosperity and distribution of income arising from a broad based growth of agriculture and related activities in rural areas can be achieved only when the 'basic demand' for a wide range of industries producing articles of mass consumption is adequately met. The policy objective was to achieve through a process of reinforcing the interaction of agricultural and industrial sectors, employment for larger number of the rural population who cannot be absorbed in the agricultural sector. Considering, the vast rural manpower and the reservoir of highly technical personnel, the new industrial policy aims at placing man at the center of planning and implementation of projects and schemes.

The salient features of the policy were:

**Small-Scale Industries:** The main thrust of the Industrial Policy, 1977 was on an effective promotion of cottage and small industries widely dispersed in rural areas and small towns. It is the policy of the Government that whatever can be produced by small and cottage industries must only be so produced. For this purpose, the list of industries which would be exclusively reserved, for the small-scale sector had been significantly expanded, and included more than five hundred and four items against about 108 items, reserved for this sector in the past.

**Tiny Sector:** While the existing definition of small-scale industries will remain, within the small-scale sector itself, special attention will be given to units in the tiny sector, namely those with investment in machinery and equipment upto Rupees one lakh and situated in towns and villages with a population of less than 50,000 according to the 1971 census. Schemes will be drawn up with a view to making available margin money assistance to tiny units in the small-scale sector as well as cottage and household industries.

**Arrangements for Provisions of Credit:** The financial assistance given to small and cottage credits under the rural industries programme will be extended to all the districts in the country within the next 4 years. In order to provide effective financial support for the promotion of small village and cottage industries, the Industrial Development Bank of India has taken steps to set up a separate wing to deal exclusively with the credit requirements of this sector. It will co-ordinate, guide, and monitor the entire range of credit facilities offered by other institutions for the small and the cottage industrial sector for which separate wings will be set up in these institutions, particularly in nationalized banks. Banks will also be expected to earmark a specific proportion of their total advances for the promotion of small, village, and cottage industries. It was the policy of the government to see to it that no worthwhile scheme of small or village industry is given up for wants of credit.

**Arrangements for Marketing:** The marketing of the production of the small-scale and the cottage industries, with its concomitants of product standardization, quality control, market surveys, etc., would receive special attention. The government would provide maximum support for these activities on a priority basis. It would encourage the purchase of the products of the small-scale by government departments and public sector undertakings with a view to supporting the marketing ofthese products.

**Promotion of Khadi and Village Industries:** The Khadi and Village Industries Commission presently has 22 village industries within its purview, but the promotional work in this area has been haphazard and the progress has been slow. It will henceforth, have to work out detailed plans for the development of these village industries by adopting modern management techniques. In this context, special programmes would be drawn upto increase the share of village industries in the total production of footwear and soaps in the country. The list of items currently under the purview of the Commission will be expanded and the organizational structure of the Commission will be revamped to make it more effective.

The Khadi and Village Industries Act, has been amended to permit the implementation of a large scale programme for the manufacture of 'Nai Khadi'. The government would provide maximum financial and marketing support needed for the promotion of the khadi programme. Along with khadi, the clothing need of the masses would be progressively met by the development of the handloom sector, which provides employment to a large number of people. To affect this, government will not permit any expansion in the weaving capacity in the organized mill and power loom sectors. It will give priority to handloom sector in the allocation of yarn spun in the organized sector. Further, in order to provide a market for handloom products, it would be ensured that the organized mill sector does not provide unfair competition to the handloom sector. The government will enforce the existing reservation of certain items of textiles for the handloom sector and further expand it to other items.

**Appropriate Technology:** It will be an integral part of government policy to ensure that the development and application of technology – appropriate to the country's social-economic conditions receives adequate attention. Special arrangements will be made to ensure an effective and coordinated approach for the development and widespread application of suitable small and simple machines and devices for improving the productivity of village industries. It will further be the government's endeavour to fully integrate such appropriate techniques of production with the broader programme of all round rural development.

**Role of Large-Scale Industries:** The role of large-scale industry will be essentially related, to the programme for meeting the basic minimum needs of the population by effecting a wider dispersal of small-scale and village industries and strengthening of the agricultural sector. These will be:

(*a*) Basic industries, which are essential for providing infrastructure facilities as well as for the development of small and village industries, such as steel, non-ferrous metals, cement, and refineries.

(*b*) Capital, goods industries required for meeting the machinery requirements of basic industries and small-scale industries.

(*c*) High technology industries requiring large-scale production and which are related to agriculture and small-scale industrial development such as fertilizers, pesticides, andpetro-chemicals.

(*d*) Other industries which are outside the list of items reserved for the development of the economy like, machine tools, organic and inorganic chemicals.

**Indigenous and Foreign Technology:** The government's policy is that the future development of industries in India must as far as possible, be based on indigenous industries. Full scope will be given to the development of indigenous technology, which would subserve the objective of efficient production of increasing quantities of the goods, which society urgently needs. The government also recognizes the necessity of continued inflow of technology in sophisticated and high priority areas, where Indian skills and technology are not adequately developed. In such areas, government's preference would be for outright purchase of the best available technology and then adopting it to the country's needs.

**Foreign Investment:** The provision of the Foreign Exchange Regulation Act will be strictly enforced as far as the existing foreign companies are concerned. After the dilution of equity,companies with direct non-resident investment not exceeding 40 per cent will be treated on par with Indian companies, except in cases, specifically notified, and their future expansion will be guided by the same principles as those applicable to Indian companies. Foreign investment and acquisition of foreign technology as necessary for India's industrial development will be allowed only on such terms as determined by the Government of India, to be in the national interest. In areas, in which foreign technological know-how is not needed, existing collaborations will not be renewed. The government will issue a revised illustrative list of industries for which no foreign collaboration, financial or technical is considered necessary, if indigenous technology has fully developed in this field. For all approved foreign investments, there will be complete freedom for remittance of profits, royalties, dividends as well as remittance of capital, subject to rules and regulations. While, as a rule, the majority interest in ownership and effective control will be in Indian hands, the government will make exceptions in highly export-oriented cases. It may even consider, permitting a fully owned foreign company to operate in India.

**Indian Joint Ventures Abroad:** The government's policy is that, at the present stage of industrial development of the country, the contribution of Indian entrepreneur to joint ventures abroad will be mainly in the form of machinery and equipment, structural, technical know-how and management expertise. If such investment is found necessary, the government will be willing to consider such investment up to a maximum limit to be prescribed for this purpose.

**Location of Industries:** No licenses will be issued to new industrial units within certain limits of large metropolitan cities having a population of more than one million and urban areas with a population with more than five lakhs as per the 1971 census. Further the State Governments and financial institutions will be requested to deny support to such new industries in these areas which do not require an industrial license. The Government of India, would also consider providing assistance to large existing industries which want to shift from congested metropolitan cities to approved locations in backward areas.

## INDUSTRIAL POLICY RESOLUTION, 1980

The Industrial Policy statement made, on 23 July, 1980 primarily seeks to harmonize the growth in the small scale sector with that in the large and medium sectors. The emphasis in the new policy is on fostering the complementarity between the small and large sectors so that the dichotomies (which are more apparent than real), between the two sectors do not distort the economic pattern. In the words of the latest policy statement : 'It will be government's endeavour to reverse the trends of the last three years towards creating artificial divisions between the large and the small industry under the misconception that these interests are essentially conflicting'.

The broad socio-economic objectives of the new policy have been set out as follows:

*(i)* Optimum utilization of installed capacity.

*(ii)* Maximizing production and achieving higher productivity.

*(iii)* Higher employment generation.

*(iv)* Correction of regional imbalances through a preferential, development of industrially backward areas.

*(v)* Strengthening of the agricultural base by according a preferential treatment to agro based industries and promoting optimum inter-sectorial relationship.

*(vi)* Faster promotion of export oriented and import substitution industries.

*(vii)* Promoting economic federalism with an equitable spread of investment and the dispersal of returns amongst widely spread small but growing units in rural as well as urban areas.

*(viii)* Consumer protection against high prices and bad quality.

An important element of the new policy is the raising of the investment limits of the tiny and small-scale sectors. These limits have been redefined in terms of investment in plant and machinery and have been fixed at Rupees two lakhs for tiny sector instead of Rupees one lakh, Rupees two lakhs for the small-scale sector instead of Rupees 10 lakhs and Rupees 25 lakhs instead of Rupees 15 lakhs for ancillaries. This step is essentially a pragmatic one and takes into account the significant price rise that has occurred in the last 5 years, following the fixation of the investment limits for the small-scale sector.

However, this decision would bring into the fold of the small-scale sector a number of technology-oriented units whose growth will have to be backed by a suitable system of incentives. The new industrial policy spells out some of these incentives which are proposed to be provided so that the small-scale sector may grow in a significant measure and contribute to the national economy.

**Financial Support to Small Units:** One of the major constraints on the growth of the decentralized sector has been the difficulty of finance which has been experienced particularly by industrial entrepreneurs in small, cottage, and rural sectors. Although, there is an adequate network of institutional finance, it is nevertheless essential to co-ordinate the flow of capital both short-term and long-term. The Government should evolve a system of co-ordination to ensure the flow of credit to the growing units in the decentralized sector at the right time and on appropriate terms, it should strengthen the existing arrangements and make such changes as may be necessary to facilitate the availability of credit to the growing units in the small-scale sector.

**Buffer Stock for Critical Inputs:** In order to assist in the growth of small-scale industries, it has been proposed to introduce a scheme for the building up of buffer stocks of essential materials which are often difficult to obtain. For this purpose, the existing set up of Small Industries Development Corporations in the States and the National Small Industries Corporation (NSIC) at the center will also be utilized. The special needs of the states which rely heavily on a few essential raw materials will receive priority.

**Marketing Support and Reservation Items for Small Industries:** Policies related to marketing support of the decentralized sectors and the reservation of items for small-scale industries shall continue to be in force, in the interests and growth of small industries.

**Village Industries:** Government is determined to promote such a form of industrialization in the country as would generate economic viability in the villages. The promotion suitable to industries in rural areas will be accelerated to generate higher employment and higher per capita income for the villagers without disturbing the ecological balance. Handlooms, handicrafts, khadi and other village industries will receive greater attention to achieve a faster rate of growth in the villages.

**District Industries Centers:** The Government has reviewed the scheme of District Industries Center's, which has not produced benefits commensurate with the expenditure incurred on them. It therefore proposes to initiate more effective alternatives. The Policy Statement of 1980 makes it clear that the existing support programme for marketingas well as for the reservation of items in the small-scale sector will continue. These form an important underpinning of the small industry development programme. It is, therefore proposed, that the existing policies will continue to operate to strengthen the small-scale sector.

The basic thrust of the new policy is to ensure a continuous growth of the small-scale sector without, at the same time, inhibiting the growth of other sectors. In this context, automatic growth for a large number of industries in the medium and large sector has been ensured so that they can grow without hindrance.A special emphasis has been laid on the establishment of 'nucleus plants' in backward districts around which a programme of ancillarization would be developed. To quote from the statement:' The proposed nucleus plants in industrially backward districts would generate a network of small-scale units, on the existing network of small scale units in an area which would acquire a faster growth by the coming up of a nucleus plant in the area. In between, the nucleus, large plants and the satellite ancillaries, the Government would permit a system of linkages for an integrated industrial development'.

## 1991, POLICY MEASURE

Over the last few decades, small enterprises emerged as leaders in industrial sector. They also played a more significant role in creating balances for economic and social development in the country. In recognition of their significance and stature, the new government announced Policy Measure on August 6, 1991 for promoting and strengthening of small, tiny and village enterprises.

Objectives:

(1) To impart more vitality and growth impetus to the small-scale sector.

(2) To decentralize and de-license the sector.

(3) To deregulate and de-bureaucratize the sector.

(4) To review all statutes, regulations, and procedures and effect suitable modifications where necessary.

(5) To promote small enterprises especially industries in tiny sector.

(6) To motivate small and sound entrepreneurs to set up new green enterprises in the country.

(7) To involve traditional and reputed voluntary organizations in the intensive development of KVI through area approach.

(8) To maintain sustained growth in productivity and attain competitiveness in the market economy, especially in the international markets.

(9) To industrialize backward areas of the country.

(10) Accelerate the process of development of modern small enterprises, tiny enterprises and village industries through appropriate incentives, institutional support and infrastructure investments.

**Salient Features:**

(1) Legislation to limit financial liability of new and non-active partners/entrepreneurs to the capital invested.

(2) Hike in investment limit for tiny sector up from Rupees two to five lakhs.

(3) Service sector to be recognized as tiny sector.

(4) Support from National Equity Fund for projects upto Rupees 10 lakhs.

(5) Single window loans to cover projects upto Rupees 20 lakhs. Banks also to be involved.

(6) Relaxation of certain provisions of labour laws.

(7) Sub-contracting exchanges to be set up by industry association.

(8) Easier access to institutional finance.

(9) Factoring services through SIDBI to overcome the problem of delayed payments, legislation to ensure payment of bills.

(10) Women enterprises redefined.

(11) Marketing of mass consumption items by National Small Industries Corporation, under common brand name.

(12) Composite loans under the single window scheme also to be given by banks.

(13) Tiny sector to be accorded priority in government purchase programme.

(14) Priority to SSIs and tiny units in allocation of indigenous raw materials.

(15) Promise to deregulate and de-bureaucratize small and tiny sector.

(16) PSUs and NSIC to help market products through consortia approach, both domestically and internationally.

(17) Janata Cloth Scheme to be replaced by a new scheme which will provide funds for loans and modernization.

(18) Compulsory quality control for products that pose risk to health and life.

(19) Legislation to ensure payment of small scale industries bills.

(20) A special monetary agency to be set up for the small-scale sector's credit needs.

(21) A new scheme of integrated infrastructural development to be implemented.

(22) A technology development cell to be set up.

(23) Incentives and services package to be delivered at the district level.

(24) An expert development centre to be set up.

(25) Khadi and Village Industries Commission (KVIC) and Boards to be expanded.

(26) Investment limit of ancillary units and export-oriented units rose to seventy-five lakhs.

(27) Traditional village industries would be given greater thrust.

## OTHER IMPORTANT ASPECTS OF GOVERNMENT POLICIES

## TINY SECTOR

The Policy Statement gives a new thrust for the development of tiny enterprises which accounts for nearly 90 per cent of all small-scale units. The investment ceiling has been raised from Rupees two to five lakhs. A significant feature of the policy is the due recognition. Inorder to strengthen the tiny sector it has been decided to recognize all industry-related service and business enterprises irrespective of their location, as small scale industries. Their investment ceiling would correspond to those of tiny enterprises.While the small-scale sector (other than tiny enterprises) would be, mainly entitled to one time benefits (like preference in land allocation/power connection access to facilities for skills, technology upgradation) the tiny enterprises would also be eligible for additional support on a continuing basis, including easier access to institutional finance, priority in the Government Purchase Programme and relaxation from certain provisions of labour laws.

## HANDLOOM SECTOR

Schemes for the handloom sector will be redesigned keeping in mind the local and regional needs. Substantial funds will be provided for modernization of looms, training, provision of better designs, provision of better dyes and chemicals and marketing assistance. Spinning capacity in the co-operative sector will be increased, National Co-operative Development Corporation will provide more assistance for this in the form of seed money, both for cotton growers, spinning mills and weavers' spinning mills.

The Janata Cloth Scheme which sustains weavers often on a minimum level of livelihood will be phased out by the terminal year of the Eighth Plan and replaced by the 'omnibus project package scheme' under which substantial funds will be provided for modernization of looms, training, provision for better designs, provision of better dyes and chemicals and marketing assistance.

The role of the National Handloom Development Centers (NHDCs) is also being enhanced. It would now be a 'nodal agency' for increasing supply of hand yarn, dyes and chemicals.For the handicraft sector, 'craft development centers' are proposed to be set up which would ensure raw materials, design and technical guidance, market support, training and procuring of related inputs in an integrated and area based manner. Measures are also proposed to be initiated to increase exports from this sector through new marketing channels like trading companies, departmental stores, etc.

## VILLAGE INDUSTRIES

Intensive development of KVI through area approach with tie-up with DRDA, TRYSEM and ongoing developmental programmes relating to weaker sections like scheduled castes, scheduled tribes and women would be extended throughout the country. The traditional village industries would be given greater thrust. Involvement of traditional and reputed voluntary organizations will be encouraged for this purpose. The new policy's success depends substantially on the quality of the service provided by bodies like Small-Scale Industries Development Organization, Prototype Development Centers, NSIC, etc., whose services in the past have not inspired much success.

## RURAL INDUSTRIES

Rural industry embraces different kinds of village and small industries. The cottage industries are an important component of rural industries. By the term 'rural industry' is meant industry appropriate for the rural areas as demarcated by the census records. The concept here has a special demographic undertone. The rural industry serves the requirements of rural people as well as other markets. By and large, the financial needs of rural industry are small.

More importantly, they function in the absence of infrastructural facilities and are environmentally friendly.

**Types of Rural Industry:** By and large rural industries are interlinked with agricultural activities,rural development and service sector. They may also be grouped into small-scale industry, tiny industry and rural artisans (self-employed). The scope for process industry is vast and unexplored.The need of the hour is the proper organization of rural industries and to ensure that they integrate well into the rural ethos and development.

**Importance of Rural Industrialization:** Rural industrialization is important not only as a means of generating employment opportunities in the rural areas with low capital cost and raising the real income of the people, but because it contributes to the development of agriculture and urban industries. Without rural industrialization, it would be considerably more difficult to solve the problem of agricultural unemployment and widespread underemployment. Rural industrialization promotes rural industry. The development of rural industries, increases the level of income in rural areas, and tends to break down the old self-sufficiency of the family and to lessen its cohesiveness, creating opportunities for youth, women and the able bodied as well in changing the pattern of leisure and work. Rural industrialization should be looked upon not merely as a way of containing the rural workers and stopping them from migrating to urban areas by providing them some kind of remunerative employment in the villages, but as a dynamic element in the process of raising the productivity and income levels of the workers in rural areas.

The main characteristics of these industries are to develop local initiative, co-operation and spirit of self-reliance in the economy and at the same time help in utilization of the available manpower for processing locally available raw materials by adopting simple techniques.These are capable of offering employment opportunities at the place of residence to a large section of population. The village industries are an antidote to the widespread problems of disguised unemployment or underemployment.

These decentralized industries require lost gestation period on the one hand and produce goods of common necessities on the other. These industries have the capacity to correct regional imbalances by initiating industrial activities on dispersed basis in the most neglected, backward, inaccessible areas where perhaps large-scale sector is unable to penetrate. Being small, these activities can ensure maximum participation of workers in management thus ensuring a feeling of involvement which is so uncommon with the large-scale sector. These industries possess an additional advantage wherein the maximum participation of women-folk can be ensured.

Rural industrialization has taken roots in the rural economy in India. This is so because simple forms of manufacture, typical of consumer goods industries and varied service industries are everywhere developed before the more complex process involved in the production of capital goods and because the size of the home market at the time of industrialization prohibits the establishment of optimum-sized plants in the production of certain capital goods.

## KHADI AND VILLAGE INDUSTRIES

The development of village and khadi industries provides opportunities for work albeit part time work in certain cases and thereby helps to mitigate the severity of rural unemployment and underemployment. With this end in view, the Khadi and Village Industries Commission (KVIC), was established in April 1957, under the Khadi and Village Commission Act, 1956.

Under the guidance of Mahatma Gandhi, provisional activities of khadi were started in 1922,when they were symbolic of the 'Fight for Freedom'. The khadi programme was thus closely linked with the struggle for freedom. The All-India Congress Committee, then known as the All-India Spinners Association (AISA) was established in 1952, to organize hand-spinning and hand-weaving. This was followed by the establishment of another organization in 1935, called the All India Village IndustriesAssociation (AIVA), to look after other village industries, such as hand pounding of paddy, ghana oil, palm gur, bee keeping, handmade paper, etc. The establishment of Khadi Commission was the culmination of the efforts to organize cottage/ village industries during the freedom movement. In 1951, the Sarva Seva Sangha took over the work of AISA and AIVA, as a part of an integrated plan for rural industrialization.

The Government of India evolved a general policy framework for the development of the seindustries. In the First Plan, these industries were treated as an integral part of agriculture and the emphasis was on the local consumption. In the Second Plan on the advice of the Village and Small-Scale Industries Committee (Karve) 1955, was in consonance with the Industrial Policy Resolution of the whole plan for the country's industrialization. The Third Plan retained the emphasis on these programmes while highlighting the need for an integrated approach. In the successive plans, the emphasis and policy were shifted from one of protection of such industries to positive forms of assistance, such as improving skills, supplying technical guidance, better equipment, and adequate credit with a view to increasing productivity and reducing cost.The government is committed to the encouragement of the production of textiles and textile products in the khadi sector.

Considering its large employment potential, it should be the endeavour of the government to make products of these sectors, more competitive and of better quality. The infrastructure for the distribution of controlled cloth, particularly in rural areas, will be strengthened and streamlined. State governments will be encouraged to open more rural outlets and exercise stricter control over distribution.

**Functions of KVIC:** The functions of KVIC comprise building up a reserve of raw materials and implements for supply to producers, creation of common service of facilities for processing, marketing, and training.

Other functions are:

(1) To promote the sale and marketing of khadi products of village industries or handicrafts. The KVIC may forge times with established marketing agencies wherever necessary and feasible.

(2) The KVIC is also charged with the responsibility of encouraging and promoting research in the production techniques employed in the khadi and village industries sector and providing facilities for the study of the problems relating to it, including the use of non-conventional energy and electric power with a view to increasing productivity, eliminating drudgery and otherwise enhancing their competitive capacity and to arrange for dissemination of salient results obtained from such research.

(3) Further, the KVIC is entrusted with the task of providing financial assistance to institutions or persons engaged in the development and operation of khadi and village industries and guiding them through supply of design, prototypes, and other technical information.

(4) In implementing KVI activities, the KVIC may take such steps to ensure genuineness of the products and to set up standards of quality and ensure that the products of khadi and village industries do conform to the standards, including issue of certificates or letters of recognition, to the concerned.

(5) The KVIC may also undertake directly or through other agencies studies concerning the problems of khadi or village industries besides experiments or pilot projects for the development of khadi and village industries.

(6) The KVIC is authorized to establish and maintain separate organizations for the purpose of carrying out any or the entire above matters incidental to its activities.

## INDUSTRIAL ESTATES

Industrial estates and ancillary industries were started in India with great hopes in their efficacy as tools of industrial dispersal, rural industrialization and to sustain growth of the small-scale industries. In India, industrial estates and ancillary industries have been utilized as an effective tool for the promotion and growth of small-scale industries. They have also been used to decentralize, industrial activity to rural and backward areas.

According to P.C. Alexander, an Industrial Estate is 'a group of factories, constructed on aneconomic scale in suitable sites with facilities of water, transport, electricity, steam, bank, postoffice, canteen, watch and ward and firstaid; and provided with special arrangements for technical guidance and common service facilities'.

The United Nations has defined an Industrial Estate as 'a planned clustering of enterprises, offering standard factory buildings, erected in advance of demand and variety of services and facilities to the occupants'.

**Types of Industrial Estate:** The service term, industrial estate covers all the four variants of the concept namely, industrial areas, industrial estates, industrial townships and galas.

An industrial area is one wherein the infrastructure facilities and services are provided but factory accommodation is constructed by entrepreneurs. In an industrial estate, both infrastructural facilities and factory sheds having accommodation and other civic amenities associated with a town are also provided.

In galas, space is provided in a big building to set up small-scale industries along with infrastructural facilities. On the basis of functions, industrial estates are classified into: *(a)* Conventional (general) type, and *(b)* Special type.

General type industrial estates provide accommodation to a wide variety and range of industrial concerns, while, special type estates attempt the establishment of industrial units, which are vertically or horizontally dependent. In India, general type estates are very popular.

On the basis of the organizational set up, industrial estates are classified into: *(a)* Government, *(b)* Private, *(c)* Co-operative, and *(d)* Municipal estates.

There are a number of other variants of industrial estates such as:

*(a)* ***Ancillary Industrial Estate:*** Only small industries which are ancillary to a particular large industry are housed in this estate, just like the one attached to the HMT Bangalore.

*(b)* ***Functional Industrial Estate:*** This is a small and fully serviced unit which serves as a reception center for displaced small firms. It also serves as a 'Pilot-cell' for small firms going into production and is a base for expansion into larger factories.

*(c)* ***The Workshop Bay:*** This is designed for very small firms and is usually meant for artisans who do mainly repair works.

*(d)* ***The Service Industrial Bay:*** This is usually located in the shopping centers to provide space for repair shops and enterprises such as job-printing.

**Objectives of Industrial Estates:** The objectives underlying the establishment of industrial estates in India are as follows:

*(i)* To encourage the growth of small-scale industries.

*(ii)* To shift small-scale industries from congested areas to estate premises with a view to increasing their productivity.

*(iii)* To achieve decentralized development in small towns and large villages.

*(iv)* To encourage growth of ancillary industries in the townships, surrounding major industrial undertakings, both in public and private sector.

*(v)* To faster the development of industry as well as entrepreneurship by providing economies and incentives

**Lessons of Experience:** According to the Development Commissioner of Small-Scale Industries, the following lessons of experience could be drawn for future:

(1) Industrial estates have to be properly coordinated with the broader development programme. They have to be not only an integral part of the industry development

programme but also of the overall economic development programme of the area/region.

(2) Industrial estates should be planned with a view to developing them into focal points of healthier industrial growth in an area rather than as a cluster of merely inward looking, group of production units. They are to be so designed and managed that theymay, later be in a position to provide necessary common service facilities, technical advice, guidance etc., to other industrial units in the area.

(3) Homogeneity (rather than heterogeneity) is to be the guiding criterion while selecting industrial units. This would lead to better planning and utilization of common facilities, inter-firm co-operation and inter-linked development.

(4) While planning an industrial estate, due consideration is to be given to 'secondary growth' effect in order to regulate any haphazard growth around the estates.

(5) Location of an industrial estate is to be decided only on techno-economic considerations. A techno-economic feasibility study should always precede the setting up of an estate.

(6) While planning industrial estates in an area uniform pattern need not be followed. The organizational structure in a particular area/region may be adjusted taking into consideration factors such as special requirements of an area, economic developments, availability of skills, talents and enterprise, level of development of the region, etc.

(7) Instead of building sheds in advance of demand, sheds may be built on the expressed demand as revealed at the time of conducting techno-economic or feasibility studies.

(8) Elaborate and costlier construction has to be avoided and instead, functional types of sheds at cheaper rates may be provided.

(9) When private initiative is ready, or the success of industrial estates has been demonstrated by one or more examples, government may confine its role to prescribing minimum factory standards, etc., and increasingly associate the entrepreneurs in the work of construction and maintenance of buildings.

(10) To keep construction costs to the minimum, adequate attention should be paid to reduce the cost by improving design efficiency, increasing the size coverage and reducing to the minimum the area allotted for on-factory purposes. The scope for reducing expenditure and non-development and administrative activities in the estates may also be explored and the consequent implications of cost of construction on rent may be kept in view.

(11) In backward and rural areas greater efforts would have to be made to stimulate local entrepreneurship. The industrial estates in such areas have to play promotional role and act as pace-setters in the process of industrial development besides guiding the entrepreneurs in selecting the right lines of manufacture. It may also be necessary to offer additional incentives for locating industrial units. These incentives may be in the shape of concessional credit, rebates, in various taxes, preferential, allotment of scarce raw materials, etc. The industrial estates in backward areas have also to be nursed over longer periods and provided with adequate inducements to counter-

balance the inherent disadvantages from which they suffer. The concessions could be given preferably as a 'package deal' on a tapering basis.

(12) The selection of products to be manufactured in the industrial estates should be in accordance with other development programme, *viz.*, mechanization of agriculture, utilization of agriculture produce, electrification, items of mass consumption, etc.

(13) While general purpose industrial estates are very useful for backward and rural areas in urban areas functional or special types of industrial estates may be preferred in view of the emphasis on modernization, ancillary developments, etc.

An industrial estate is a method of organizing, housing and servicing industry for an orderly development. It is considered as a multipurpose tool supposed to take care of provision of suitable factory premises utilities, facilities and services, economy in the investment on social overheads and the increased scope for inter-servicing and inter-trading development of complementarity in production and creation of the spirit of co-operation, decentralization of industry for development of backward areas, more industrialization, achieving a specific locational pattern, town planning, etc. In short, it accelerates the integrated development of small-scale industries in the country.

## ANCILLARY INDUSTRIES

A balanced industrial development consistent with social justice calls for diffused ownership and control and also decentralized growth of industries. This is possible only if new entrepreneurship is developed. The process ancillarization is one of the handiest methods of encouraging new entrepreneurs to set up small-scale units. This is so because the running of ancillary industry does not give rise to complex problems which the uninitiated new entrepreneur will have to face, if he is to run an independent manufacturing unit. Also, ancillarisation makes it possible for him to establish a coherent relationship with small and large units. It is in these circumstances that ancillaries can provide a strong and widespread base for industrial development.

A major problem faced by ancillary units is their vulnerability to variations in demand. When the large scale manufacturer producing end product face slackness in demand the ancillary unit supplying the components is hit hard and may have to remain practically idle until the demand for the end product revives. Since the production apparatus in the ancillary units is highly specialized and tailored to meet the requirements of a particular assembly, it is not possible to switch over toany other item without incurring losses on account of machinery installed.

An ancillary unit, therefore, is a 'Captive unit' with no alternative outlet. Its difficulties are often aggravated by delay in the payment of bills. During times of financial stringency, there is a tendency on the part of the parent firms to squeeze the ancillary units by giving "themselves the credit through non-payment of bills. A survey of industries in Japan revealed that only eight per cent of the firms received payment in 60 days and that the remaining 92 per cent receivedit after the lapse of 60-150 days. In this particular respect, there foreancillary units are in more vulnerable position, than small-scale industrial units. A small-scale industrial unit producing consumer items or other products will be able to make quick adjustments in its production plan as well as product design in order to minimize the adverse impact of a fall in demand. It may consider diversifying its activity with marginal addition to its machinery and/or equipment. It may even supply its products to other markets if the traditional markets fail. But ancillary units are tied to the 'apron strings' of one or two specific large-scale units and often find it extremely difficult to make such adjustments. As a result, they get adversely affected.

While ancillary units suffer from these disabilities, they are free from the usual worries about the marketing of their products. An ancillary unit produces for a pre-determined market because its production is effected against advance orders. It may be provided with scarce raw materials or even finance by the parent firm depending upon the type of relationship between the two and during periods of rising demand and plentiful orders, the ancillary unit can continue to operate with hardly a problem.

In India, unlike other countries, the ancillaries sponsored by large units, suffer from a majorhandicap. They lean too heavily on the large units. This dependence may be, unavoidable in theinitial stage of development, but the ancillary should be able to stand on its own legs after a time, which would be possible only if the accent is placed on product improvement, cost reduction andthe development of export outlets, especially when the ancillary product is able to meet therequirements of the replacement market abroad.

**Factors Affecting Ancillarization:** A series of rapid developments in the industrial structure in the country has led to a trend toward ancillarization is growing.

The various factors affecting ancillarization are:

(1) The size of the operations of several industrial units has increased enormously, with the result that they are compelled to sub-contract some of the items of production to ancillaries. During the 1950s, these industrial units were set up, so that the production of all the components against the stipulated targets might be met in terms of the licenses granted to them. In those days, there were few ancillary units adequately equipped to produce the components according to specifications. But during 1960s, a large number of small-scale units, which were capable of producing a variety of items emerged with the result that large-scale manufacturers developed enough confidence in them to assign the production of specific items to these units.

(2) It was more convenient for large-scale manufacturers to get the ancillary units to produce certain items for them with the growing complexity of management, the large scale manufacturer can now concentrate on the problems of organization, marketing, finance, etc., rather than fritter away his energies on finding raw materials and framing production plans for the manufacture of the several minor items which go into the final assembly. Example: A bicycle manufacturer does not have to bother about buying and stocking of rubber used in the production of pedals; he prefers to get this item supplied to him by an ancillary unit.

(3) Large-scale manufacturers can economize on transport costs, storage space, etc., by sub-contracting rather than by producing the same components themselves.

(4) It is economic to have some items manufactured by ancillary units because the cost of these items is higher when they are fabricated by large-scale manufacturers.

(5) By sub-contracting, a large-scale manufacturer is able to insulate himself against fluctuations in the prices of raw materials over a period of time by entering into contracts for the supply of these items.

A more accurate assessment of the input cost as well asthe returns on manufacture is possible is if the components are available at fixed price.

All these facts underscore the point that the development of ancillaries and their growing popularity have been well supported by economic and management considerations.

*****

# 14

# Role of Agencies in Entrepreneurship Development

- *Introduction*
- *Entrepreneurship Development Institute (EDI)*
- *Small Industries Service Institute (SISI)*
- *National Institute of Entrepreneurship and Small Business Development (NIESBUD)*
- *National Entrepreneurship Development Board (NEDB)*
- *District Industries Centre – A Case of Tamil Nadu*

## INTRODUCTION

The basic objective of the Industrial Policy pursued by the Tamil Nadu Government is to achieve massive increase in employment by promoting Small Industries and Rural Industries. The Government is of the firm belief that given the magnitude of unemployment and the number of persons living below the poverty line, the touch stone of all industrial schemes and investments ought to be their employment potential especially in the short term.

For this purpose, a thrust has been given to establish, promote and develop the rural industries which are also called the cottage industries and village industries or small industries including tiny and household sector, particularly in backward areas where it is essentially needed. The Government is also in active move in promoting Self-Employment opportunity in Urban and Rural areas by extending financial assistance through banking sector for the establishment and development of small industries.

The policies and programme of Government for the development of rural industrialization based on the utilization of local resources and raw materials and locally available man power and skill are translated into action through the various agencies under the Industries Department which are primarily concerned with the promotion of Small and Rural Industries. Provisions have been made to provide infrastructure facilities. Assistance is provided and growth centers have been promoted. Institutions like Tamil Nadu Industrial Investment Corporation along with Small Industries Service Institute of the Government of India and Nationalized Banks assume the responsibility for providing necessary inputs to this sector. This will go a long way in reducing unemployment.

Since agricultural sector has been fairly saturated, it is necessary to develop secondary sector of economic activity in order to improve the overall economy of the district, as well as to solve the mounting unemployment problem towards this objective. Hence, a new scheme, namely,

NEW ANNA MARUMALARCHI THITTAM has been introduced with a very purpose of imparting thrustto the Agro based industries in each Block of this state.The District Industries Centre is the institution at the district level, which provides all the services and support facilities to the entrepreneurs for setting up small and village industries. This includes identification of suitable schemes, preparation of feasibility reports, arrangements for credit facilities, machinery and equipment, provision of raw materials and extension services. The District Industries Centre, Viluppuram has been pursuing the basic objectives by assisting for optimum utilization in existing industries, faster promotion of new small-scale industries and Village Industries with a rural bias and by increasing the employment opportunities in industries sector.

The Small entrepreneur required various types of assistance right from the selection of an item for manufacture, inputs like credit, raw materials, power, land and building, etc. Under the new scheme of District Industries Centre, the entrepreneur can get all such assistance through one agency.

General Manager heads the District Industries Centre assisted by Manager (Economic Investigation) to look after the survey and statistical work, Cottage Industries and Village Industries and administration and Manager (Materials) to look after Materials and Infrastructure, Exports, Entrepreneurial Development Programme and Training, exclusively for Women and of course, with other supporting staff.

The main functions of District Industries Centre are:

1. Conducting motivation campaigns in Block level.
2. Counselling and guiding the entrepreneurs.
3. Issuing provisional registration for small-scale industries, manually.

*I. Online provisional registration for small-scale industries, through authorized Browsing Centers.*

4. Conducting Single Window Committee meeting periodically to get the clearances fast from different agencies like Power, Local body, etc.
5. Preparing technical feasibility report, whenever the financial institutions ask for.
6. Issuing permanent SSI registration for the industry which commenced production.

7. Issuing registration certificates for Cottage Industries.
8. Issuing registration certificates for Handicrafts Industries.
9. Counselling and guiding the entrepreneurs to start under New Anna Marumalarchi Thittam (NAMT).
10. Granting subsidy on Low Tension Power Tariff at 30, 20, and 10 per cent for the first 3 years, respectively, for the industries set up under NAMT.
11. Granting export compensatory subsidy for leather and electronics industries.
12. Conducting Task force committees to select the beneficiaries under Rural Employment Generation Programme of Khadi Village Industries Commission and tying up with financial institutions for loan assistance.

*II. Conducting Task force committees to select the beneficiaries under Prime Minister's Rozgar Yojana scheme for the educated unemployed youth block wise, train them and tying up with financial institutions for loan assistance.*

13. Conducting Entrepreneur Development Programme at selected institutes to the probable entrepreneurs.
14. Conducting exclusive Entrepreneur Development Programme for women – under five lakhs women entrepreneur training scheme.
15. Conducting seminars, and workshops, etc., on industrial development-related subjects.
16. Formation of industrial co-operative societies in the district.
17. Recommending the industries for awards of state and central governments.
18. Identifying the sick units and declaring them through District Sick Unit Declaration Committee.
19. Assisting the SSI units to get their long pending dues from their borrowers through Regional Industry Facilitation Council.
20. Recommending SSI units to get actual users certificate to obtain concession in the rate of customs duty while importing capital goods.
21. Assisting the entrepreneur to get scarce raw material.
22. Assisting the entrepreneur to get the industrial license, if needed.
23. Assisting SC/ST entrepreneurs under twenty point programme.
24. Conducting regular meeting with local SSI units to solve any particular problem of SSI.
25. Assisting the banks in recovering the dues from the PMRY beneficiaries by conducting regular recovery campaigns.
26. Associating with various departments/Government agencies like TAHDCO, TABCEDCO etc., for the uplift of the entrepreneurs belonging to the socially weaker sections.
27. Assisting and guiding the entrepreneurs in exporting through the proposed export cell.

## INDIAN INSTITUTE OF ENTREPRENEURSHIP (IIE)

### About The Institute

With an aim to undertake training, research and consultancy activities in the small industry sector focusing on entrepreneurship development, the Indian Institute of Entrepreneurship (IIE) was established in the year 1993 at Guwahati by the erstwhile Ministry of Industry (now Ministry of Small-Scale Industry), Government of India as an autonomous national institute. The institute started its operations from April 1994 with North East Council (NEC), Government of Assam, Arunachal Pradesh and Nagaland and SIDBI as other stakeholders. The policy direction and guidance is provided to the Institute by its Board of Management whose Chairman is the Secretary to the Government of India, Ministry of Small-Scale Industries. The governing council of the institute is headed by Chairman, NEC and the Executive Committeeis headed by the Secretary SSI and ARI, Government. of India. The Institute is located at Lalmati, Basistha Charili, 37 NH bypass. It is 5 km from Dispur Capital complex, 10 km from Railway Station and 30 km from LGBI Airport.

### Objectives

- To organize and conduct training for entrepreneurship development.
- To evolve strategies and methodologies for different target groups and locations and conduct field tests.
- To identify training needs and offer training programmers to Government and non-Government organizations engaged in promoting and supporting entrepreneurship.
- To document and disseminate information needed for policy formulation and implementation related to self-employment.
- To identify, design, and conduct training programmers for existing entrepreneurs.
- To prepare and publish literature related to entrepreneurship and industrial development.
- To organize seminars, workshops, and conferences for providing a forum for interaction and exchange of views by various agencies and entrepreneurs.
- To conduct research for generating knowledge to accelerate the process of entrepreneurship development.
- To act as a catalyst for development of self-employment/entrepreneurship, industry/business.
- To evolve, design, and help in the utilization of various media for creating entrepreneurship.

### Activities

The activities of the Institute include identification of training needs, designing and organizing programmers both for development functionaries and entrepreneurs, evolving effective training strategies and methodologies for different target groups and locations; organize seminars, workshops, and conferences for providing foray for interaction and exchange of views by various agencies and entrepreneurs, undertaking research on entrepreneurship development, documenting and disseminating information needed for policy formulation and implementation on self-employment and entrepreneurship. The Institute acts as a catalyst for entrepreneurship development by creating an environment for entrepreneurship in the support system, developing new entrepreneurship, helping in the growth of existing entrepreneurs and propagation of entrepreneurial education.

## SMALL INDUSTRIES SERVICE INSTITUTE (SISI)

### Aims and Objectives

'Imparting greater vitality and growth impetus to the small, tiny and village enterprises in terms of output, employment and exports and instilling a competitive culture based on heightened technologyawareness'.

The Small and Medium Enterprises (SME) sector is one of the fastest growing industrial sectors all over the world. Many countries of the world have established a SME Development Agency (SMEDA) as the nodal agency to co-ordinate and oversee all Government interventions in respect of the development of this sector. In the case of India, though a separate medium sector is not defined, the Office of Development Commissioner (Small-Scale Industries) also known as Small Industries Development Organization (SIDO) functions as the nodal Development Agency for small industries.

SIDO functions under the Ministry of SSI (Ministry of Small-Scale Industries).SIDO was established in 1954 on the basis of the recommendations of the Ford Foundation.

Over the years, it has seen its role evolve into an agency for advocacy, hand holding and facilitation for the small industries sector. It has over 60 offices and 21 autonomous bodies under its management. These autonomous bodies include Tool Rooms, Training Institutions and Project-cum-Process Development Centers. SIDO provides a wide spectrum of services to the small industries sector. These include facilities for testing, tool mending, training for entrepreneurship development, preparation of project and product profiles, technical and managerial consultancy, assistance for exports, pollution and energy audits, etc. SIDO provides economic information services and advises Government in policy formulation for the promotion and development of SSIs. The field offices also work as effective links between the Central and the State Governments. Consequent to the increased globalization of the Indian economy, small industries are required to face new challenges. SIDO has recognized the changed environment and is currently focusing on providing support in the fields of credit, marketing, technology, and infrastructure to SSIs. Global trends and national developments have accentuated SIDO's role as a catalyst of growth of small enterprises in the country.

The small-scale industry sector output contributes almost 40 per cent of the gross industrial value added 45 per cent of the total exports from India (direct as well as indirect exports) and is the second largest employer of human resources after agriculture. The development of small-scale sector has therefore been assigned an important role in India's national plans.

In order to protect, support, and promote small enterprises as also to help them become self supporting, a number of protective and promotional measures have been undertaken by the Government.

The promotional measures cover:

- Industrial extension services.
- Institutional support in respect of credit facilities.
- Provision of developed sites for construction of sheds.
- Provision of training facilities.
- Supply of machinery on hire-purchase terms.
- Assistance for domestic marketing as well as exports.
- Special incentive for setting up enterprises in backward areas etc.
- Technical consultancy and financial assistance for technological upgradation.

While most of the institutional support services and some incentives are provided by the Central Government, others are offered by the state governments in varying degrees to attract investments and promote small industries in varying degrees to attract investments and promote small industries with a view to enhance industrial production and to generate employment in their respective States.

## NATIONAL INSTITUTE OF ENTREPRENEURSHIP AND SMALL BUSINESS DEVELOPMENT (NIESBUD)

The National Institute for Entrepreneurship and Small Business Development (NIESBUD) was established in 1983 by the Ministry of Industry (now Ministry of Small-Scale Industries), Government of India, as an apex body for coordinating and overseeing the activities of various institutions/agencies engaged in Entrepreneurship Development Particularly in the area of small industry and small business. The Institute which is registered as a society under Government of India Societies Act (XXI of 1860) started functioning from 6th July, 1983. The policy, direction and guidance to the Institute is provided by its Governing Council whose Chairman is the Minister of SSI. The Executive Committee consisting of Secretary (Small-Scale Industry and ARI) as its Chairman and Executive Director of the Institute as its Member Secretary executes the policies and decisions of the Governing Council through its whole-time Executive.

### Activities

- To evolve standardized materials and processes for selection, training, support, and sustenance of entrepreneurs, potential and existing.
- To help, support, and affiliate institutions, organizations in carrying out training and other entrepreneurship development-related activities.

- To serve as an apex national level resource institute for accelerating the process of entrepreneurship development ensuring its impact across the country and among all strata of the society.
- To provide vital information and support to trainers, promoters and entrepreneurs by organizing research and documentation relevant to entrepreneurship development.
- To train trainers, promoters, and consultants in various areas of entrepreneurship development.
- To offer consultancy nationally/internationally for promotion of entrepreneurship and small business development.
- To provide national/international forums for interaction and exchange of experiences helpful for policy formulation and modification at various levels.
- To share internationally experience and expertise in entrepreneurship development.
- To share experience and expertise in entrepreneurship development across National frontiers.

## GUIDELINES FOR NATIONAL ENTREPRENEURSHIP DEVELOPMENT BOARD (NEDB) SCHEME

### Objectives

The main objective of the National Entrepreneurship Development Board (NEDB) Scheme is promotion of entrepreneurship for encouraging self-employment in small-scale industries and small business.

### Salient Features

The scheme covers the following activities:

To identify and remove entry barriers for potential entrepreneurs (first generation and new entrepreneurs) including study on entrepreneurship development.

*(i)* To focus on existing entrepreneurs in micro, tiny and small sector and identify and remove constraints to survival, growth and continuously improve performance.

*(ii)* To facilitate the consolidation, growth, and diversification of existing entrepreneurial venture in all possible ways.

*(iii)* To support skill upgradation and renewal of learning processes among practicing entrepreneurs and managers of micro, tiny, small, and medium enterprises.

*(iv)* To sensitize to support agencies in the area of entrepreneurship about the current requirement of growth.

*(v)* To act as catalyst to institutionalize entrepreneurship development by supporting and strengthening state level institutions for entrepreneurship development as

most entrepreneurship-related activities take place at the grass-root level and removing various constraints to their effective functioning.

*(vi)* Setting up of incubators by entrepreneurship development institutions and other organizations devoted to the promotion of entrepreneurship development.

*****

# 15 Problems of Small-Scale Industries

Despite of several strengths of SSIs, the entrepreneurs are facing several problems, constraints or challenges. The small industry is confronted with number of problems, constraints, handles, hazards, limitations, and rigidities, but of which some are old and chronic whereas the others are new and complicated. The worldwide industrial and economic environment and particularly New Policy regime had also affected the small-scale industries in the state.

In a nutshell, the following problems relating to small industry have been identified:

*(i)* Raw material constraints.

*(ii)* Organizational problems.

*(iii)* Social and cultural value system.

*(iv)* Environmental pollution and other problems.

*(v)* Technological problems.

*(vi)* Manpower development related problems.

*(vii)* Quality-related problems.

*(viii)* Marketing-related problems.

*(ix)* Export-related problems.

*(x)* Financial problems of entrepreneurs.

## Diagnosis of Emerging Problems

As the Indian industry entered into the third millennium, the most daunting challenge it has to encounter in a liberalized global trading system relates to the attainment and maintenance of technological competitiveness while a vast network of technological infrastructure has been built in the country and considerably progress has been achieved in the industrial and scientific arena since independence, many industries, mostly in the small-scale sector still suffer from technological obsolescence as compared to that of the international level. More importantly, any technological innovation has not trickled down to the desired extent to the small-scale and rural industries. It has been observed that the linkages between R&D and SSIs, and also between on parallel units and SSI's, are weak. Similarly, the linkages between trade consultants, media, websites, trade fairs, industry associations, on the one hand and SSIs, on the other hand, are simply moderate. This is because of the fact that institutional research is not demand-driven and there is mismatch between institution's orientation towards basic research and industry's needs for new or improved products.

With gradual industrialization and advancement of workers having basic workers having basic skills in the trades starting to place strict competition from their competitors, who used advanced technology, modern machines, new designs, etc. This is one of the some very strong reasons of deterioration of their overall condition. There are millions of workers in the state of Uttar Pradesh living in rural areas, suffering from illiteracy, superstitions and financial weakness and unable to enjoy the benefits of technological development. Neither were they brought close to the new technology nor did the technology reach them

Some of the infrastructural inadequacies affecting the SSI sector are absence of design centers, evaluation and demonstration facilities, lack of services and feasibility studies, poor assistance for pilot plant trials, inadequate testing facilities, high cost of maintenance, environment cleanliness, including effluent treatment and disposal facilities, absence of common facilities, non-availability of developed tool rooms and standards for ensuring quality and accuracy of the work/product, proper storage and handling facilities.

Lack of infrastructural facilities has hampered efforts towards attainment of technological self-reliance for small-scale industries.

The SSIs lack indigenous technological capability, improved traditional technologies to reduce dependence on advance countries and to export some technologies for striking a better bargaining position for imported technologies. In this context, even IT sector is found to be weak mainly due to: (i) inadequate management skills, (ii) lack of access to technological information and consultancy services, (iii) relative isolation from technology hubs, (iv) inadequate quest for technological advancements, (v) inadequacy of financial capability, (vi) low levels of investment in R&D, (vii) inadequate adaptability to changing trends, (viii) non-availability of technically trained human resources.

An industrial production is associated with the problem of disposal of effluents. However, the leather, chemical, sugar, and tannery industries have been singled out as pollution intensive industries. There is belief that the large-scale unplanned tanning actively can erode the soil. The leather industry is one of the major industries that discharge toxic pollutants like sulphide, phenolic compounds, chromium and other mineral salts, dyes, solvents, etc. Out of which, chromium contributes a major share to the potentially hazardous nature of tannery effluents, owing 15 above hazards a stringent environmental regulations is at present posing an important threat to the growth of leather industry. Most of the tanneries in India are century old with no drainage facilities and no adequate measures to recycle or diffuse the effluent.

Small enterprises are presently handicapped in comparison with large units by an inequitable allocation system for scarce raw materials and imported components. The SSI sector has not shared proportionately, the growing supplies of scarce raw materials. In village industries, raw materials account for more than 60 per cent of the total cost of the product, and in some industries, like leather, oil, metal products it is even higher than 80 per cent. New enterprises face problems in obtaining raw materials in the absence of a proper and equitable policy of raw material distribution.

There has been a decrease in availability of many of the materials needed for craft manufacture and a decline in quality in many of the still available materials. The materials facing the most severe shortage today are wood, cane, silk, scrap, and virgin metal. The costs of some of these are rising faster than the Wholesale Price Index.

Importantly, many of the agro-based industries find it difficult to obtain the right type of raw materials at the right time and at moderate prices. Agricultural produce are seasonal products. Agro-based industries suffer from this problem due to their poor financial position. They cannot stock adequate raw materials when they are available. Agro-based industries obtain their inputs from agricultural sector. The output of agricultural sector depends upon the soil, climatic conditions, rainfall, use of fertilizers, pesticides etc. Therefore, agricultural output cannot be increased according to the demands of agro-based industries. Therefore, agro-based industries fall the problem of inadequate raw materials.

Lack of finance has been a serious problem by the small-scale industries. This problem becomes acute after 1972-73 policy in terms of modernization and expansion of industries. In the state of Uttar Pradesh, the small business entrepreneurs rely on traditional sources of finance such as personal or family sources or local moneylenders. Credit available through financial institutions is either availed by large entrepreneurs and the smaller ones are deprived of it due to illiteracy, lack of awareness, tedious procedure, followed for obtaining loans, or due to local petty politic king. Large industrial institutions with enormous resources take fuller advantage and keep growing further. If this problem is not checked now, the large business entrepreneurs may eat up the small industrial entrepreneurs.

Capital is one among the four factors of production. No industry can function without capital. Capital is necessary to carry on productive activities. Capital is also necessary for development and expansion. Therefore, capital is the lifeblood for every business owners of agro-based industries. They cannot obtain adequate financial assistance from the financial institutions, because they do not have right type of security which is demanded by the financial institutions as collateral security. So far their financial requirements, they often go to many lenders who charge exorbitant rates of interest. Small industries face the problem of the irregular supply of power. In many towns and villages, power is not available. So the small agro-based industries have to use manpower to its optimum level and produce the commodities. Thus, the cost of production is very high. At the same time, they are unable to sell their products at a profit. Small industries also face the problem of poor transport facilities. Development of transport facilities is inadequate. In many towns, there are no proper roads to transport the output of industries. The cost of transport also results in an increase in prices. Hence, the products are sold in local areas at low price.

The industries are facing too many visit and inspections by the Government officials regarding sales tax formalities and other such regulations and over-emphasis by Government for implement specifications for buildings, trading to high investment. One of the major problems which entrepreneurs face today is related to availability of labour. The non-availability of qualified technical manpower is emerging, as a major impediment in the speedy growth of industries.

The small industries suffer from administrative difficulties. Applications for access to almost any form of governance service involve the endless filling of forms. The complexity of procedures, the multiplicity of required clearances, and the low salaries of the junior clerks who are involved at every stage result in wide spread corruption.

As conventional trade barriers disappear in the world economy, a new set of concerns, laudable in themselves, are often extremely difficult to address satisfactorily in developing countries. Child labour is a case in point. Although there are many cases of gross, even criminal, exploitation of children in India, there are also difficult types of child labour. In the small industry, one of the most important obstacles of development is the existing system of raw material distribution and marketing of products. Presences of middlemen in the intermediaries are agents with vested interests are problematic especially for tiny business entrepreneurs. Inadequate market intelligence is another problem faced by the small industrial entrepreneurs. Absence or improper market intelligence reduces the foreign exchange earning capacity of the industry. This processes more and more sophisticated finished products for exports.

From the marketing aspect, the main problems identified are: (i) packaging, (ii) pricing, (iii) selling, (iv) promotion, (v) transport, (vi) market information. Although many exploit the vulnerabilities of their suppliers, there are also a good number of entrepreneurs who are committed to improving the lives of crafts persons, and who conduct their enterprises with integrity and dedication. A number of these people have established businesses that are recognized as true pioneers in the field. Exporters complained about the difficulty of obtaining credit. The problems they face are in fact, similar to those faced by crafts producers. Procedural complexities, inefficiencies and corruption of government officers are perennial problems being faced by business entrepreneurs. Export procedures from India are complex. It is very difficult for an individual buyer on a short trip to find economical ways of shipping home a small order. Most agencies work on a container basis, even if they agree to accept a smaller order, they will charge extremely high rates. Individual crafts producers, NGOs and small retailers cannot offer this kind of service, which means that visiting buyers can purchase from them no more than they can fit into their unit case.

Globalization has brought on some qualitative charges. Export potentials generally enable easier credit flow and financing. Nevertheless, the export market continues to be characterized by some disturbing features. There is usually a very wide differential between manufacturer's price, export price, and retail price for all hand-made products. The carpet is an established trade. In relatively new products, the differential can also arise from lack of information on the part of buyers about the true manufacturing costs. Importantly, limited information and finance restrict access to three key means of value addition: training in skill up gradation, design input and technical advancement. Insufficiencies in accessing and understanding viable new markets pose another challenge.

Rapid globalization and changing domestic preference have brought the industries face to face with a unique set of challenges. The problems these industries face is not one of universal unqualified obsolescence in the face of competition from mechanized industries. To the contrary, the demand for handcrafted goods has the potential to expand together with growth of world and domestic tourism, and with spending on interior decoration. While exportly–share grown, the pattern of change in the domestic market has been complex. By and large, the Indian consumers show an increasing preference, for factory made goods and particularly products of MNCs. Factory made products or MNCs products have the advantage of uniform quality, while quality of small manufacturer's item is inconsistent. Large manufacturers and MNCs have ample budgets for market research, product development, and advertising, which allow them to keep in tune with consumer needs. Factory made and MNCs products can usually be sold at the lower price because of reduced cost of production due to use of improved sophisticated technology of production and managerial efficiency. The small industrial entrepreneurs face the problems of increased competition from organized sector as well as access to infrastructure, credit, technology, markets, and retailing.

Thus, globalization, liberalization and marketization of economy have posed challenges to SSI sector which need to be faced with preparedness. Business process re-engineering, R&D, technological upgradation, enhancing competencies of human resources, enhancing financial creditability, widening the scope of marketing, policy support in terms of credit, raw materials, technology transfers, prices, trade tax excerption, etc., need immediate attention of policy makers to revive the industrial productivity and enhancing the managerial efficiency.

## Problems of Small and Medium Enterprises

Small and medium enterprises face problems relating to project implementation, production, marketing, finance, administration, etc.

The identified problems may be summarized as:

**I. Problems relating to project implementation**

- Non-availability of land at the selected site.
- Non-availability/difficulty in procuring construction materials like cement, steel, etc.
- Delay in delivery of machines.
- Difficulties/delay in tying up financial arrangements with other financial institutions and banks.
- Inability of the promoters to bring in funds to the extent proposed.

- Delay in disbursement of assistance due to non-compliance of the major terms and conditions of the loan agreement.
- Delay in getting power connection, water connection, permission of concerned authorities to discharge effluents, etc.
- Changes in certain project concepts due to subsequent detailed advice received from collaborators/consultants.
- Increase in project cost under different heads due to price escalation, underestimation of cost, etc.
- Siphoning of funds by the promoters from the project by unfair practices.

**II. Problems relating to production**

- Non-availability of raw materials or increase in the price of raw materials without a corresponding increase in sale price of the products.
- Non-availability of important infrastructure facilities like power, water, transport etc.
- Unsatisfactory performance of certain machines resulting in low production due to lack of routine and preventive maintenance leading to frequent breakdown.
- Lack of coordination between marketing and production planning.
- Obsolescence of the manufacturing process following technological development.

**III. Problems relating to marketing**

- Introduction of better substitutes.
- Entry of many new manufacturers leading to cut–throat competition.
- Dependence of the unit on one buyer/ very few buyers.
- Poor quality of products.
- Lack of sales promotion.
- Poor delivery schedules and lack of proper distribution system.

**IV. Problems relating to finance**

- Low promoters contribution.
- High debt-equity ratio leading to high interest burden.
- Inadequate bank finance.
- Lack of proper follow up action for realization of debts.
- Lack of proper planning to pay creditors.
- Diversion of working capital funds for acquisition of fixed assets.

**V. Problems relating to management**

- Dissension within the management.
- Absence of manpower planning.

- Poor industrial relations.
- Lack of coordination and control.
- Non-availability of skilled manpower.

## Various Organizations for Assisting Small and Medium Entrepreneurs

Various organizations have been set up by the central and state governments and banks to support the development of the small-scale enterprises.

The main organizations are as follows:

**I. Central Government**

1. National Board for Micro, Small, and Medium Enterprises.
2. Small Industries Development Organization (SIDO).
3. Micro, Small, and Medium Industries Services Institute.
4. National Small Industries Corporation Limited (NSIC).
5. National Institute for Micro, Small, and Medium Enterprises (NIMSME).
6. Entrepreneurship Development Institute of India (EDI).

**II. State Government**

1. District Industries Centers (DIC).
2. State Financial Corporations (SFCs).
3. State Industrial Development Corporations/ State Industrial Investment Corporations (SIDC/SIIC).
4. State Small Industries Development Corporation (SSIDC).
5. Khadi and Village Industries Commission (KVIC).

**III. Financial Institutions/Banks**

1. Small Industries Development Bank of India (SIDBI).
2. Commercial Banks.
3. Regional Rural Banks.
4. Cooperative Banks.
5. National Bank for Agriculture and Rural Development (NABARD).

**IV. Organizations promoted by the Government/ Banks/Financial Institutions**

1. Technical Consultancy Organization in various states.
2. India SME Technology Services Ltd.
3. SIDBI Venture Capital Ltd.
4. Credit Guarantee Fund Trust for Micro and Small Industries.
5. India SME Asset Reconstructing Company (ISARC).

**V. Industry Associations**

1. Confederation of Indian Industry (CII).
2. Federation of Indian Chamber of Commerce and Industries (FICCI).
3. Associated Chamber of Commerce and Industries in India (ASSOCHAM).
4. Consortium of Women Entrepreneurs in India (CWEI).
5. World Association of Small and Medium Enterprises (WASME).
6. Federation of Association of Small-Scale Industries (FASSI).

Technology upgradation for Small-Scale Industries

The Government of India has decided to continue the following four schemes during the 11th Plan period (2007–2012) to assist small-scale industries for technology upgradation though various schemes.

1. Credit Linked Capital Subsidy Scheme for Technology up-gradation of Small Industries (CLCSS).

2. Technology upgradation Fund Scheme (TUFS) for Textile and Jute Industry.

3. Scheme of technology upgradation/setting-up/modernization/expansion of food processing industries.

4. Integrated development of leather sector scheme (IDLSS).

Recommendations and Strategies for revival of SSIs Manufacturing capabilities should be developed to a level where products are competitive across global markets in terms of price, quality, technology, delivery of services. To achieve this, Indian firms should be enabled to access the latest technology from across the globe, indigenous research and development innovation need to be encouraged and a passion for manufacturing needs to be created while infrastructure, public services and utilities should be improved and made more efficient to assist manufacturing growth. Government, industry, research institutions and academicians should be facilitated and encouraged to work in collaboration to improve industry capabilities. Moreover, firms should be able to obtain funds easily and cheaply, and be encouraged to invest in developing technology.

To improve standard of living through manufacturing growth, workers should be enabled to move from lower value added to higher value added jobs. SSIs and cottage industries should be encouraged to grow and become competitive. Moreover, education should focus on fostering a culture that encourages innovation and manufacturing so that people are training for alternate avenues of employment.

Government must eliminate all reservations in SSI sector, standing with 63 items which constitute over 80 per cent of the total output of SSI sector. State governments and industry bodies have to take a lead to identify SSI clusters, promote cooperation between business and local authorities for cluster development, and formulate policies that attract investment to these clusters.

One hundred per cent FDI should be allowed in all except a few strategic sectors. FDI restrictions in retail need to remove to support by actions in associated areas like granting tax benefits, enabling ease of technology transfer, easing labour regulations, removing SSI restrictions, facilitating easy setting up of business, and enabling infrastructure in the country.

Considering the urgency of taking an early lead in attaining technological competitiveness of SSIs, both in the domestic and industrial markets, it is important to stimulate and usher in a technological revolution among SSIs. Attainment of international competitiveness of SSIs through technological upgradation should be treated as priority and a mission by the state government. The ultimate aim of State Technology Mission should be to enable the SSIs to assimilate new technologies though appropriate utilization and modification and also to strengthen indigenous technological infrastructure including R & D institutions and enterprise linkages, industrial engineering design, consultancy services, etc. It can be very useful if it deals with identification of new products and technologies and proper transfer of the same, advice and information of product innovation, design, better management practices, financial resources, marketing research, process automation and last but not the least tying up with MNCs and large Indian companies as ancillaries for outsourcing their requirement from SSIs along with technology packages.

It is recommended that a State Technology Development Fund for small industries be established in the state to act as the main conduct of transmission mechanism of the Sate Mission on Technology. The fund should be routed through SIDBI because it is the principal financial institution for SSIs. The fund should support SSI units in absorbing technology transfer costs, meeting with initial ground work related expenditure. The fund should initiate efforts at the earliest to set up technology packages, clusters for SSIs in important zones to promote induction of new technologies, incremental innovations and effective transfer.

The industrial estates can provide the following facilities in addition to developed plots and buildings such as — (i) common utilities like power, water, electricity, industrial gas, compressed air, etc., (ii) offsite facilities like water tanks, storages, fuel supplies etc., (iii) common effluent treatment and disposal, (iv) communication facilities, (v) secretarial facilities, (vi) staff housing, (vii) transport facility, (viii) medical facility, (ix) fire protection services, etc.

It is recommended that central facilities should be established for small and tiny sectors for liaison work and market development. These SSIs should also be availed the benefits of product exhibition for export.

It is also recommended that State Technology Information Bank should be established in the state to make a mission of spreading knowledge about every aspect of technology to all small-scale industries situated at every part of the state. It should act as a central Document Centre by sourcing, collecting, and disseminating information regarding the availability of technology developed technologies as well as technologies available in the country and abroad.

Fiscal incentives should be provided to SSIs for technical modernization. Exemption from excise duty on goods manufactured by SSIs, tax holiday and tax reduction to SSIs sponsoring research and technological development, zero customs duty for all goods imported to use in R&D projects by SSIs, providing equity capital to SSIs and providing financial support for research and development institutions to transfer technology. Excise duty waiver on indigenous equipment spare parts, consumables and prototypes produced by commercial entities in the small-scale sector as against currently limited to non-commercial scientific and industrial research organizational needs. Policy attention, providing financial assistance to such research and development institutions engaged in developing indigenous technology or adaptation of improved technology for commercial application in SSIs on soft terms may also be considered.

There has to be change in the mind set of individual entrepreneurs to recognize the changing reality and to move as far as possible to change and adopt. This can be catalyzed by efforts by industry associations. The associations and other forms of intermediate local government structure in step with needs of local industry play a pivotal role in aiding government to develop a cluster approach. It is necessary that the industry associations help in establishing both backward and forward linkages for sustenance and development of small industries.

The recommendations of the various circulars and committee reports of RBI should be implemented minimize the financial problem, authorities can minimize the time taken for loan sanctioning and ensure the collateral free loans at the time of requirement.

The following promotional measures are suggested for SSI sector (i) ban on entry of medium and large units into the manufacture of such products which are served for small scale sector, (ii) excise duty and sales tax exemptions/concession, (iii) government and PSU should make their purchase for SSI sector, (iv) adequate infrastructure facilities like land and building, technical consultancy and finance, (v) small units can adopt a group approach to ensure efficient management with a view to reduce the cost of production, and (vi) to make the climate attractive to industrialists for investment.

## Strategies for Revival of SSIs

1. To encourage private and government participation in industrial and social development.
2. To create industrial friendly atmosphere for industry.
3. Developing necessary infrastructure.
4. New small-scale and tiny units should be given capital subsidy equal to 10 per cent of this investment subject to a maximum of ₹ 5 lakh. A capital subsidy fund of ₹ 250 lakh should be created for this purpose.
5. New small-scale and tiny units have to be given interest subsidy of 5 per cent (subject to a maximum of ₹ 2.5 lakh annually) for 5 years on loan from banks/financial institutions.

6. Creation of an industrial estate infrastructure development fund which should be at the disposal of a committee comprising of entrepreneurs.
7. Purchase of technology and provision of common facility centers must be managed through ASIDE scheme.
8. Publicity should be made through an interactive website by the greater use of information technology.
9. Monthly teleconferencing/video conferencing must be organized enabling entrepreneurs throughout the state to interact with senior officers and professionals.
10. Small-scale and tiny units should be exempted from land-use change charge for change of agriculture land to industrial purpose.
11. Policy guidelines must be to ensure cluster based industrial development.
12. A system of providing testing and certification facilities to small scale and tiny units, especially those which want to contribute in the field of exports, should be established by the State Government.
13. Adequate steps must be adopted to sustain and strengthen the traditional knowledge, skills and capabilities of weavers, to revitalize the institutional structure to enrich human resource skills and capabilities.
14. There is almost a total vacuum in the field of reliable data in the handloom sector making it imperative to establish an effective MIS for the sector. Giving priority to this work, a detailed database needs to be created.

A close supervision and follow up is necessary to take corrective steps at the appropriate time. Following suggestions can be considered for avoiding or tackling the problems of SMEs:

- Proper appraisal of the project.
- Implementation of the project according to the time schedule.
- Disbursements of funds according to the requirement of the project.
- Modernization/expansion/diversification of the project.
- Detection of sickness and taking corrective steps at the incipient stage.

Small-scale industries in India could not progress satisfactorily due to various problems that they are confronted with while running enterprises. Inspite of having huge potentialities, the major problems, small industries face are given below:

1. *Problem of skilled manpower:* The success of a small enterprise revolves around the entrepreneur and its employees, provided the employees are skilled and efficient. Because inefficient human factor and unskilled manpower create innumerable problems for the survival of small industries. Non-availability of adequate skilled manpower in the rural sector poses problem to small-scale industries.
2. *Inadequate credit assistance:* Adequate and timely supply of credit facilities is an important problem faced by small-scale industries. This is partly due to scarcity of capital and partly due to weak creditworthiness of the small units in the country.

3. *Irregular supply of raw material:* Small units face severe problems in procuring the raw materials whether they use locally available raw materials or imported raw materials. The problems arise due to faulty and irregular supply of raw materials. Non-availability of sufficient quantity of raw materials, sometimes poor quality of raw materials, and increased cost of raw materials, foreign exchange crisis and above all lack of knowledge of entrepreneurs regarding government policy are other few hindrances for small-scale sector.

4. *Absence of organized marketing:* Another important problem faced by small-scale units is the absence of organised marketing system. In the absence of organized marketing, their products compare unfavourably with the quality of the product of large- scale units. They also fail to get adequate information about consumer's choice, taste and preferences of the type of product. The above problems do not allow them to stay in the market.

5. *Lack of machinery and equipment:* Small-scale units are striving hard to employ modern machineries and equipment in their process of production in order to compete with large industries. Most of the small units employ outdated and traditional technology and equipment. Lack of appropriate technology and equipment create a major stumbling block for the growth of small-scale industries.

6. *Absence of adequate infrastructure:* Indian economy is characterized by inadequate infrastructure which is a major problem for small units to grow. Most of the small units and industrial estates found in towns and cities are having one or more problems like lack of power supply, water and drainage problem, poor roads, raw materials, and marketing problem. Thus absence of adequate infrastructure adversely affects the quality, quantity and production schedule of the enterprises which ultimately results in under-utilization of capacity.

7. *Competition from large-scale units and imported articles:* Small-scale units find it very difficult to compete with the product of large-scale units and imported articles which are comparatively very cheap and of better quality than small unit's product.

Besides the above problems, small-scale units have been constrained by a number of other problems also. They include poor project planning, managerial inadequacies, old and orthodox designs, high degree of obsolescence and huge number of bogus concerns. Due to all these problems the development of small-scale industries has not been as envisaged.

*****

# 16

# Causes of Sickness in Small Industries

- *Causes of Sickness*
- *Reasons for Sickness*
- *Signals of Sickness*
- *Remedies*
- *Curative Measures*

Industry is a Latin term meaning 'diligent and industrious.' Hence, the word industry refers to the manufacturing of a good or service within a category. The key industrial economic sectors are: the primary sector, largely raw material extraction industries such as mining and farming, the secondary sector, involving refining, construction, and manufacturing, the tertiary sector, which deals with services (such as law and medicine) and distribution of manufactured goods. Sickness refers to constituting an unhealthy environment for those working.

Industrial sickness refers to sickness of an industry which means that the industry is suffering from any of the ailment – be it finance, production, technology, marketing, etc.

Definition of a sick unit is given by Sick Industrial Companies Act, 1985. According to the act 'the sick industrial company is a company which has at the end of any financial year accumulated losses equal to or excluding its entire net worth and has also suffered cash losses in that financial year and in the financial year immediately preceding it'.

Industrial sickness is growing at an annual rate of about 28 and 13 per cent, respectively, in terms of number of units and outstanding number of bank credit. It is reckoned that as of today there are more than 2 lakhs sick units with an outstanding bank credit of over ₹ 7,000 crore nearly 29,000 units are added to sick list every year. Industrial sickness especially in small scale has been always a demerit for the Indian economy, because more and more industries like – cotton, jute, sugar, textile, small steel, and engineering industries are being affected by this sickness problem.

## CAUSES OF SICKNESS

Most of the Indian authors and researchers have classified the different types of industrial sickness under two important categories. They are: internal causes and external causes.

Internal causes pertain to the factors which are within the control of management. This sickness arises due to internal disorder in any one or many of the areas mentioned below:

1. **Lack of Finance:** This including weak equity base, poor utilization of assets, inefficient working capital management, absence of costing and pricing, absence of planning and budgeting, and inappropriate utilization or diversion of funds.
2. **Bad Production Policies:** The another very important reason for sickness is wrong selection of site which is related to production, inappropriate plant & machinery, bad maintenance of plant & machinery, lack of quality control, lack of standard research & development and so on.
3. **Marketing and Sickness:** This is another part which always affects the health of any sector as well as SSI. This including wrong demand forecasting, selection of inappropriate product mix, absence of product planning, wrong market research methods, and bad sales promotions.
4. **Inappropriate Personnel Management:** The another internal reason for the sickness of SSIs is inappropriate personnel management policies which includes bad wages and salary administration, bad labour relations, lack of behavioural approach causes dissatisfaction among the employees and workers.
5. **Ineffective Corporate Management:** Another reason for the sickness of SSIs is ineffective or bad corporate management which includes improper corporate planning, lack of integrity in top management, lack of coordination and control, etc.

External causes refer to reasons beyond the control of the management. These include:

1. **Personnel Constraint:** The first for most important reason for the sickness of small-scale industries are non-availability of skilled labour or manpower wages disparity in similar industry and general labour invested in the area.
2. **Marketing Constraints:** The second cause for the sickness is related to marketing. The sickness arrives due to liberal licensing policies, restrain of purchase by bulk purchasers, changes in global marketing scenario, excessive tax policies by government and market recession.
3. **Production Constraints:** This is another reason for the sickness which comes under external cause of sickness. This arises due to shortage of raw material, shortage of power, fuel and high prices, import-export restrictions.
4. **Finance Constraints:** Another external cause for the sickness of SSIs is lack of finance. This arises due to credit restrains policy, delay in disbursement of loan by government, unfavorable investments, fear of nationalization.

## REASONS FOR SICKNESS

Production related reasons:

- Faulty product mix.
- Backlog of production.
- Poor quality of end product.
- Delayed delivery schedule.

Financial reasons:

- Low profitability.
- Low fund generation.
- Poor liquidity.
- Step cost structure.
- Lack of financial resources.
- Lack of credit facility.
- Faulty credit utilization.
- Low share value.

Market reasons:

- Poor marketing strategy.
- Imbalance between production and marketing.
- Wild market shifts.
- Lack of awareness of consumer's preferences.
- Lack of specific market segmentation.
- Poor distribution network.
- Poor market performance.

## SIGNALS OF SICKNESS

The following actions of the unit indicate that the unit is sick or going to be sick:

- Continuous irregularity in cash credit accounts.
- Low capacity utilization.
- Profit fluctuations, downward sales and fall in profits followed by contraction in the share market.
- Failure to pay statutory liabilities.
- Larger and longer outstanding in the bills accounts.
- Non-submission of periodical financial data/stock statement, etc. in time.

- Financing capital expenditure out of funds provided for working capital purposes.
- Rapid turnver of key personnel.
- Existence of large no. of law suits against a company.
- Rapid expansion and too much diversification within a short time.
- Any major change in the share holdings.

Effect of sickness:

- Industrial sickness contributes to high cost economy. This in turn, will affect the competitiveness of the economy at home and abroad.
- Dead investment is a burden on both banks and budgets and ultimately consumers should pay the high cost.
- Money locked up in sick units gives no returns and effects the availability of resources to the other viable units.

## REMEDIES

Majority of sick units are retrievable. In order to tackle the problem of sickness, the role of three agencies assumes significance:

- The government.
- Financial institutions.
- Industry associations.

*Role of Government:* If the number of units in the country has increased some 10 times since independence and if we have diversified industrial structure with wide spread entrepreneurship the credit for this largely belongs to government. Second area where the government can be helpful is *vis-à-vis* industrial licensing. The very existence of licensing and monopoly regulation legislation implies that there is a stampede to 'to get in' whenever licensing is liberalized for an industry or an economy as a whole.

*Role of Financial Institutions:* The following are the ways by which sickness can be prevented by financial institutions:

- Continuous monitoring of unit.
- Careful project appraisal.
- Professional institutional response to unit's problems.
- Required systems at client units.
- Incentives to units to remain healthy.

*Role of Industry Associations:* A good practical review by each industry association of installed and usable capacity in the industrial units, capacity utilization, growth trends, problems if any should be useful for the potential new entrants for deciding whether to enter the industry or not. The industry can have some sort of first-aid cell which could consist of professionals who could go to the aid of a unit that is beginning to fall sick with the offer of managerial and technical help.

## CURATIVE MEASURES

These measures include how to cure the sickness after it has crept in. There are lots of agencies which help cure Industrial sickness. There is Industries (Development and Regulation) Act, 1951, which provides for the takeover of a sick unit by the Government of India. Before resorting to a takeover, other alternatives like rehabilitation through the concerned state government and financial institutions or for the merger of a sick unit with a healthy unit could be explored. Then there is the Sick Industrial Companies (special provisions) Act, 1985, which was passed by parliament and received the assent of president in January 1986. It was amended in December 1991 so as to bring government companies within the preview of the Act. Further, there is the Industrial Reconstruction Bank of India (IRBI) which came into being on 20 March, 1985 by converting the erstwhile Industrial Reconstruction Corporation of India. It provides assistance for reconstructions and rehabilitation of the sick industrial units by granting those loans and advances, underwriting shares and debentures etc. For the sick units in the small-scale sector, separate facilities are available. State Finance Corporations and commercial banks will be asked to devise a scheme for the rehabilitation of sick units in the small-scale sector, and the assistance given by them for the revival of such units will be eligible for refinancing by the IRBI at the confessional rate of interest. The Government must not only provide facilities, but also ensure proper implementation of policies so that not only the efforts of the government bear fruits but also the common man benefits.

*****

# PART III : STUDENT SUPPORT

1. Exercises
2. Success Stories
3. Appendices
4. Additional Reading

# EXERCISES

1. Who Am I?
2. Entrepreneur Self Test
3. Check Right Entrepreneurial Personality Type
4. Identifying Entrepreneurial Talent
5. Building Your Game Plan
6. Questions for Creative Thinking
7. Understanding Just WHAT is PROFIT?
8. Creativity-Innovation-Problem Solving
9. Visualize Your Future – Activity
10. Developing Skills for Ethical Decision-Making

# EXERCISE 1

**Who Am I?**

Name: ____________________________________

| Who Am I? | What I Do? |
| --- | --- |
| What I Bring? | What I Expect? |

*****

# EXERCISE 2

# ENTREPRENEUR SELF TEST

This assessment is designed to help an individual identify and understand his/her entrepreneurial potential. The test can be used at the individual level/community level for profit and non-profit sector/services and potential entrepreneurs.

## Scoring the Test

Not all questions carry the same value and weight. The following scoring approach is recommended:

- First two questions under motivation:
  2 questions × 10 pts = 20 maximum pts × factor of 1 = Score of 20
- Remaining questions under motivation:
  10 questions × 10 pts = 100 maximum pts × factor of 0.25 = Score of 25
- Capacity – skill questions:
  9 questions × 10 pts = 90 maximum pts × factor of 0.25 = Score of 22.5
- Capacity – Networking/Partnering Questions:
  6 questions × 10 pts = 60 maximum pts × factor of 0.25 = Score of 15
- Support questions:
  5 questions × 10 pts = 50 maximum pts × factor of 0.25 = Score of 12.5

## Score Sheet

Low potential 0 to 25 score.

Some potential 26 to 50 score.

Moderate potential 51 to 75 score.

High potential 76 plus score.

---

The *Entrepreneur Self-Test* consists of three sections: motivation, capacity, and support.

## Motivation

( ) Evaluate your overall motivation to start and operate your own business. Score on a 1 to 10 scale, where 10 indicate strong agreement with the statement and 1 indicates little or no agreement with the statement.

( ) Perceive opportunities – I am constantly seeing business opportunities or ideas that have potential commercial value.

( ) Growth oriented – I like growing or building business, or taking ideas and make something of them.

( ) Creative – I am creative and I am regularly coming up with new ideas on how to do things better or more efficiently.

( ) Innovative – I am innovative and I am able to find solutions to challenges and problems.

( ) Resourceful – I am resourceful and I am able to find solutions to challenges and problems.

( ) Dynamic – I am a dynamic person providing vision, hope and energy to those I am working and partnering with.

( ) Hard working – I am a hard working person and I do what it takes to succeed.

( ) Flexible – I am flexible and I am able to adapt to changes and surprises quickly and successfully.

( ) Risk tolerant – I am risk tolerant and I am able to successfully manage risk associated with creating and growing a business.

( ) Open to learning – I thrive on learning and I am constantly seeking out new information that can help me with my business.

( ) Competitive – I am motivated by success and driven to do well.

( ) Collaborative – I believe in working with others who can help me make my dream a reality.

## Capacity

Evaluate your capacity related to the following *business skills*. Consider not only your own capacities, but also the capacities of the other members of your management team. Rate yourself on a scale of 1 to 10 with 1 being no capacity and 10 being high capacity.

( ) Ability to assess market opportunities.

( ) Ability to develop products or services.

( ) Ability to provide products or services.

( ) Marketing and communications capacity.

( ) Fiscal management.

( ) Ability to acquire financial capital.

( ) Personnel or team development and management.

( ) Ability to develop and sustain partnerships.

( ) Quality control.

Evaluate your ability to network and partner with other organizations and individuals. Score on a 1 to 10 scale where 10 indicate strong agreement with the statement and 1 indicates little or no agreement with the statement.

( ) I am comfortable seeking out information from others.

( ) I regularly network with others to gain information for my business.

( ) I have an extensive resource network that I am constantly building.

( ) I am comfortable with partnerships.

( ) I have two or more partnerships associated with my business.

( ) I have learned how to deal with the challenges of partnering with others.

## Support

Evaluate the level of support you feel from your family and community as you pursue your business opportunities. Score on a 1 to 10 scale where 10 indicate strong agreement with the statement and 1 indicates little or no agreement with the statement.

( ) I am challenged and happy in my work building a business.

( ) I believe there is good balance between my work and my personal life.

( ) My family and friends are supportive of my work and encouraging to me.

( ) My community is supportive of me and my business undertakings.

( ) My community is actively helping me build my business.

*****

# EXERCISE 3

## CHECK THE RIGHT ENTREPRENEURIAL PERSONALITY TYPE

It takes an entrepreneurial fire in your belly to start a business – and make it succeed – and not everyone has it. How do you know if you have what it takes to start a business? There's really no way to know for sure. But I do find things in common among the emotional and family fabric of people ready to consider an entrepreneurial venture. You don't have to fit all seven of these categories to be a good candidate for entrepreneurship. But it probably wouldn't hurt. In general, the more you have in common with these characteristics, the closer you probably are to being ready to try going out on your own.

1. You come from a line of people who couldn't work for someone else. I don't mean that in a negative way. People who are successful at establishing their own business tend to have had parents who worked for themselves. It's usually easier to get a job with a company than to start your own business, people who strike out on their own often have the direct example of a parent to look to.
2. You're a lousy employee. No need to sugar-coat this one. People who start their own businesses tend to have been fired from or quit more than one job. I'm not saying you were laid off for lack of work or transitioned from one job to a better-paying one – you were asked to leave, or you quit before they could fire you. Think of it as the marketplace telling you that the only person who can effectively motivate and manage you is yourself.
3. You see more than one definition of 'job security'. I'm truly envious of the few people I know who've stayed with one employer for 25 or 30 years. They look incredibly secure. But how many people do you know who are able to stay with one company for that long? In a rapidly changing economy, job security can be frighteningly fleeting.
4. You've gone as far as you can go, or you're not going anywhere at all. Sometimes the motivation to start a new venture comes from having reached the top of the pile where you are, looking around, and saying, 'What's next?' Early success can be wonderful, but early retirement can sometimes drive energetic and motivated people totally batty.
5. You've done the market research already. Don't even talk to me about your great business idea if you haven't put the time into figuring out if there's a market for your product or service. As the people behind any number of failed Internet ventures will tell you, 'cool' doesn't necessarily translate into 'profitable'. Don't bother building it if you haven't figured out whether there's a good chance the customers will come.
6. You've got the support of your family. Starting a business is stressful under the best of circumstances. Trying to do it without the support of your spouse or other significant family members or friends would probably be unbearable.
7. You know you cannot do it alone. You might excel at promoting a business. May be you love running the financial end of the enterprise. You could be someone who starts a business because you have unique creative or technical know-how to create a product.

Any of the above is possible, but it's unlikely that you are going to excel at all of these tasks – or at all of the tasks involved in running any business. Forget all that 'lone wolf' stuff. No matter how 'go-it-alone' your philosophy is, you're going to need some help sometime. The willingness to get that help – having employees, partners or consultants for those areas in which you are not an expert – is one indicator of likely future success. 'No successful entrepreneur has ever succeeded alone,' and 'the person who is most capable of enlisting the support of others is the most likely to succeed'.

*****

# EXERCISE 4

# IDENTIFYING ENTREPRENEURIAL TALENT

This tool has two parts. First, the **Entrepreneurial Talent Checklist** provides descriptive characteristics for different types of entrepreneurial talent and should be used as a resource as you map students/trainee entrepreneurs. Second, the **Entrepreneurial Talent Mapping Worksheet** provides space for you to identify and classify specific students/trainee entrepreneurs according to your understanding of their entrepreneurial talent. Remember, you may move entrepreneurs from one place on the worksheet to another as you interact and learn more about them.

## Part 1: Entrepreneurial Talent Checklist

### Potential Entrepreneurs

#### Aspiring

[ ] Actively considering going into business.

[ ] Actively researching a business idea.

[ ] May be attending business workshops.

[ ] Networking and testing ideas with others.

[ ] Motivated toward a life change.

#### Dreamers

[ ] Have a business idea that is not fully developed.

[ ] May be experimenting with the idea in some way.

[ ] May not yet be motivated to try to make the dream a reality.

[ ] May not have articulated the dream to others yet.

#### Start-ups

[ ] In the process of starting a business.

[ ] May or may not have been in business before.

[ ] May or may not have a good plan.

[ ] Motivated to make this life change.

[ ] May or may not have the necessary skills.

### Youth

[ ] Interested in learning new career opportunities and paths.

[ ] May already have a business, *e.g.*, yard care, pet sitting.

[ ] May have been exposed to entrepreneurship in school or clubs.

## Business Owners

### Survival

[ ] Struggling to make enough income to sustain their families.

[ ] Doing multiple things to generate enough income.

[ ] Have difficulty seeing opportunities, such as new markets.

[ ] Often stressed.

[ ] Reluctant to seek out help.

### Re-Starts

[ ] Have been in business before with limited success.

[ ] In the process of starting a new business.

[ ] Recognize weaknesses in business skills.

[ ] Motivated to succeed this time around.

[ ] Willing to seek out help.

### Lifestyle

[ ] Generally successful.

[ ] Often well established.

[ ] Not actively seeking to change business model.

[ ] Not actively seeking to grow.

[ ] Have established and comfortable goals.

### Transitional

[ ] Currently in business with a probable history of success.

[ ] Want to leave the business, creating opportunity for another entrepreneur.

## Growth Entrepreneurs

### Growth Oriented

[ ] Successful in business.

[ ] Have a growth orientation and drive.

[ ] Actively seeking new markets, services, and products.

[ ] Open to new ideas and seeking new insights.

[ ] Seeking to be more competitive.

**Entrepreneurial Growth Companies (EGCs)**

[ ] Experiencing rapid growth in employment or sales.

[ ] Reaching new markets.

[ ] Developing new products and services.

[ ] Experiencing growth in customers or users.

[ ] Innovative and dynamic leadership and workforce.

**Serial**

[ ] History of creating and growing more than one business.

[ ] Tend to move on to a new business idea quickly.

[ ] Often sell a business start-up once it is up and running.

[ ] Generally on the lookout for new ideas and opportunities.

[ ] May have multiple business interests going at one time.

## Part 2: Entrepreneurial Talent Mapping Worksheet

| | |
|---|---|
| Youth | Aspiring |
| Dreamers | Start ups |
| Survival | Re-starts |
| Lifestyle | Transitional |
| Growth oriented | Entrepreneurial growth companies (EGCs) |
| Serial | Others? |

*****

# EXERCISE 5

# BUILDING YOUR GAME PLAN

**Step 1: Clarify purpose**

**Agree on what you want to focus. Do you want to strengthen skills, nurture entrepreneurship, involve youth, and refine organization's priorities or __________?**

**Step 2: Construct a vision**

A. Using your purpose as a starting point, consider what you would like to have happen in the next several years. Share your vision of the future with members of your team.

B. What common themes emerge from these snapshots of the future?

**Step 3: Identify strategies**

Look at many different strategies. What strategies will you need to implement in order to achieve that future?

**Step 4: Define success**

Discuss how you will know you are successful. What will change? What indicators will help you determine the degree of change?

**Step 5: Specify the audience**

Who are the stakeholders you need to convince?

Who will be at your table – the people you will need to work with to achieve success (*e.g.*, youth, leaders, practitioners, network partners, ____________)?

Who are your customers – who will you serve (*e.g.*, youth, student community, children, and general public ____________)?

**Step 6: Write an implementation or action plan**

Using the form on this page, identify the specific tasks that need to be accomplished to achieve your goals, who will do those tasks, and when they need to be done. Consider a 6-month time period. Be realistic in defining and assigning your tasks. Double-check whether they are achievable so that you can experience some early success and build momentum for your efforts.

| Actions or Tasks | Person(s) responsible Date | Expected completion Date | Actual completion |
|---|---|---|---|
| | | | |
| | | | |
| | | | |

*****

# EXERCISE 6

## QUESTIONS FOR CREATIVE THINKING

Use some of the following questions to guide your thinking about starting a business:

A. What kind of business would you start if your family would lend you ₹ 5,000 to get it started?

B. What kind of business would you start if you and two classmates had access to a loan for ₹ 100,000?

C. What kind of business could you start if you want to do business with another country?

D. What type of business could you start while still going to school?

E. What type of business could you start using the skills you have now?

F. What type of business could you run while also working in a part time job (to provide the security of a salary while the business grows)?

G. How could you start a business and then later make it into your own franchising business for purposes of expansion?

After developing your business plan you will want to discuss your ideas with the class or an advisor to improve your plan and determine what you learned in the process of preparing a business plan. Now that you are thinking like an entrepreneur you may find these same questions pop up about many different business possibilities as you experience new opportunities in life.

*****

# EXERCISE 7

## UNDERSTANDING JUST WHAT IS PROFIT?

Understanding profit is essential to anyone interested in starting their own business. It is also important for anyone who works in a business that seeks to make a profit. Much of the misunderstanding about profit is related to a lack of understanding of the terms used in business that explain financial decisions.

For example, return on investment means the percentage you make each year on the money you invest. If you put ₹ 10,000 in a savings account at the bank you will earn interest probably around 5-6 per year. If you put that same ₹ 10,000 in stocks you will hope to earn dividends as well as have the value of the stock go upto give you a return on your investment. Now, if you invest that ₹ 10,000 in your business you will hope to be able to make even more as a return on your investment than just putting it in the bank. In that case you would expect to make an annual profit that is greater than about ₹ 500 (5 per cent of ₹ 10,000). After all, the higher the risk the greater return the entrepreneur would expect for the investment.

Next we need to define profit or better yet what profit is not.

Profit is not included in the amount of money a business owner pays himself/herself. Many new entrepreneurs forget to count the costs of their time and take out a regular salary. Or when times are tough the salary is the first thing they forget.

Profit is not the difference between the costs of the product or service and the price being charged for it. In addition to the costs of the product sold you must account for the fixed costs that are paid regularly each month no matter what. These include such items as rent or mortgage payments, utilities, regular salaries, insurance, etc.

Next you must remember to plan for the variable costs of running the business that fluctuate with the success of the business and resulting needs for advertising, staffing, supplies, etc. The fixed costs and the variable costs together are known as overhead. Overhead, as well as the costs of the products sold, is subtracted from the income from sales before profit can be made.

Finally you must pay taxes out of the income before actually determining your profit from your business. These include federal, state, and local taxes which are based on a percentage of your income minus expenses. After all these costs, the owners' profit is what is left.

What are the decisions that affect profit?

For any small business there are many day-to-day decisions that change the possible profit the business might make. For example, consider what each of the following choices might do to your profit:

- Pay employees more.
- Hire more employees.
- Buy new furniture.
- Buy a new truck.
- Find a cheaper source of products.
- Increase the advertising budget.
- Give your daughter money to buy a new dress.
- Select a cheaper long distance phone service.
- Remodel your building.

All of these decisions increase, or decrease your cost of operations affecting what is left as profit.

When deciding how to price the goods or services to be sold, the owner must take into consideration the costs of all decisions made. Some decisions will result in higher sales which will more than make up for increased costs. It is thought that appropriate advertising will do this. Or if you pay your employees more they may be willing to work harder and increase sales. However, nothing is really sure about these decisions and their effect on profits.

So business owners often decide to use a percentage of the product costs in determining their selling prices. The percentage is based on distributing the costs of running the business (overhead) and profits in an equal manner to all items sold, based on the product costs. This is called markup. Think of markup as the share of the consumer's price that is necessary to run the business, plus what is left over as return on the owner's investment. The markup on all the products sold, added together, is designed to cover the costs of running the business and making a profit.

Business owners use past experience and experience of similar businesses to determine the expected overhead costs and profit they hope to make. This is called their margin...the amount of money available after the costs of products sold are deducted from the income from sales. If your sales equal $1 million and your product costs are $200,000, your margin is $800,000. Remember, this is not your profit. We hope by now you can explain why this is so.

*****

# EXERCISE 8

# CREATIVITY-INNOVATION-PROBLEM SOLVING

Creativity and innovation consists of...

- SEEING what everyone else has seen,
- THINKING what no one else has thought,
- DOING what no one else has dared!

Innovative thinking is the key to becoming a successful entrepreneur. Whether you actually invent a new product or process, or you use creativity to find a better way to market existing products or services, you will need to learn how to think like an inventor.

## START WITH THE CUSTOMER OR END USER

The customer is always your first and most important creative challenge. Listen! Try to see the customers' problems and needs from his or her point of view. Restate the problem and the customers' needs in their terms until a consensus is reached. Ask not only what the problems are, but what special methods are presently used to solve them.

Work with the end user or customer. Use fictitious product descriptions to stimulate ideas and discussion. Remember that effective market research and sales strategy requires just as much creativity, enthusiasm and perfection as does product development.

## IMPORTANCE OF ASKING THE RIGHT QUESTIONS

The problem as first stated is rarely the true problem. Ask at least five times. Always restate the problem as many ways as you can; change the wording, take different viewpoints, and try it in graphical form. Describe the problem to laymen and also to experts in different fields.

Don't try to learn all the details before deciding on a first approach. Make the second assault on a problem from a different direction. Transforming one problem into another or studying the inverse problem often offers new insights. If you don't understand a problem try explaining it to others and listening to yourself. Test the extremes. If you can't make it better, try making it worse and analyzing what happens. Visualize a new way to solve your problem.

'Why are we so much better at answering questions than at answering the right questions? Is it because we are trained at school and university to answer questions that others have asked? If so, should we be trained to ask questions?' [Or trained to ask the complete set of right questions in the right way?] Trevor Kletz (Analog Science Fiction, January 1994, p. 195).

## GETTING GOOD IDEAS FROM EVERYONE AND EVERYWHERE

Asking once is rarely effective, you have to ask many times in many ways. Look at all possible sources of good ideas: your customers, your competition, your peers, the literature, patents, and your own subconscious. Give others some examples, this serves both to illustrate what you're talking about and encourages them to suggest improvements to your ideas.

Tell them also what [you believe] you don't want and which solutions [you believe] won't work. Remember that breakthrough innovations often come from the outside. Work with high performers in fields related to your own to identify and adopt their relevant methods, tools and 'tricks of the trade.' Trade ideas with all.

## SEARCH FOR MULTIPLE SOLUTIONS

'Nothing is more dangerous than an idea when it is the only one we have'. The first solution found is usually inadequate or not the optimum. There is usually more than one acceptable solution. Suspend judgment and criticism when first collecting ideas. Studying multiple problems jointly often generates unique solutions. Look for solutions using combinations of ideas from different or evolving technologies. Even if you have one optimum solution it may be necessary to get patent coverage for all other effective solutions so as to protect your market.

*****

# EXERCISE 9

# VISUALIZE YOUR FUTURE – ACTIVITY

All students should have an opportunity to dream about their future while they are still preparing for it. This activity can be used with youth of any age, but will need some modification regarding the number of years from now they are to think about for their future.

## PROCEDURES

1. Students will sit with their eyes closed and visualize themselves as a grown person in response to questions asked by the teacher.
2. After visualizing the future students should take 5-10 minutes to write down the answers to the 'Questions About My Dream.' Encourage them to think seriously about their ideas.
3. Now divide the students into groups of about 5 and ask them to compare their ideas about the future. Each group should identify one person to report to the whole class in a summary of what the group as a whole learned in the process of visualizing their futures.

## INSTRUCTIONS FOR THE STUDENTS

Students will be asked **to listen** and **to dream** in the first part of the activity. Then you will write your ideas on a form I will give you that will help you analyze your ideas. Finally, you will get together with a group of students to talk about what you each learned from this activity.

- You must listen carefully to others and not talk until told to do so later.
- Your dream can be as big as you wish.
- Please think about as many details as possible in answer to my questions.

## INSTRUCTOR READS THE FOLLOWING SCRIPT SLOWLY, ALLOWING TIME FOR THINKING

'Let us close our eyes and picture a relaxing scene and remain quiet for a few moments'.

## PAUSE

'Now you will imagine your life as you would like it to be 10 years from now when you are grown up and out of school.'

## PAUSE

'Now it is morning and you have just awakened.' What do you see?

**PAUSE**

'Now you go to your closet to get dressed. What do you see in your closet? What do you choose to wear to work today?'

**PAUSE**

Now you are eating breakfast. What do you see?

**PAUSE**

You are now ready to leave for work. Where do you go? How do you get there?

**PAUSE**

Who do you see in your workplace? What are they doing?

**PAUSE**

What are your feelings about the work you are doing?

**PAUSE**

It is now lunchtime. What are you doing? How long do you take for lunch?

**PAUSE**

You are now at work and it is close to the end of the day. What are you doing? What time is it?

**PAUSE**

Where are you going now that work is finished? How do you feel about the day?

**PAUSE**

Now let's take a few minutes to review the day. What were your most important thoughts and ideas during this dream?

### QUESTIONS ABOUT MY DREAM

1. What were my most important feelings about this day?
2. What type of work did I choose for myself? Why?
3. Did I work with people, ideas or things?
4. Did I use interests/hobbies/skills that I am developing now?
5. Did I work for someone else, or was I in charge of the business?
6. Was I satisfied with the job I chose? Why or why not?

**Notes:** As the students discuss this activity some of the types of information they will want to include are these questions. How many of them owned their own business? How many drove a fancy car? How many owned their own house or apartment? What does this mean about the amount of money they are earning? How many used skills or aptitudes that they have already started to develop? Were they happy with this life? What did they learn about themselves in this activity?

*****

# EXERCISE 10

## DEVELOPING SKILLS FOR ETHICAL DECISION-MAKING

The day-to-day operations of a business require everyone to make decisions all the time. Practice in developing a code of ethics and then applying it to situations is important to establishing an ethical business image.

Ask the class to form small groups of about eight persons to work on ideas for ethical decision-making. Provide them with information about a business to use for the activity. This could be a local business, a business idea of your choice or theirs, or a business plan sample that they have been working with in the class. Ask each group to do the following:

1. Identify problems the entrepreneur might encounter in running this business in an ethical manner.
2. Develop a 10-point code of ethics for the business.
3. Discuss policies and procedures appropriate for this business that would support the code of ethics.
4. List as many ethical problems as possible that might be faced by employees during a normal work day. Discuss the possible solutions for the problems. Consider how a procedure guide might help employees to make the best decisions.
5. Members of the group should then role-play the process of handling an ethical issue with a customer, with a supplier, with a competitor, and with the son of the owner. Discuss the results of the role-playing exercise. If necessary you may want to modify your code of ethics at this time.
6. Each group should present their code of ethics to the class and discuss major outcomes of their discussion.

*****

# SUCCESS STORIES

| Serial No. | Title |
|---|---|
| 1 | The Oberois |
| 2 | Decorail |
| 3 | Shehnaz Hussain |
| 4 | Mesco |
| 5 | Brahma Builders |
| 6 | Ekta Kapoor — The Queen of Indian Soaps |
| 7 | Bicon India Ltd. |
| 8 | Ramoji Film City |
| 9 | Vijay Mallya — The Spirit Behind the Kingfisher Brand |
| 10 | Sunil Mittal — Bharati Group |
| 11 | Edupreneur Gupta — Sharda University |
| 12 | Agripreneur — Lashko |
| 13 | Asmaa — Women Entrepreneurship |
| 14 | Technopreneur — IdeaForge |
| 15 | E Joseph Cossman — Entrepreneur with a Mission |
| 16 | Achelis's — A Vision for the World of Financing |
| 17 | Dr. Hauck — Curiosity Made the Difference |
| 18 | George Gerpheide — The GlidePoint® Guru |
| 19 | Labourer to Market Leader — D.N. Kathuria |
| 20 | Russell Cox — Creating Art Source |
| 21 | Professional Entrepreneurship — Vikas Verma |
| 22 | A Nutritious Business |
| 23 | Dream Houses — Entrepreneurial Journey |
| 24 | Doctor But Entrepreneur |
| 25 | Essence of Enterprise |

**Note:** These success stories are compiled from published sources, and are intended to be used as a basis for class discussion to inspire, motivate and create entrepreneurial spirits.

# 1. The Oberois

It is not often acknowledged that Raj Bahadur Mohan Singh Oberoi, 100, chairman of anempire of 29 hotels spanning most of the world's landmass is also the man who pioneered India as abrand, way back when it was only a bazaar of begging bowls and exotica. At 90, he looked back insomething close to awe and said, "I often wonder how I did it."

Certainly he did not give much of the credit to luck. True, he stood at the right time at the right place to confront his destiny, but this was just physical circumstances. What he did with the situation was amazing for a man from the boon docks of Bhaun, with little education, and really not to the manor born.

Indeed, if anything the Rai Bahadur made his fortune out of calamity. If his father hadn't died of cholera when he was only an infant, his mother would not have returned to the ancestral home which gave Oberoi the connections and contacts that helped him raise money later to buy his first hotel, the Clarke's at Simla. If he hadn't flunked the interview for his first job as clerk with the Government of India, he would never have made his way to the Simla Mall, gazed in wonderment at the glitter of the Cecil and made up his mind that he would work there. If a fatal bug in the water supply, hadn't laid low Calcutta's mighty Grant Hotel. It would never have been up for grabs. Again Oberoi just chanced tohear about it at the Delhi railway station when he was leaving to return to base in Simla. He simply changed his ticket and his direction and went to mint millions out of wartime Calcutta-another catastrophe. Life served his lemons regularly but with even greater regularity did the Rai Bahadur make lemonade.

The story of Rai Bahadur is all the more impressive because there was nothing in his background to suggest that he would be able to create the world-class ambience and sophistication for which the group is now celebrated, that he would be able to foresee India's current positioning in the global market, while doffing a deferential hat to history when it was demanded.

For instance, when other hotels were cramming their lobbies with brassbound chests and colonial nostalgia, Oberoi created the first international business hotel, the Oberoi Intercontinental in Delhi. However, in the Mena House, Egypt, and the Windsor, Australia, he went to extraordinary lengths and expense to produce authenticity to the last detail, including country-wide searches for memories and memorabilia. In order to replicate the flooring in the Windsor, he tracked down the original supplier of the tiles in distant Stoke-on-Trent, England.

Celebrating his 100th birthday, with his mind almost as clear as it was 50 years ago, perhaps the one philosophy responsible for his grand success might be his dictum. "I never worry. It clutters the brain. The problem may not happen, and even if it does, worrying will only come in the way of aclear-headed solution."

## QUESTIONS

1. "Nature and nurture play a key role in entrepreneurship development." Explain with reference to above case study.
2. In your opinion, what are the significant determinants in the making of Oberoi's entrepreneurial career?

*****

## 2. Decorail

He claims to have saved over 25,000 trees in eight years. Ravindra Jain has achieved this by selling his 'Decorail' curtain carrier systems to people who would otherwise have got pelmets. An arts graduate, Jain worked in banks for 16 years and as an administration manager for Muscat-based Construction Company for another six before deciding to return home and set up his own business.

"My wife and I used to collect any new thing we saw while we were in the Gulf," he recalls. "We saw this product there, and decided to manufacture it in India."

Active in the Students' Federation of India while at college, Jain still believes in creating employment in rural areas. So after coming back to Pune in 1986 and surveying the market for two-and-a-half years, he searched for a place where there was no industry, and bought land at Gauddara off the Bangalore highway. All his 40 employees today are locals. In this composite project to make curtain rods, tape and hooks, lack of knowledge of either textiles or engineering proved to be a plus point. "I might not have ventured into it had I been an engineer," he says. Today, Jain's Windecor products makes and exports a range of rope operated drapery systems-Roll-on-rail, Draperail, Minirail, Fast Track, and Easyline Track, besides the original Decorail.

All of them, except Fast track which was developed for heavy-duty use in hotels, hospitals and public places, are telescopic: there are four basic sizes, which provide rust-resistant, powder-coated rods between 90 cm and 4.5 ms in size.

With 13 components to make, Windecor needs 150 press-shop operations with 250 different dies. Everything is done in-house, from shaping and punching the mild steel strips to powder-coatingthe finished rods and hooks, and weaving of the polypropylene and cotton ropes which open andclose the curtains. Jain is especially proud of the fact that he is the only Asian manufacturer of thetape used for his systems and he points out "Unlike the normal curtain tape, which becomes flaccid after washing, this stays stiff so that the curtain retains the right fall."

Another division, to make the 'tie bags' used to pull the ropes, was set up as a separate company in collaboration with British Trimmings in 1994. Jain employs only women in this unit, and intends to stick to this policy even after an impending expansion. "Every family in the village has at least one woman who has been widowed, or deserted, or faces other problems," he explains.

In developing a dealer network, Jain did not want established businessmen. Most of his 150 dealers today are people who started with Decorail. About 30 of them are women; and the others involve their families in business, because he insists that every dealer must also offer a curtain stitching service: "The customer wants the curtains, not the rod" he remarks. Along the way, he has also set up three centres to train his dealers' wives and family members for this purpose. The advantage, he points out, is a close dealer — customer rapport, so much so that there are instances where the dealer's son fell in love with and married-the customer's daughter! Obviously, the dealers are happy — each sells about 100 units a month, earning between ₹ 10,000 and ₹ 15,000 from commission, cloth and stitching, and fitting charges.

Jain insists he has no competition because he keeps his products at least 25 per cent cheaper than other systems. Sales have grown 20 per cent a year since Decorail entered the market in 1991, barring the last year-and-a-half which saw a slump in new housing. His is the only company fromPune besides Telco and Bajaj Auto to advertise on national television, with a monthly advertisement spend of ₹ 2 lakhs; but Jain prefers to participate in exhibitions catering to middle class people rather than thoseheld in five-star hotels. The strategy works. "Today, people ask for even ordinary curtain rods asdecorail," he adds. So, will decorail soon become generic for curtain rods?

## QUESTIONS

1. What factors, in your opinion, helped Ravindra Jain make his brand virtually a generic name in curtain systems?
2. List the major entrepreneurial competencies you find in Ravindra Jain.

*****

## 3. Shahnaz Husain

US magazine Success's "World's Greatest Woman Entrepreneur-" there are perhaps few others who can stand testimony to the truth of these words, as Shahnaz Husain, India's pioneer in herbal cosmetics. Credited for single-handedly placing Indian herbals on the world cosmetic map, her success story — of a young girl from a conservative Muslim family who rose to become an international trailblazer in the field of herbals — is by now a legend.

President of CIDESCO, she is the first Asian to enter Selfridges in London and break a 40-year-oldsales record. GQM Commitment to Quality award, FICCI's outstanding woman entrepreneur, US magazine Success's "World's Greatest Woman Entrepreneur" the list of accolades and achievementsis endless.

An entrepreneur in the truest spirit of the word, the lady has 80 per cent of the domestic herbal market, and sales counters in the best stores internationally, be it the Seibu chain In Japan, Bloomingdales in the United States, Galleries Lafayette in Paris, Harrods and Selfridges in London.

One looks at the high priestess of herbals, one is struck by the fact that Shahnaz wears the accolades with the confidence of a person who deserves them — there is no self-effacing embarrassment when she discusses the more than humble beginnings of the Shahnaz Husain Empire. "Though I was married at a very young age, I always knew that I was made for something more," begins Shahnaz. Not prepared to sit back as a housewife and mother at the age of 16, the young Shahnaz setabout writing for magazines to earn money so that she could fund her education. Staying with husband Nasir in Tehran, Shahnaz found the ideal opportunity in the international beauty schools there. After studying cosmetic chemistry in international beauty schools in centres including London, Paris and Denmark for close to eight years, Husain hit upon the idea of exploring the 4,000-year-old Indian Ayurvedic system, so that she could research and develop herbal cures and treatments.

"I had seen the debilitating effect of synthetic cosmetic abroad; there was no doubt in mymind that the herbal system would work," recalls Shahnaz.

She returned to India to set up a shop in one room, with a start-up investment of ₹ 35,000, borrowed from her father. The going was tough — Shahnaz had priced her product well above the existing market."I began with just one product — Shalife, a massage cream. My facial was priced at ₹ 100,while you get one in the market for a paltry ₹ 6," reminisces Husain. However, that did not stop the crowds from coming and soon Shahnaz had more clients she could handle.

The lady invented a marketing style uniquely her own; she decided to make the brand a personality-driven one, flying into various cities to lecture on herbals and Ayurveda, inaugurating Shahnaz franchises and salons, and returning the same day. It worked. Today there are more than 600 salons in India and abroad.

The Shahnaz Husian group of companies has acquired a global presence, with exports to 132 countries including those in the Middle East, South-East Asia, Australia and all over Europe. Recently, a Fortune 500 investment company to explore business opportunities has approached the company.

Interestingly, Shahnaz has never advertised her product, a fact that had Harvard in the US wanting to use her marketing system as a case study. In retrospect, Shahnaz attributes her success to her "sheer grit and determination." "I do not believe in destiny — the word "fail" does not exist in my dictionary. I never fail, because I never stopped trying," says she. That she doesn't is obvious — 17 herbal lines, with many more in R&D, Husain is busy expanding her empire by adding health resorts, signature garments, accessory lines and more to her portfolio.

Having completed 25 years in the business, the self-taught marketing miracle reveals her formula for success. "In life, you get what you negotiate. Any woman has the capacity to do what I did- it doesn't matter what you want, what matters is how badly you want it."

*****

## 4. Mesco

Rita Singh, the founder of Mesco Company with an annual turnover of ₹ 1,500 crore had to put hard labour to reach to the pinnacle of her success. When she was just 7 years old, her father retired from the post of lecturer. She got married with an Air Force officer at the age of 19 years. When she felt boredom after marriage, she planned to start a milk dairy. She started it with three buffaloes at Hindon near Ghaziabad. She started earning profits from selling milk and thought to expand herdairy business. Her husband was, meanwhile, transferred to Sarwana. Like most of the Indian wives, she joined her husband at Sarwana but certainly with her innate enterprising attitude.

That place and situations do not deter one from marching ahead in accomplishing one's mission was certified by Rita Singh by installing a sugar plant a Sarwana. She was so strong in her mission that she dared to do on her own even the risky jobs like driving tractors packed with sugarcane. There came yet another trial for her. Her husband had to retire 20 years before his superannuating age as he was prey to paralysis. Now, there was no other option for Rita Singh but to struggle. This struggle period sparked an altogether new business idea in her head. Rita Singh started thinking of venturing into the export business that was least known to her. She was firm on it and her ardent effort brought an order for 5,000 tons of Tepeo (a kind of cattle fodder) to supply to Germany and America.

Rita Singh somehow complied with the order without sufficient capital at her disposal and toured Germany all alone. Though she did not earn any profit out of her business tour to Germany, she could well understand the complex procedure involved in export business. This came as a turning point inher life. Then, there was no looking back for Rita Singh.

The Hindi word 'Singh' means lion. The name 'Rita Singh' symbolizes 'lion'. She was as strongin strengths and serious in efforts as lion is. Today, the outcomes of Rita Singh's tireless hard labour to achieve greater and greater things in life are the Mesco pharmaceuticals, steel plant, leather goods, footwear, and airlines. There is no denying of the fact that to erect such a gigantic business empire and to reach to her self-actualization stage, Rita Singh underwent through every trialand struggles. Her success founded on series of struggles has made Rita Singh inclined to simple life and ordinary things, though she likes to look after her business empire by travelling abroad in her helicopters. She likes to pass her holidays in her home in Mauritius. In fact, her likings are bundles of contradictions. While she likes to be adorned with diamonds and pearls, she loves to remember her days of struggle by looking at people travelling in rickshaws and in jam-packed DTC and blue linebuses while travelling in her costliest Rolls Royce on the heavily crowded roads in the national capital city of Delhi. This is not the end of her likings. Last time, she also contested from the Ghaziabad parliamentary constituency, which she lost. She wants to live life with fulfilment for which she is always ready to take any risk. Rita Singh believes: "Risk needs to be taken in life because it is impossible to climb the stairs of success without taking risks."

## QUESTIONS

1. In your opinion, which theory of motivation does apply to Rita Singh?
2. Discuss the major entrepreneurial competencies that you find in this case.

*****

# 5. Brahma Builders

Despite coming from a family, which had three generations of businessmen, Surendra Kumar Agarwal had to virtually start from scratch and has struggled his way up in life. His fore fathers were well settled in Batala Punjab. They had the business and foundries, non-ferrous rolling mills, and machine toolunits. In 1957, Agarwal's father decided to separate from his family and shift to Bhandara, nearNagpur. There he started Paras Metal Works in partnership with a local businessman to manufacture non-ferrous utensils.

Agarwal did schooling in Bhandara and joined the Benaras Hindu University. Having graduated with a bachelor's degree in mechanical engineering in 1968, he took over his father's business, only to find that the income from the business was barely enough to sustain his large family of four brothers and a sister. He also realized that most of the raw materials like brass scrap, copper andzinc came from the western region of Maharashtra, mainly from Mumbai and Pune. Even large chunkof the finished products, that is, brass utensils, were sold — in this region. So, in order to save on transportation costs and come closer to his markets, Agarwal decided to shift to Pune.

In 1969 he bought a piece of land at Vadgon on the city's outskirts for ₹ 30,000 and invested another ₹ 4 lakhs 'in building and machinery to set up Vishnu Metal Works, his first major business venture and flagship company for a little over a decade. In the first two years it was an uphill struggle and he barely broke even. "I used to work 18 hours a day in the factory and even stayed with my family on the premises in a small 500-square-foot house," he reminisces. "But the speciality of the brass utensils we manufactured was that they was light-weight and had a super finish. As a result, the price per piece of our products was the lowest in the market. We could thus quickly establish ourselves and the demand for our products grew," he adds.

The business grew rapidly and, in the next five years, the turnover touched ₹ 25 lakh. Agarwal now needed to expand his operations and so, in quick succession, he started Five Star Metal Works, B.T. Rollings, Bramha Metal Works, and Radhan Rollings at different locations in and around Pune.

## The First Diversification

The business continued to grow and, by 1980, Agarwal's companies were producing 500 kg of utensils per day and the group turnover had reached ₹ 75 lakhs. In 1980 Agarwal diversified into the manufacture of HDPE bags and set up yet another company called Pawgir Jute Mills, which contributedin no small measure to the group's turnover. However, at around the same time, the brass utensils business began to be threatened by the growing popularity of stainless steel, which had by then become more widely affordable. Housewives preferred stainless steel to non-ferrous utensils because they were easier to clean and saved them the hassle of periodic tinning.

Agarwal quickly realized that he would eventually have to close down all his facilities unless hequickly diversified into another line of business. The opportunity presented itself in the form of a courtauction of a plot of land. Agarwal's lawyer S.K. Jain knew the owners of the land and advised him to buy the plot, as it was a prime property located in the heart of the city. The 60,000 square feet plot cost him ₹ 32 lakh and he entered the construction business as Brahma Builders. The new company's first project consisted of 24 residential flats and 20 shops, and the turnover was over ₹ 1 crore. "We made good money from our first project. Also, that was the time when there was a boom in realestate. So we decided to concentrate on the construction business," says Agarwal. Ultimately heclosed down his other business, including Vishnu Metal Works, and sold off some of his other factories to invest in real estate.

Turnover increased at the rate of 50 per cent annually, and Brahma Builders soon became oneof the leading builders in Pune and during the next decade or so, completed 14 projects and sold 660 flats, 16 bungalows, 28 offices, and 75 shops. By 1990, turnover had crossed ₹ 10 crores. Meanwhile, in 1986, Agarwal had bought a beautiful British mansion, which stood in a plot of land spread over 7 acres located near the Pune railway station. Five years later he started the Residency Club at thislocation because there was a dearth of good clubs in Pune and it was tough to become a member ofany of the existing clubs because of long waiting lists.

Residency Club has a swimming pool, a well-equipped health club, a good restaurant, 20 residential rooms, and large banquet area. When membership opened the response was overwhelming.

The initial fee of ₹ 20,000 has gone up to ₹ 1 lakh. Today, the club has over 2,000 members andis one of the leading clubs in Pune. Looking at the demand for the 20 rooms at the club, Agarwalthought of building a hotel. Accordingly, he bought a two-acre plot at a prime location just behindPune railway station in an auction by the income tax authorities, at a throw away price of ₹ 4.2 crore (all adjoining plots of similar size were subsequently sold to someone else for ₹ 30 crore).

Thus, Brahma Bazaar Hotels Ltd. came into existence in 1995. Agarwal roped in Hafeez Contractor, the well-known architect, to design his five-star hotel. Says Agarwal, "I knew Hafeez Contractor personally and, though he was a leading architect in the building line, he had never got the opportunity to design a five-star hotel completely and he had many new ideas which we liked very muchand we not only contracted him to do the exteriors and interiors of the hotel, but he was also responsible for installing the utilities like air-conditioning, boilers, plumbing, etc." This made co-ordination easierand the whole project was completed in a record time of two-and-a-half years at a cost of ₹ 70 crores. The management contract was given to Le Meridian and the hotel opened on 18 March in 1999.

Agarwal's Le Meridian has many unique features. It is the largest five-star hotel in Pune with 178 rooms, which are more spacious than those in conventional five-star hotels. Each has an interactive TV and the hotel is perhaps the only one in India to have video-conferencing facilities and squash court. It has a full floor devoted to banquets and one of the conference halls can accommodate asmany as 1,200 people, making it one of the largest banqueting facilities in Maharashtra. It has four layered glass windows to make it completely sound proof.

The architecture is a unique fusion of classical Rajasthani palace style blending superbly with unobtrusive European charm. Inside the hotel are exquisite carvings in marble and wood, especially handcrafted by over 300 artisans from Jaipur. Within 2 months of its opening, the occupancy rate is 45 per cent and this is expected to reach 80 per cent within the next 2 months (the break-even is 50 per cent). The expected turnover in the first year was ₹ 35 crore for the hotel and ₹ 40 crore forthe group.

With an asset base of ₹ 100 crore, Agarwal now plans to open more hotels in Pune, Mumbai, and Mahabaleshwar, once Le Meridien Pune starts generating profits. He has come a long way, and he's still going places.

### Question

1. Go through the case, analyse the factors making Agarwal's diversification a successful venture.

*****

## 6. Ekta Kapoor — The Queen of Indian Soaps

"Seeing your own production being aired is a great kick and the fact that most of them figure among the top ten TRP rating makes me feel wonderful" Ekta Kapoor, Creative Director, Balaji Telefilms.

Kahani Teri Meri, (The Story of You and Me) Ekta Kapoor's (Ekta) latest offering was aired in January 2003 on Sony Entertainment Television at 9:30 pm. It was touted as the Devdas of the small screen and said to be "much larger and far more lavish than any serial currently airing on television."

The serial replaced another production of Balaji Telefilms Limited (BTL), Kutumb (Family), in the same time slot. But despite the grandeur of the set and the added advantage of being Ekta Kapoor's pet project, the serial was not able to make a mark. Even after 3 months on air in a prime time slot, the television rating points (TRPs) were lower than expected, leaving analysts wondering whether the Ekta magic was on the wane.

Ekta, the face and brain of BTL, was almost completely responsible for the position BTL was able to achieve in the television software market. The program listings on various channels in 2002 show the hold BTL had on television viewers. Her serials are aired on channels like Star Plus, Zee TV, Sony Entertainment Television (SET), Doordarshan and Metro TV, as well as regional channels like Gemini, Sun, Vijaya TV, Udaya TV, etc. BTL grew rapidly since 1994, when it first began operations.

The rate of growth increased after the company went in for a public issue in 2000. From a modest beginning of 8.5 programming hours per week in 2000, BTL achieved about 35 programming hours perweek across all channels in 2002. Most of the achievements of BTL could be traced back to Ekta, thecreative director at BTL. In 2001, Ekta was selected by the Confederation of Indian Industries, (CII), tohead the committee on entertainment. She also received a number of awards over the years. Someof the awards are: "Ernst and Young Entrepreneur of the Year" (in 2001), "Corporate Excellence" from Bharat Petroleum (in 2002), "Rajiv Gandhi Award" (in 2002). In 2001, Asia week magazine included her in the list of "Asia's 50 most Powerful Communicators".

### The Making of an Entrepreneur

Ekta Kapoor is the daughter of Ravinder Kapoor (popularly known as Jeetendra), a Hindi movie star from the 1960s to 1980s. Her mother, Shobha Kapoor, is the CEO of BTL and her younger brother Tushar Kapoor is an actor in Hindi movies. According to Ekta, she had a childhood, which was "materially easy but emotionally difficult. During her childhood she was extremely obese and suffered from low self-esteem. She was a much pampered child and was never oriented towards any kind of achievement. A student of Bombay Scottish School and Mithibai College, Ekta was a poor studentand content with getting the minimum passing grades. Her family wanted her to enrol in an MBA program but she was not interested in a the oretical education and had no clue about what she wanted to do in her life. "I was fat, lazy and absolutely aimless in life. I had no direction or focus. I did not believe in excellence or hard work," she said. According to Ekta, she had a childhood which was "materially easy but emotionally difficult.'

Her only interest was watching television, which she did whenever she could. She says she felt guilty about disappointing her parents, but was not able to do much to rectify the situation. On completing her higher secondary education, she joined FAR Productions, an advertising agency, and worked as an assistant model co-ordinator for a short time in an attempt to do something worthwhile.

The turning point in Ekta's life came in the early 1990s (she was about 19 years old then), when Ketan Sommaya (a non-resident Indian) requested her father to produce some television software, fora channel he was starting. Ekta's father, understanding her craving to do something worthwhile, asked her to get involved in the production of the necessary software. At that time, she knew nothing about television production, but she produced six pilots, each with about three episodes, at a cost of roughly ₹ 5 million. The channel unfortunately did not do well and was later sold to Zee TV. Not wanting her efforts to be wasted, she started looking for buyers for the software she had developed.

Her first pilots were not successful, but her father encouraged her to make more software. In 1994, Ekta's father set up BTL as a private limited company. The first serial Mano Ya Na Mano (Believe it or Not) was aired in 1995. This was followed by Dhun Dhamaka (Music Explosion), a music based show on DD Metro; the show was moderately successful. Ekta's first major success camewith Hum Paanch (We Five), a family-based weekly comedy. Hum Paanch had a successful run of 5 years on Zee TV. In those initial years, all her working hours were dedicated to television. She worked relentlessly, even foregoing holidays, thinking out concepts, casting, discussing scripts, shooting and carrying out the many activities connected with television software development. Her efforts finally paid off. By the end of 2002, her programs had become so popular that she was in a positionto dictate terms. Her serials regularly featured in the top ten programs of the week and got the highest TRP ratings.

## QUESTIONS

1. Do you consider Ekta as an entrepreneur in the traditional sense? If so, why and if not, why not?
2. What makes Ekta click and can success be sustained?
3. What, according to you, are the critical factors contributing to the success of Ekta?

*****

## 7. Bicon India Ltd.

Biocon India (Biocon), the number one biotech company in Asia in terms of revenues and market capitalization, was founded in the backyard of a suburban house in Bangalore in 1978 as asmall operation of enzyme extraction. The woman behind Biocon — Kiran Mazumdar Shaw (Kiran) who dreamt of starting her own business with just ₹ 10,000 in hand and a degree in brewery — is now the richest woman in India.

### Businesswoman of the Year 2004

In November 2004, Kiran Mazumdar Shaw (Kiran), the Chairperson and Managing Director of Biocon India Limited (Biocon) received the 'Businesswoman of the Year Award,' from 'The Economic Times of India, ' a leading Indian business daily. This award was to be given to a person who "was global in nature and would have shareholders' good uppermost in mind. The person should have followed her heart and vision relentlessly, broken all glass ceilings and pioneered the cause of womenin business." It symbolized the increasing importance of the role of women in the Indian businessarena.

One of the most successful business women in India, Kiran had received several awards during her career of over 25 years. She founded Biocon as an enzyme extraction company in a rented garage in 1978. By 2004, Biocon had emerged as the #1 biotech company in Asia, and #16 in the world in terms of revenues and market capitalization. The company made its initial offer of shares tothe public in March 2004. The shareholders earned handsome returns on their investments as the stock, which was offered at ₹ 315, touched a high of ₹ 780 in early November 2004. Reportedly,Kiran had to break through the 'glass ceiling' effect on several occasions being a woman entrepreneurin the traditional Indian society. She believed that Indian women can do well in business even if they do not belong to a business family or have political influence or immense wealth. Kiran believed thatwomen in India were not meant for only certain kind of jobs like teacher, nurse or personal secretary, or for running a small or cottage industry at the most. She considered herself a representative of themodern women who could work shoulder-to-shoulder alongside men and build mega businesses.

Expressing a deep desire for equality, she said in her award acceptance speech, "I do hope that inthe not-too-distant future, there will be one award for men and women alike — the Businessperson ofthe Year Award."

### The Entrepreneur

Kiran was born and brought up in Bangalore in the state of Karnataka, India. She hailed from amiddle-class family, which encouraged her to pursue higher education. Following the footsteps of herfather, who was chief brew master in United Breweries, she went to Ballarat College in Melbourne, Australia, to specialize in Malting and Brewing Technology to become India's first woman brew master.

Kiran came back to India in 1975 expecting to get lucrative job offers. However, she did not receiveany. Though she possessed the required technical qualifications, her chosen profession was completely male-dominated one. After staying for two years as a consultant in India, Kiran went abroad and found a job in the UK. There she met Leslie Auchincloss (Auchincloss), the owner of Biocon Biochemicals Limited, an Ireland-based company. Auchincloss was planning to start a business in India. The Irish company wanted to establish its operations in India to produce simple bio-products from indigenous raw materials.

From being repeatedly denied a job for which she was qualified, Kiran now had an opportunity to start her own company in India. However, she did not get much support when she decided to establish a biotech company in India. She was advised not to give up her job abroad in order to set up a company in an unknown industry. Kiran was also warned about the difficulties involved in doing business for a woman in India. However, thanks to the support of her parents and her strong willpower,

Kiran did not give up the idea of establishing her own business. Arranging for the required finances was a major challenge for Kiran. She had just ₹ 10,000 in her bank account. When Auchinclosscame to India, Kiran contributed her share of ₹ 0. 1 mn.

Thus, Biocon came into existence to produce enzymes for beer, wine, paper, animal feed and detergents in an office located in a house garage. Incorporated on November 29, 1978, at Bangalore, Biocon was the first biotechnology company in India. Kiran owned 70 per cent and Auchincloss owned 30 per cent equity stake in Biocon. Kiran became the Chairperson and Managing Director ofthe company. The initial operations of Biocon included extraction of enzymes and their export to theIrish company. Though the initial infrastructure was set up for Biocon, Kiran faced problems in financing regular operations and hiring staff for the company. Yet today, Biocon is one of the successful and pioneering enterprises in the field of Biotech and Kiran is recognized for her enterprising spirit.

## QUESTIONS

1. Trace the Biocon history.
2. Comment on Kiran Mazumdar Shaw's entrepreneurial dream.
3. Bring out the characteristics of Kiran as a professional entrepreneur.

*****

# 8. Ramoji Film City

Ramoji Rao started his career in the early 1960s in Delhi with an advertisement agency Ad Crafts. In 1962, he opened the first branch of Margadarsi — a chit fund company in Hyderabad. Realizing the advertising needs of Margadarsi, Ramoji Rao established an ad agency — Kiron Ads — named after his eldest son, Kiron. It was the first accredited ad agency in Hyderabad. After a few years, thesecond branch of Margadarsi was opened in Visakhapatnam (Andhra Pradesh). The setting up of Dolphin Hotel in Visakhapatnam followed this in the late 1960s; Ramoji Rao also started a magazinefor the farmers called 'Annadata' in Telugu. Commented Ramoji Rao, "My heritage lies in the soil andmy forefathers were all farmers. But I sold off all my property and to atone for this and to do somethingspecial for the farmer community I started a magazine in their language"

## Introduction

In April 2001, Ramoji Group's Film City, hosted its first English production, 'Quicksand', produced by Ramoji Rao and directed by Sam Firstenberg. Thus, Ramoji Film City brought international (Hollywood) attention to Hyderabad. Ramoji Rao incorporated the Ramoji Group in 1962, with Margadarsi Chit Fund Ltd. By 2001, the ₹ 15 billion Ramoji Group became one of the biggest business houses in India. The group had interests in newspapers and magazines, hotels, films andtelevision, investment companies, condiments and confectioneries, a 1,000-acre film city, apparels, and handicrafts. Over the years, the Ramoji Group under the entrepreneurship of Ramoji Rao, seemedto have set standards in the print, television and the film industry. Analysts felt that Ramoji Rao's excellent business acumen, sharp insight and an eye for spotting out opportunities, made him asuccessful entrepreneur.

In 1974, Ramoji Rao entered the print media by launching Eenadu, a Telugu newspaper in Visakhapatnam. Ramoji Rao explained, "I focused on the region which I thought was most relevant tothe people." The Hyderabad edition was launched in 1975, followed by the Vijayawada (Andhra Pradesh) edition in 1976. In the early 1980s, Ramoji Group entered the foods business with Priya Pickles. The Priya brand was later extended to culinary pastes and powders. The Group then made a foray into films with Ushakiron Movies. The Group established Mayuri Film Distributors to distribute its filmsand Mayuri Audio to market the audiocassettes of the films. In the early 1990s, Ushakiron Movies diversified into satellite television with ETV — the Telugu channel.

In 1992, the Ramoji Group started a handicrafts division under the narne 'Kalanjali'. The division was set up with a view to promote the sale and export of handicrafts, cottons and textiles of Indian craftsmen. The Group set up a showroom in Hyderabad. From April 1993, the division started exportsof various goods under the trademark of 'Kalanjali'.

On September 9, 1997, The Ramoji Group inaugurated its most innovative creation — The Ramoji Film City based on the maxion — "Walk in with your script and walk out with your print". Spreadover 1000 acres, the Film City had gardens, temples, a sprawling country-side, a fort, hotels, citystreets, railway stations, a palace, an airport, a mobile kitchen etc., It had all the technical support tomake a film — 40 studio floors, a fully equipped prop shop, a set design and construction division, state-of-the-art equipment, experienced production staff, and hi-tech digital editing, dubbing andsound-recording facility. Said Ramoji Rao, "The idea is to save time, energy and resources and focuson creative excellence, executional quality, economical schedules and meticulous planning." The USP of the Film City was claimed to be its ability to rebuild any place for a shoot. Producers had choice of flexible locations. For instance, a song could be choreographed in any or all of the locations. Later changes could be made to the fountain's appearance, the layout of the street or the facades ofthe buildings in the streets or the shape of the multi-dimensional pond, to create a totally different locale.

In the late 1990s, the Group started an Internet edition of its newspaper - Eenadu. The Internetversion was designed to give the same look as the original newspaper. Content was designed toprovide local news about Andhra Pradesh. The group claimed that the website received a phenomenal response from the Telugu populace abroad. Within three months of its launch, the site achieved the landmark figure of a million hits a day. In April 2000, ETV launched ETV Bangla. The channel telecasta combination of entertainment and news programs in Bengali. In July 2000, ETV Marathi was started followed by ETV Kannada in December 2000.

In mid-2001, the Group entered the world of fashion with Margadarsi Apparels. The company planned to introduce garments for both men and women. The garments were segmented as formalwear, work wear, and casual wear for all the age groups. The company expected to manufacture 30,000 garments per day and is expanding day-by-day. Today the group is a successful businesshouse.

## QUESTIONS

1. Trace the landmark left behind by Ramoji Rao.
2. What is the unique aspect of this entrepreneurial venture?
3. Bring out the characteristics of Ramoji as an entrepreneur.

*****

## 9. Vijay Mallya — The Spirit of Kingfisher Brand

**Achievement:** Chairman of the United Breweries (UB) Group; Launched a new domestic airline called Kingfisher Airlines; Rajya Sabha M.P. Vijay Mallya is the Chairman of the United Beverages (UB) Group. He recently launched a new domestic airline called Kingfisher Airlines which is making great waves. Vijay Mallya is famous for his flamboyant and flashy lifestyle.

Vijay Mallya is the son of a famous industrialist Vittal Mallya. He assumed the Chairmanship of the United Breweries (UB) in 1983 and took the company to great heights. Under his dynamic leadership the group has grown into a multi-national conglomerate of over sixty companies. During this processUnited Breweries acquired several companies abroad. The UB Group has diversified business interestsranging from alcoholic beverages to life sciences, engineering, agriculture, chemicals, information technology and leisure.In 2005, Vijay Mallya established Kingfisher Airlines. In a short span of time Kingfisher Airline has carved a niche for itself. It was the first airline in India to operate with all new aircrafts. KingfisherAirlines is also the first Indian airline to order the Airbus A380.

Vijay Mallya has other interests too apart from business. He has won trophies in professional car racing circuits and is a keen yachtsman and aviator. Vijay Mallya has also won numerous trophiesin horse racing including several prestigious Derbies.In 2000, Vijay Mallya entered politics superseded Subramaniam Swamy as the president of Janata Party. Presently, he is a Rajya Sabha M.P.

Vijay Mallya, the flamboyant CEO of United Breweries — the company that owns the Kingfisher brand — is one of the most flamboyant CEOs in Asia. Vijay Mallya believes in leading his brand fromthe front by leveraging his personality.

Vijay Mallya is referred to as India's Richard Branson. A great part of the personality of the Kingfisher brand is based on Mallya's personality. He is credited with having single handed changed the image of his beer brand from a commodity to a lifestyle brand. The Kingfisher brand commands a 29 per cent share of the beer market in India and is sold in over 52 countries.

Vijay Mallya has built a reputation for splurging his money in the public. He is the key sponsorto many of India's top derby championships, he owns a yacht once owned by Elizabeth Taylor, fliesa personal Boeing business jet, owns super stylish homes in London, US, Dubai, and India. Vijay Mallya is a diehard party animal, and is seen as the personification of a luxurious life! Vijay Mallya's associations with the rich, trendy and the luxurious have rubbed on his business venture and thebrands. Similarly to Richard Branson, he recently launched Kingfisher Airlines, which draws a lot ofits brand equity from Mallya himself. Vijay Mallya is a classic example of how Asian CEOs can leadtheir brands by being the most vocal ambassadors of their brands to build and sustain brand equity.

## QUESTIONS

1. Discuss and analyse the characteristics of the entrepreneur, enterprise, and entrepreneurship.

2. "Entrepreneur is the brand of the enterprise." How true is this?

*****

## 10. Sunil Mittal — Bharti Group

**Achievement:** Mr. Sunil Mittal, Chairman and Managing Director of Bharti Group, India's largest GSM — based mobile phone service provider; IT Man of the Year Award 2002 from Data quest and CEO of the Year, 2002 Award from World HRD Congress.

Sunil Mittal can be called as originator of cellular phone revolution in India. He is the founder, Chairman and Managing Director of Bharti Group and runs India's largest GSM — based mobile phone service. Sunil Bharti Mittal's father was an M.P. Sunil did not follow his father's footsteps. After graduating from Punjab University in 1970s, he set up a small bicycle business in Ludhiana in partnership with his friend. By 1979, Sunil Mittal realized that his ambitions could not be fulfilled in Ludhiana, so hemoved out to Mumbai from Ludhiana.

He spent a few years in Mumbai and in 1982; Sunil Mittal started a full-fledged business selling portable generators imported from Japan. This gave him a chance to acquaint himself with the nitty gritty'sof marketing and advertising. His business was running smoothly but later on, the government banned the import of generators as two Indian companies were awarded licenses to manufacture generators locally.

In 1986, Sunil Bharti Mittal incorporated Bharti Telecom Limited (BTL) and entered into atechnical tie up with Siemens AG of Germany for manufacture of electronic push button phones. Gradually he expanded his business and by early 1990s, Sunil Mittal was making fax machines, cordless phones and other telecom gear.

In 1992, when the Indian government was awarding licenses for mobile phone services for the first time, Sunil Mittal clinched Delhi cellular license in collaboration with French telecom group Vivendi. In 1995, Sunil Mittal founded Bharti Cellular Limited (BCL) to offer cellular services under thebrand name AirTel. Soon, Bharti became the first telecom company to cross the 2-million mobile subscriber mark. Bharti Cellular Limited also rolled out India's first private national as well as international long-distance service under the brand name IndiaOne. In 2001, BCL entered into a joint venture with Singapore Telecom International for a $ 650-million submarine cable project, India's first ever undersea cable link connecting Chennai in India and Singapore. Bhartihas grown successfully in partnership with various leading companies of the world like — Singapore Telecom, Vodafone, Warburg Pincus, British Telecom to name a few. Today, Sunil Mittal runs a successful empire with a market capitalization of approximately $ 2 billion and employing over 5,000 people. He has been honoured with severalawards. Sunil Bharti Mittal was chosen as one of the top entrepreneurs in the world for the year 2000and among 'Stars of Asia', by 'Business Week'. He also received IT Man of the Year Award 2002from Data quest and CEO Of the Year, 2002 Award (World HRD Congress).

### Other Activities

Sunil has been nominated to serve on several distinguished boards, committees and councils:

- Prime Minister's Council on Trade and Industry
- Prime Minister's Task Force for Economic and Social Development of Jammu & Kashmir.
- National Council and Steering Committee of Confederation of Indian Industry (CII)
- Indo-British Partnership (Co-Chairman)
- Board of Global GSM Association (GSMA)
- "International Enterprise (IE) Singapore", a statutory board under Ministry of Trade & Industry, Government of Singapore.
- Singapore-India Partnership Foundation.
- Organizing Committee of Commonwealth Games, Delhi 2010(Deputy Chairman).
- Boards of Governors of Indian Institute of Management (IIM), Lucknow and Indian Instituteof Technology (IIT), Mumbai.
- International Advisory Board of "Center for the Advanced Study of India (CASI)", University of Pennsylvania (UPENN).
- Bharti School of Telecommunications Technology and Management (Bharti School), a postgraduate school of IIT, Delhi (Co-Chairman)
- INSEAD Global India Council

## Recognitions

- "Star of Asia for the Year 2001" — Business Week
- "Businessman of the Year, 2002" — Business India
- "CEO of the Year, 2002" — World HRD Congress
- "India's Best People CEO. 2004" — Hewitt Associates
- "Asia Pacific CEO of Year, 2004" — Frost & Sullivan
- "Ernst & Young Entrepreneur of the Year, 2004"
- "Best Asian Telecom CEO", 2005 — Telecom Asia
- "Business Leader of the Year, 2005" — Economic Times

### QUESTIONS

1. Trace the entrepreneurial journey of Mr. Mittal.
2. What have been the criteria for success of Bharti Group?

*****

# 11. Edupreneur Gupta – Sharda University

## Sharda Group of Institutions 'the story of edupreneurship'

Education is more than just the memorization or learning of theories, it is the pathway of gaining access to a better life and in the bigger picture it leads to a better human society. Mr. P. K. Gupta has been privy to this fact for some time now and as Founder Chairman of the Sharda Group of Institutions is among the leading educational reformers in India. As the entrepreneur behind Sharda University he has revamped the way education is imparted in his colleges and in educational institutions across India.

**Business Idea** – Unlike most other institutions of formal learning Sharda University stresses upon not what they are teaching but whom and how... It is 'An education system which would inculcate an application based approach in the young students enlightened the thought of opening up educational institutions which would focus more on nurturing the talent & develops curiosity of young individuals'.

**Target Market** – Every young mind looking for quality education factoring in your average and not so average students should take a look at their offerings. From the Hindustan Institute of Science & Technology to the Hindustan Institute of Management & Computer Studies, they cover a large spectrum of subjects. They also set up Anand Engineering College in 1998 and Babu Mohanlal Arya Samarak (BMAS) Engineering College in 1999 to meet the growing demand for quality education.

In 2000, Anand College of Pharmacy was established and by 2005, the first of its kind Faculty Development Institute was also founded. Between 2005 to 2008 few more colleges have been added under the group's umbrella like, Hindustan Institute of Dental Sciences, Hindustan Business School, Hindustan Institute of Technology, HAERT, & Hindustan Institute of Allied Health Sciences & Research.

### What sets them apart?

Apart from Mr. Gupta's altruistic vision Sharda University is also known for application oriented methodology. Mr. P.K. Gupta is also well known for providing and championing the cause of higher education to the girl child. Sharda University has a 90 per cent scholarship for girls whose family cannot afford to pay their tuition fee because of Mr. Gupta's interest in reducing gender inequality.

**Future Plans** – The group is looking at expansion on a global scale and has recently announced their intentions. SGI, under the leadership of Mr. P. K. Gupta, is set to realize a new dream of setting up campuses in UK, US, East Asia, and Latin America with a family of 1 lakh students by 2020.

**His Entrepreneurial story-** Mr. P.K. Gupta believes that the true rewards of entrepreneurship are not the kind that can be counted or weighed. He explained what has been most important in his entrepreneurial journey saying. It was not just an intention to be successful or the idea of huge profits that motivated me to foray into the higher education sector. In fact, I was genuinely concerned as I saw the drive in the youth around me. They wished to excel in higher education and it was my good fortune that I was able to provide students in north India with quality education right at their door step. In a way, being an entrepreneur in the education sector also allows me to fulfill my duty towards serving the society. Imparting education is gratifying in itself.

It's a matter of great pride to be able to provide the means for shaping the youth of India'. Born on 9th December 1959, in Agra, Mr. Gupta was brought up in a family with strong values and dedication towards social service. His grandfather, the Late Shri Mohan Lal Arya, was an eminent personality and a freedom fighter in India's Independence struggle. His father, Mr. A.S. Gupta, who traded in medicines, was a businessman who was involved in the cause of social service. Like any other child, Mr. Gupta, was more interested in the playground than his books. His interest in studies came from the inspiration and motivation that the principal of his school was able to impart. This later made him realize the importance of a teacher in shaping the future of a child.

On completing his graduation from Victoria Engineering College, he started his career with HNT as a contractor in 1979. By 1980, he was an entrepreneur and had started his business of manufacturing and supplying engineering equipment to various Educational and Research Laboratories. He diligently spread his business from North India to South India and travelled all over meeting his clients. On his business trips he observed that his co-passengers were mostly students who were travelling from north India to south India for their education. In those days, students had to struggle for admissions in the engineering colleges due to which they travelled to South India.

This observation sowed the seeds of what was to come.

In 1985, he shifted to Chennai and through his business networks came across many educators and institutions which were running their colleges in small rented buildings. Realizing the absence and need of infrastructure in an engineering college, he decided to set up a college in Agra.

From then on whenever he met any faculty or visited any institution, he would observe their methods of running an educational institution. He would go through the strengths and weaknesses of the colleges running in Chennai and focused on the teaching pedagogy prevailing in that area. In 1995, he established the Sharda Education Trust under which he opened up an engineering college by 1996 in Agra, well known as Hindustan Institute of Science & Technology. In 1997, he opened up a second college for students of management and computer science by the name of Hindustan Institute of Management & Computer Studies.

His journey was not bereft of challenges or trails, but his perseverance and vision helped Sharda University to be ranked among the best. M. Gupta says 'Our biggest challenge was that of establishing a world class university with one of the best and most flexible education systems in the country. For this, we adopted the best of international standards. We run a credit-based system at Sharda University'.

'This system offers students the flexibility to choose subjects from other streams, which provides them with the opportunity to be exposed to domains other than their core electives. This in turn helps them to develop analytical, logical and reasoning skills'. 'Initially, there was resistance, but I have always believed that challenging the rules with logic creates new rules which lead to innovation. Now, in our very first year, we have witnessed an encouraging response from the community. Parents and students alike have welcomed the university's initiative towards re-defining the teaching methodology. I can confidently say that we are growing by leaps and bounds'.

Looking at the huge response and demand for colleges, he opened up Anand Engineering College in 1998 and Babu Mohanlal Arya Samarak (BMAS) Engineering College in 1999. In 2000, Anand College of Pharmacy was established to diversify into other areas of education.

By 2005, the first of its kind Faculty Development Institute was set up in the Greater Noida Campus. This establishment was started based on the vision of shifting the management from theory based learning to application based learning. The change was witnessed within the classrooms but the traditional examination system created a resistance in realizing the vision.

Thus, the need of a fully innovative system was felt and the idea to set up a university began to come into existence. The inception of Sharda University in Greater Noida has been a step towards changing the teaching pedagogy to a stress free environment with a flexible credit based teaching providing dual degree courses. 20-30 per cent of the faculties are being appointed from UK to US to provide an international exposure of teaching for the students.

Today, under the umbrella of Sharda Education Trust, with 160 students in 1996 Sharda Group of Institutions have grown to a family of 20,000 students. Over 10,000 students have passed out since the inception. Over 6,000 students have been placed in the best organizations across the nation and almost 4,000 of these students have become entrepreneurs owing to the relevant exposure to entrepreneurship.

In addition to the various educational institutions Mr. Gupta has also set up Maxwel Hotel Private Ltd, Agra, Sharda Hospitals Private Ltd, Agra, Sharda Software Solution Private Ltd, Delhi and Maxwel Products, Agra.

**Recognition gained** – Aside from being known as Sharda University's founder and guiding light, P.K. Gupta has also found time out of his busy schedule to help society. He is a founding member of the National Chambers of Education Promotion Society of India. At many conferences he has also championed the cause of educational reforms with leaders like Yashpal Sharma, Dr. Abdul Kalam and many other prominent personalities.

He had also submitted a report on educational reforms to the Ministry of HRD and many of his suggestions have been implemented by the Planning Commission. He is an active member of the Agra Club, the Rotary Club (Agra), and the National Chamber of

Commerce and Industries. In 2001, Mr. P.K. Gupta was honored with the Udyog Ratna award and a year later with the Uttar Pradesh Ratna award for his many years of service to society.

**Entrepreneurial Lesson** – The reformer within Mr. P.K. Gupta has advice which he believes every future entrepreneur should pay heed to. He says 'I would like to suggest to the young entrepreneurs to Be job creators instead of job seekers so that you can serve mankind.

- Try to earn profits through products of excellence in every field.
- Money is the byproduct of excellence in your field.
- Never say I am working very hard, always work passionately you will never get tired – Do what you enjoy never choose a career by force.'

*****

# 12. Agripreneur - Lashko

## Securing Food for Coming Generations

He believed that land fertility needed a relentless plough and firm plougher in order for its fruits to bloom all the time. Therefore, he decided to plough it in order to plant a tree in every place for this generation to eat and the coming generations to benefit. Businessman Nasser Lashko brings to mind this vital sector that has always been the subsistence resource for all nations and an inexhaustible store for coming nations, that is, the investment in agricultural sector.

## Securing Food for Coming Generations is His Aim

### Start

Nasser bin Abdullah Lashko (b. 1938) is the executive president of Nasser Lashko Group for Trading and Contracting. The first seed was in 1963 when he invested in the contracting field. He was specialized in building government institution starting with Oman Sports Club, a number of VIPs houses, and a number of civil buildings. His first project was by Omani hands. At that time, his company had 80 Omani workers.

His experience outside Oman helped him to start despite the meager amount he had, only 1.000 RO. He used the profits to extend his basis until he reached the top.

## Extension by Profits

The life of Nasser Lashko was a matter of continuous work. Once he has some profits he used to exploit them in a new project. Thus, his works extended and he established many companies. After spending many years in contracting, he thought to extend his work into other sectors. He established many companies and gained many government tenders, especially in sectors of tourism, industry, trade, public services, and others. His Group started in building government buildings, people's houses, hospitals, and villas.

Moreover, he extended his work into the industry of ships, gases, and oil company services.

Work developed in the fields of contracting, industry, and tourism until he established the first gas factory in Wadi Kabir, Oman Gases Company, with 150 thousand Omani Rials. In the tourism sector, there was Lashko Hotel that was the first hotel in Corniche Street in addition to a number of tourism agencies and Bush House auto washing.

## Agricultural Investment

He wanted to invest in the soil of his country. Thus, he thought of agricultural sector. He says, 'I started investments in agricultural sector in 1975 at Al-Khadraa Farm in As-Suwaiq, that is, Nasser Lashko Model Farm. It was the first farm in Oman to produce all vegetables in a scientific manner. It had more than 20 kinds of vegetable. It was the first farm to grow zucchini, cabbage, watermelon and potatoes that were sold in local market and the returns were big'.

He started to develop work in the agricultural field through the establishment of a company to reclaim and develop lands under the BOT system. Pursuant to this, a company for digging wells and procuring agencies for water pumps was established.

This was the first company to gain the tender of the Ministry of Agriculture to provide chemical fertilizers under farmers' support system for 5 years from 1975 to 1984. Each year was for nearly half a million RO. He then thought to invest in huge specialized projects. He established Barka Poultry Company in 1985. Lashko says, 'We started by producing (12) million eggs per annum then we extended work to reach (36) million eggs then (75) million and now we produce (100) million eggs annually.

The current investment in this regard has reached 5 million RO. The company is ISO certified both locally and internationally. It used the latest international technologies in producing eggs. We are currently studying the extension of work to produce (150) million eggs per annum and to export 205 to UAE and Qatar. The area of the farm is 25 feddans and it is rented from the Ministry of Housing'.

Then came Nizwa Company for Poultry Mothers in 1997. Lashko speaks about this company saying, 'We bought it from Oman Development Bank.' It was for the production of carnivorous poultry but we turned it into the production of fertilized eggs and chicks. We fulfill the requirements of the local poultry raisers and export our production to the neighboring countries.

This is the first specialized company in this field in Oman. It has the best international breeds and provided after-sale services. Now, we are studying the establishment of an automatic slaughterhouse for poultry with a capacity of 2.000 chickens per hour. The problem of raisers is marketing, and this slaughterhouse shall be a marketing outlet for the producers and raisers. This slaughterhouse shall be established in Al-Musanah with a total cost of (600) thousand RO under the name 'Modern As-Sawadi Poultry Company'. It is expected to start operations within one year. This company shall be specialized in carnivorous poultry with a capacity of one million chickens per year. We shall use the latest equipment and devices in this field.

## Investment Basket

Out of his experience in agricultural field, he realized that the diversity of crops should result in rich and high quality harvests. He also believed that diversity in investment would result in developing projects and avoiding losses. Therefore, he directed his interest to the emerging sectors of long-term investments. He built Al-Burj International Hotel, a 3-star hotel in Ruwi (44 rooms) that has all hotel services. The occupancy rate there is 80 per cent. Moreover, 30 rooms shall be added to that hotel. He also thinks of building a tourism resort in Al-Batinah. He also established the Fiber Glass Division for Boats in 1987 to build boats and fish refrigerators from fiber glass. He has also real estate investments and camel and cattle farm. He thinks of establishing a specialized institute in training and qualifying staff in the agricultural field.

*****

# 13. Asmaa – Women Entrepreneurship

## Scratch to Renowned Business

Through persistence, strong will and self-reliance Asmaa Al-Awadi managed to be one of the successful Omani business women in the field of trading and contracting. Although she studied sociology and geography, she excelled in business administration. Her willpower enabled her to make success and distinction in its path that started from zero. She now runs one of the biggest corporations where 100 employees work and strikes deals valued more than thousands of Omani Riyals.

She occupies the position of chairperson of Falaj Al-Qabail Trading and Contracting, and a member in Tourism and Real-Estate Investment Committee in OCCI branch in Sohar. She is one of the female business pioneers in Batina region.

### Growth

Asmaa Al-Awadi was born in wilayat of Sohar, Batina Region amongst a family that pays attention to trade. Her father was one of the most prominent merchants in Batina Region. He had got a lot of commercial relations with other merchants in the markets of Gulf, India and the rest of Arab region through import and export. All that made her thinks from the early childhood about following her father's footprints in the field of trading. She was brought up with the fondness of Determination and self confidence were here tools for success trade as she realized that her responsibility in a very early stage and started to think in establishing her independent business by entering the world of money and business from the widest gate.

### The Beginning

Asmaa Al-Awadi started her journey in businesses three years ago. She managed during this short period to make good money and business. She started with RO 150,000 as a capital for establishing Falaj Al-Qabail Trading and Contracting Co. now the company works in various commercial businesses including land transport, contracting, and stores for electronics and building materials. Her capital grew throughout three years to be about RO 3 millions.

### Main Challenges

Asmaa Al-Awadi says that the main challenges that faced her at the beginning were her status as the first woman to strike deals in the field of building contracting in Batina Region. The society observes her with wonder and lack of trust. They cannot believe that a woman can lead a major company and execute many big building protects. She managed to succeed in the businesses that many people think they are only for men.

Asmaa said that after I managed to jump over this stage and confirmed my success, the company received several projects in many areas not only inside Batina Region but also in several other governorates and regions across the Sultanate including Muscat, Buraimi, and Musandam and in the future I will reach Dhofar too. I also faced the challenges of making a plan to the administrative work of the company in a way that match the growing number of contracts and projects. Through training, qualifying and consulting those of expertise, I managed to draw the administrative framework of the company. Now our company becomes amongst those of expertise who offer consultation to others who work in the same field.

## Asmaa Vs. Crisis

'The financial crisis slightly influenced my business due to some contracts with international companies that also were affected by the current crisis' Asmaa said, about the influence of the world current crisis. 'We can say that due to the wise leadership of His Majesty Sultan Qaboos bin Said and his view that put the Omani economy amongst the strong world economies, we are now in a good condition, thanks God' Asmaa added, indicating that the company takes balanced steps and plans that cope with the current economic condition.

## Overview about Future

Asmaa always thinks about the future that put obstacles in front of the businessmen. Some businessmen might not be able to pass over these obstacles. For this purpose, she put future plans by getting the best use of other businessmen's experience. She thinks that it is necessary for those who want to enter the field of trade to put the right basis to confront the possible future obstacles. She also sees that man should be optimistic and avoid pessimism. She believes that attention and care about any thing would result in success but that also requires us to avoid frustration that rises in the initial failure. This frustration and initial failure is the test that faces any person at the beginning of the business. After passing over this stage, the person can determine his path in the field of money and business.

## Message to Woman

Asmaa Al-Awadi sends a message to the woman calling her to enter the field of trade by imitating Sayyida Khadija (may Allah bless her) who was an example of a Moslem woman in this field. I would like to tell the Omani woman that there are many opportunities and options to enter the world of trade. There is no thing impossible in front of self-confidence, strong willpower and firm steps. Believe in God would guide us to jump over all the obstacles that might confront our path towards success. There is an apparent example, the productive families who managed to found small businesses that now offer them good return.

## Special Agenda

I like travelling to countries where there are historic and cultural sights as that enables me to know more about the cultures and habits of other people. I seek to participate and attend the commercial exhibitions that benefit me in my business. I like to watch discovery, cultural and economic TV shows particularly those related to my business. I like voluntary, social and charity contributions even if they are limited due to my busy agenda. I like to take risks but they should be planned. I like to follow the woman's fashion and I enjoy my time in shopping. I am looking forward to be successful in everything, as there are no limits to my ambition. I have economic trends and I have future plan to enter the industrial sector.

*****

## 14. Technopreneur – IdeaForge

As a kid, he dreamt of the impossible. When he saw Superman, he wanted to be like him and do whatever he did. At school, his teacher told him his ideas were good, but there is still a lot more to learn. He started thinking about the mechanics of engines very early in life, wondering how they worked and how processes could be changed to make things work better. His father used to have long chats with him everyday on the achievements of great inventors like Albert Einstein and Thomas Edison. This made a profound impact on him and fuelled his imagination further. 'Why can't I be an Einstein?' he wondered. The ability to question and probe everything was his motivation to keep moving forward.

This deep interest in engineering brought Ankit Mehta to the Indian Institute of Technology. Ankit, a top ranked student at IIT Bombay, did not attend a single placement interview when his friends got the greatest offers from the best of companies. For him, it was a pursuit of ideas, a journey to achieve what he had always dreamt of. 'The journey was tough, it took us an year to actually give shape to the start-up company. The lack of experience, opposition from parents, and financial problems made it tougher to get started,' Ankit says.

But the strong belief in the idea and support from friends, Rahul Singh and Ashish Bhat, and a grant from the government led to the birth of Ideaforge in 2007 when Ankit Mehta was just 24 years old. Ideaforge got started with its pioneering work at the Technology Business Incubator, SINE at IIT Bombay. 'I have been very fortunate to get like-minded people like Ashish, who has been innovative and designing electronic gadgets ever since he was a schoolkid, and Rahul who gave up a plum post to be a part of this start-up,' Ankit says.

Today, Ideaforge develops human powered cell phone chargers and fully automated Micro Air Vehicles (MAVs). With these chargers, you can charge your phone while in a car, bike, etc. Ankit lives with an idea bank and that's why he calls his company Ideaforge. 'The joy of creating a product gives the satisfaction which no high-paying job can,' he says happily. It gives him immense pleasure to work even if it means working till the wee hours. For him, every day is a chance to strive harder and make his dreams come true. He has no regrets about giving up the luxuries, which many of his classmates are used to. 'A start-up is a great way to be selfish,' he adds.

Ankit Mehta, managing director, Ideaforge, reveals more about the exciting world of entrepreneurship and also gives hints regarding formal approached to KM.

With an initial investment of ₹ 1.5 lakh (₹ 150,000) and a government grant. The company was registered in February 2007 and it got incubated at IIT.

The day starts at 10-11 and our work goes on till 1-2 am. With a team of 10 members, the core team working late the work goes on. People see it as a great opportunity to work in a start-up. It gives them a sense of fulfillment, which no other job can give. There are parallel roles, people love the challenge. The risk and rewards too are equally exciting.

Education at premier institution like IIT plays a huge role in overall development. It boosts confidence, to become better than the best. The environment is very competitive, yet friendly. The atmosphere opens up the brain so much. Education plays a vital role. Education gives tremendous confidence and knowledge is essential for making products.

The effort is to popularize clean technology products and lead the way to an environment-friendly world. Their mission is to make energy sources available everywhere .... be mobile.

The amount they invested less than ₹ 1 crore (₹ 10 million) so far. They have developed a mechanical energy storage and release device and applied for a patent. It will take about 18 months to get the patent for this. They have about seven different types of charging devices, which include a mechanical charger, a USB charger, a bike charger, a car charger and even a wall charger. These chargers can be used with any handset. They have also developed fully automated Micro Air Vehicles (MAVs) like a small helicopter that can fly, take photos and videos. While on the on GPS-hold mode, it acts like a virtual pole in the sky streaming high quality live video to the ground station with all camera controls in user's hand. These can be trained to even go inside buildings and take photos. In the age of increased surveillance, these products come in handy.

The major milestones achieved are of establishing a good distribution network. Their national distributor is Brightpoint India Pvt Ltd. Today, products are available through major retail chains like eZone, Hot Spot, RPG Cellucon, The Mobile Store and Exide's retail outlets and sites like eBay, indiatimes, homeshop18, et cetera. They have also started a pilot project with the Tatas so products will be available in Tata stores as well and will soon tie up with Airtel. They have been able to reach out to the rural areas with a tie-up with ITC's e-choupal.

According to the CEO of IdeaForge , innovation is vital for any entrepreneurship to succeed and it is absolutely essential to create value with new ideas and offer a product that the market requires. An idea pays and it is the stepping stone to success. The product should have a good market value.

The most important things that entrepreneurs must have to succeed are patience to go on, perseverance of the goal. Impatience also as it helps to get things done faster. A great team is essential. One must be able think differently. One has to believe in the idea and it should, of course, have a logical end. Make the right use of opportunities. There are billion ways of doing the same thing. One must make the right choice. Make sure to get finance and see to it that there is someone to bail you out in the event of a crisis. Ability to listen to others' ideas, and be receptive to new ideas is the key to succeed and for these ingredients there is a need to adopt the formal approach to knowledge management.

*****

## 15. E. Joseph Cossman – Entrepreneur with a Mission

Experience, and the ability to apply so many diverse experiences, enabled E Joseph Cossman to become a millionaire many times over. Perhaps you haven't heard of 'The Messiah of the free enterprise system' (Wall Street Journal) because he has not specialized in one single product or specialty throughout his life. His specialty is **MARKETING.**

Since emerging as a soldier in the Second World War, Joe has proven that taking calculated risks is fun and profitable. He didn't have a fancy college marketing degree; in fact he started into business with his high school degree from Braddock, PA and his experiences growing up in his father's neighborhood grocery store. Three years in the army in Europe was another kind of experience that led him to think about exporting as his first entrepreneurial opportunity.

His first 'risky venture' resulted from reading in a classified ad in the newspaper that soap powder was available in quantity. He knew that this was valuable to postwar Europe and other countries, so he made contact with people he had met and ended up with an order for $180,000 ... and no soap. His efforts to make this sale work demonstrate his ability to make things happen, a story in itself, but the net result was he did it, and netted $30,000 at a time when he was earning $35/week at his regular job.

Mail order is the field that is most closely aligned with this entrepreneurial thinker. When he started his business in 1947 there was very little activity in the mail order field. But soon it was growing fast because it met a definite need of people who were hungry for scarce products. When he began there were no credit cards or 800 numbers or computers, and people read the newspapers for mail order product availability.

Cossman moved to California and set up his office on Sunset Boulevard in Hollywood with the dream of working for himself and becoming a 'millionaire.' His philosophy 'There are many ways of taking a product, and by giving it a twist you can turn it into a money-maker' is demonstrated in the 20+ products that he took to market and sold atleast a million of each. He was the first to market 14 balloons for $1.00, not as balloons but as five giant animals...an idea with a 'twist'. You may remember the Plastic Ant Farm, the Spud Gun, Fly Cake, etc. Each product has its own story and experiences that helped develop my personal 'philosophy of business'.

Each year he sought out a new product to introduce at the national trade fairs as an innovative toy or aid to your lifestyle. Some didn't do so well. For example, he bought the entire inventory of 4 million high quality prints of 48 of the world's greatest paintings that had been sitting in a warehouse since 1937. And although he offered them for only $.50 each it took a number of years to find a market. At the same time he found phenomenal success with selling plastic Shrunken Heads for $2.98. The ideas that did succeed far outweighed the losses. And the experience was the real teacher.

One story he tells is about the billboard he set up outside his office on Sunset Boulevard. There he put out a new message every week that demonstrated his humor and salesmanship, an image that he encouraged. Whenever big company executives came to visit, they were publicly welcomed on the sign. Many of his sayings have become famous and can be found on the Internet when you search his name. For example:

- 'Obstacles are things a person sees when he takes his eyes off his goal.'
- 'Love is a friendship set to music.'
- 'Middle age is when your broad mind and narrow waist begin to change places.'
- 'Luck is what happens when preparation meets opportunity.'
- 'To be without some of the things you want is an indispensable part of happiness.'

Cossman believes that 'ideas are a person's greatest asset'. He quotes Harvey Firestone, the great industrialist who said,

'Capital isn't so important in business. Experience isn't so important. You can get both of those things. What are important are ideas. If you have ideas, you have the main asset you need, and there isn't any limit to what you can do with your business and your life. They are any man's greatest asset- ideas'.

Cossman says 'Most of our products are the result of our own ideas. In the long run, you're on your own, so let your judgment be your guide. But keep this in mind. A new idea is a delicate thing. It can be killed by a sneer or worried to death with a frown. Treat your own ideas like children – coddle them, keep them away from the chill of adverse criticism, have faith in them – and they'll grow up into strong, mature products to support you in your old age'.

Sharing his marketing ideas is the 'mission' he has demonstrated through so many of his actions in later life. Joe decided to retire from his search for products that built his entrepreneurial empire when he was only 50. But it didn't take long to learn that sitting in the sun is no way of life for an entrepreneurial mind.

So he wrote two books to share his experiences and in promoting the books learned that others wanted him to share his experiences personally. Thus he started his first seminar in 1963 that had standing room only in fact people were backed up in the hallways. And this new career resulted in presenting live seminars to over 50,000 people all over the US and selling the course for home study purposes.

Leading universities offered Cossman's '10-Step Entrepreneur Program' to their students. At the same time Joe decided to fulfill his lifelong dream of going to college. Showing their respect for his expertise, Pepperdine University gave him credit for his years of experience, and enrolled him in a master's degree program. Joe conducted a research study of program graduates at Pepperdine to see if his course had made any difference in the success of these students. He was pleased to discover that those who reported being successful entrepreneurs also reported being more likely to have completed all the work of his course and used what they had learned in his program. The Regents of the University awarded E. Joseph Cossman a Master of Business Administration degree in 1977.

Graduates of his programs like to share the motivation and creative ideas they discovered in his courses. Joe's students are the success stories that he enjoys telling now. Since he 'retired' in 1963 Joe has taught and advised thousands of today's entrepreneurs. He created the Future Millionaires Club in a number of cities to bring his graduates together on a regular basis to support each other.

He has published several books including How I Made $1.000.000 in Mail Order (And You Can Too), a real recipe for success. (Published by Fireside, Simon, and Schuster).

'I am constantly encouraging people to clear off their kitchen tables and start an enterprise that they can control, not one that controls them. Lack of education, lack of money, lack of business connections, lack of business knowledge are not important.

What is important is that we live in a country where over 200 million people speak the same language, 200 million people use the same currency, and you can ship a package from Los Angeles to New York without going through one foreign border or paying any duty on that package. This country is conducive to making money. Once you learn this lesson and make your first deal, you really appreciate the tools available to you in the United States'.

## QUESTIONS FOR DISCUSSION

1. How did the experiences of his life help Joe become a successful entrepreneur?
2. What type of business was Joe pursuing in his career?
3. What does he think is the most important thing a potential entrepreneur can have?
4. Discuss the reasons Joe thinks doing business in the United States is such a great opportunity.
5. How would you describe the personal characteristics of this successful entrepreneur?

*****

# 16. Achelis's – A Vision for the World of Financing

## Founder

Steve Achelis (pronounced a-kay-lis) started his company, Equis International, in 1983. He was heavily involved in investing his own money, and was always looking for ways to get better returns. Originally bootstrapped from the basement of his home in West Valley City, Utah, Steve has grown Equis into one of the world's leading developers of investment charting and analysis software. From the beginning, Steve has had a vision of how computers would change the way people invest their money. Long before personal computers became popular, he clearly saw that computers would be the great equalizer for investors everywhere – the average investor would have the same information and analysis tools that only the large Wall Street firms could previously afford.

At that time, Steve had absolutely no experience with computers. But he believed in his vision of the computerized investing market. So he took the first of many future business risks by purchasing a computer (an original Apple II+) and teaching himself how to write programs that would eventually change the world of investing forever. As he started to build a company around this new breed of software, Steve's only business assets were his energy and enthusiasm. He would sit in front of the computer and write code for days at a time (often in his bathrobe, eating all his meals at his desk), making sure that what he was creating would have real value for investors.

As a result, Equis helped to create an all-new industry: computerized investing. Equis has customers in over 70 countries, and 140 independent user groups spread across the world. Since 1983, Equis has sold more than $25 million in investment software and data. His products have received numerous awards, including *PC Magazine's Editors' Choice Award,* the Readers' Choice Award from *Stocks & Commodities Magazine* (the industry bible) every year since its inception, and many others. Plus, the financial press continues to give Equis software rave reviews, including *Barron's, The Wall Street Journal,* and many others. Steve's company is so highly regarded as the leader in its industry; it was recently acquired by Reuters - the global leader in financial news and information. His success with Equis stems from two very important attributes: (1) Steve has the ability to see technology trends, and then turn that vision into products for customers, and (2) Steve can then motivate, organize, and lead his employees to build that vision.

Giving back to the community has always been a priority for Steve and his wife Denise. In 1990, they created The Achelis Foundation to donate money to charitable organizations throughout Utah. Equis was also a charter member of the Utah Information Technology Association (UITA) – one of the largest technology organizations in the country. Equis is actively involved in sharing business ideas with smaller UITA members to help them grow and develop as Equis has.

## Getting to the Vision

In the early 1980s, Steve was actively trading the markets while working as a mechanic. While reading a popular investment book, he realized that one day all of the charts and calculations being shown could be done by anyone with a personal computer. So Steve decided to risk it all. He quit his job, bought a computer, and taught himself to write software. His wife, Denise, worked as a bookkeeper while the couple struggled to build the business.

Steve's original vision was to enter what was then a very narrow vertical market and create a product for it as if it were a horizontal market. The main competitor was selling their product for $1,900 with a manual printed on a dot-matrix printer. Steve priced his product at $195 and provided his customers with high-quality packaging, documentation, marketing materials, and product support. He worked out of his house to keep overhead down. He also wanted his employees to share in the growth of Equis, so he compensated them based on the company's performance – something he still does today.

Steve's core management belief is that if you trust people, they'll perform. 'I'm not naïve enough to think that everyone is rewarded for their good deeds,' says Achelis. 'But I'm certain that what comes around goes around. If you treat people – employees, customers, and business partners – right, they'll reward you'. In those days, computerized investing was a new industry. The challenge was to educate people and sell them at the same time. 'Many of our marketing efforts – advertisements, trade shows, user groups, and brochures – were really educational pieces hidden in a sales wrapper,' Achelis says. 'We tried to use every marketing tactic available,' Achelis continues. 'One of our biggest successes was to create unique packaging that people would be proud to display, and which would get the attention of their friends'. This high-quality packaging has also won numerous awards over the years.

As he read industry publications, Steve created a database of industry influentials – almost a Who's Who of investment software. Then, every day, he wrote personal letters to different people in the database to build relationships and position Equis as the company that really was trying to help investors. Many of those relationships are still valuable to Equis today. Even though Equis is now a strong industry leader, Steve still strives to instill the customer-oriented attitudes that helped his company get where it is today. This is particularly important as Equis takes advantage of the new opportunities presented with the acquisition by Reuters and the explosive growth of the Internet.

## Equis Product Line

Equis was created with one central vision: to help people make better investment decisions with their computers. Steve's ability to grow and develop Equis into a world leader is largely a result of his ability to stay focused on this vision. Through the years, he has had many opportunities to take the company into different directions. But he's always stuck with what he knows best-investment software.

Here's a complete look at the Equis product line:

*MetaStock* is the star of the Equis product line. It helps investors chart and analyze their investments to reduce their risk and maximize their profits. Clearly the market leader in its category, MetaStock continues to win industry awards and rave reviews. ($349)

*MetaStock RT* gives investors all of the charting and analysis tools found in MetaStock, but is used by professional traders to track the markets in real-time. With MetaStock RT, users can plot price quotes as fast as they are released by the stock exchanges. ($495)

*The DownLoader* is a program designed to be used with MetaStock and other similar software. Investors use The DownLoader with their modem to retrieve stock quotes at the end of each trading day and save them on their computer. Then they can analyze those quotes with MetaStock. ($99)

*Pulse Portfolio* helps investors keep track of all their actual investment transactions, their portfolio value, their return rate, and more. It handles nearly every type of investment available - even futures, collectibles, and real estate. ($195)

*The Technician* is similar to MetaStock. But instead of charting individual stocks and other investments, The Technician helps investors monitor the direction of the overall stock market to determine whether or not it's a good time to invest overall. Equis also maintains the database to which users of The Technician can subscribe. ($49, plus $10/month for database subscription)

## Innovative Approaches

Early on, Steve knew that he needed a strong staff to help him accomplish his goals with Equis. So he developed a variety of ways to make Equis the best company in the world to work for: bonus trips to Hawaii, cruises, and cash. He also instituted a quarterly profit bonus plan that gets paid to every employee, from top-level managers to part-time shipping clerks. Steve even provides free health insurance to all employees.

When the company was at only 20 people, he had the foresight to hire a full-time in-house Public Relations staff to promote Equis around the world. It's been a valuable tool to access the influential people in the industry, such as the press, user groups, business alliances, and industry VIPs. In the last year alone, the number of independent Equis user groups has grown from 65 to 140 – largely through the help and attention of the PR staff.

Steve knows that helping customers is the best way to succeed. 'Treat them fairly, and help them become better investors' is still the bottom line in most company meetings.

Equis customers are active investors who need access to accurate investment information. Steve recognized the importance of partnering with key information providers in the industry to make it easier for customers to get access to that information. So Equis created a software product called The DownLoader and positioned it as the information 'faucet' for historical investment information. In fact, the DownLoader gives customers access to more data suppliers than any other software program of its kind.

These partnerships gave Equis customers access to high-quality data, competitive prices, and a wide variety of information. It also brought Equis significant new revenue in the form of data royalties that helped the company continue to grow. With data royalties, Steve was also able to keep the price of his software affordable and increase market share.

Through the years, one of Equis' main strengths has been superior product development. In fact, Equis' flagship product, MetaStock, was far ahead of its time in the mid-1980s with an easy-to-use interface that let the customer track his investment charts in individual chart windows within the program. Equis customers were benefiting from this well-designed graphical user interface well before Microsoft or IBM got into the 'Windows' game. And it was all implemented in the DOS operating system.

When Achelis saw that Windows was becoming mainstream, he developed products built around an object oriented interface - a trend that is just now surfacing throughout the industry. As a result, it places Equis far ahead of competitors in the development race.

## Future Plans

Achelis sees a very simple plan for Equis: to help people use technology to make better investment decisions, from top-tier investment firms to the average next-door-neighbor investor.

He plans on accomplishing this through combining the company's strong product development skills, existing business partners, and new opportunities available through the recent Reuters acquisition.

These plans include:

Leverage Equis' core technology strength by tailoring products that appeal to both ends of the investment spectrum: mass market individual investors and high-end institutional investors. This is why he chose to partner with Reuters, because it gave him better access to both of these important markets.

A strong Internet presence - not only as an online storefront, but more prominently as a software solution to investors who want to analyze the investment information they find on the Internet.

Give customers access to more types and sources of investment information. This not only pleases customers, but increases Equis revenues.

By constantly monitoring what Equis customers are looking for and then giving it to them, Achelis will continue to position Equis as the industry leader. And he has the track record to prove he can do it.

## Facing Risks

*'Entrepreneurism is all about the willingness to take controlled risks'.*

And Steve's developed a keen sense of how to use risk in his favor over the years. In the start-up days, Steve was willing to risk it all by quitting his job as a mechanic to devote all of his time and attention to creating great software. Through the ensuing growth years, he faced the challenge of constantly changing technology, which created an environment where a false move would result in sure failure. In his private life, Steve enjoys adventure sports such as back-country snowboarding, mountaineering, and windsurfing.

When hiring employees, *Steve looks for three* qualities *he thinks are* crucial to success. He wants employees who are *honest, hard-working,* and *willing to learn.*

As overachieving employees contribute more to the success of Equis, Steve rewards them with more responsibility and accountability. That's how he's grown his team of key management employees. By careful promotion from within Equis, Steve ensures that every member of the key management team is familiar with Equis as a company, how it's run, how it fits in the industry, what the strategic issues are, and how it can succeed in the future. The Equis management structure is very flat, and is shared by many important employees. For strategic planning, key management members include:

**Mike Denison, Vice President of Sales and Marketing.** With experience as a writer and an MBA degree, Mike has helped grow the company's marketing for the past six years. His contributions include building the direct mail efforts into a vital revenue source for Equis, increasing the marketing scope by creating an in-house advertising department, and leading the charge into electronic marketing through email and the Internet.

**Ken Hunt, Programming Manager.** Ken has a wealth of experience from his days as a military simulations programmer, combined with his 7 years at Equis developing state-of-the-art investment charting and real-time data handling software. Ken is actively involved in creating new Equis software and manages the team of software engineers.

**Allan McNichol, MetaStock Evangelist.** As a broker and trader, Allan's insight into how customers use Equis software is priceless. He plays a vital role in designing product interfaces and features. In addition, Allan travels the world speaking to Equis user groups about MetaStock and other Equis products.

**John Slauson, Technical Writer.** With nine years of Equis experience, ranging from Technical Support Manager to creating all product documentation to managing the company's Internet presence, John rounds out the key management team with unique insight into the Equis market. He currently helps develop the company's key business partners and industry VIPs into revenue-generating relationships.

## Attitudes about Capitalism

Steve readily admits to being a capitalist, and that he creates products that support capitalism.

He says that, 'growth comes from risk, and the system must therefore reward risk'. But he's quick to follow with his belief that the system doesn't adequately support people on the lower end of the social strata, and that everyone has an obligation to help the people that aren't supported by capitalism.

That's one of the reasons he and his wife, Denise, created The Achelis Foundation. Through this charitable foundation, Steve and Denise have contributed significant amounts of money to the Guadalupe School in Salt Lake City, Utah. The Guadalupe School focuses on helping children, through early intervention, develop the skills they need to succeed in our society.

'I've spent a lot of time searching for different ways to personally fulfill my responsibility of making this world a better place. One of the best ways I've found is through the influential work being done at the Guadalupe School'.

Steve has also helped local students at Murray High School get a glimpse of life in the business world. Through a program designed to link successful local companies with ambitious students, Equis has helped several of these students understand not only how to get a job in the real world, but how to stand out and excel.

How does Steve summarize his views on helping others? 'Everyone deserves the opportunity to succeed; and everyone carries the responsibility to see that those opportunities exist'. Through his own actions, he strives to make this happen every day.

## QUESTIONS FOR DISCUSSION

1. What questions did Steve probably ask himself in order to come up with his ideas for Equis International?
2. How would you define his management style? Why?
3. What did you learn about the investment industry by reading his case study?
4. What attitudes does Steve have about risk?
5. What did you learn about Steve as a person and his development as an entrepreneur?
6. How would you describe the responsibilities of Steve's key personnel and which of the jobs would you enjoy? Why?

*****

## 17. Dr. Hauck – Curiosity Made the Difference

Meet a 101-year-old entrepreneur whose favorite question was WHY? What is special about Dr. Frederick Hauck? When he was nineteen years old, he was told by doctors that he had a bad heart and would die within a year or so. At the age of 102 he was still taking the bus daily to his office in downtown Cincinnati and looked forward to opening his mail every day because it always was full of new opportunities. Chemistry was his favourite school subject. It is not surprising that he described himself as a scientist and not as an entrepreneur. However, from what we know about entrepreneurs, he fits the entrepreneurial profile perfectly. Dr. Hauck learned about entrepreneurship early in his life. His grandfather came from Germany and started a successful brewery. His father became president of the Brewers Bank. But Dr. Hauck did not want to become a banker. He worked there in 1912 when you had to add all the numbers by hand (no calculators or computers of course) and he found it boring. So he decided to become a salesman instead. He said, 'No man can succeed in a line of endeavor which he does not like'.

He became a scientist by accident. He was selling medical equipment and supplies. His family had invested in a mining company in Mexico that was going bankrupt. Dr. Hauck volunteered to go there and with his usual questioning approach, he found out what the real problems were, made friends with the Mexican workers, and took over the failing company. From mining copper he continued to explore uses of other minerals. He founded Continental Mineral Processing Co. in Cincinnati to produce titanium dioxide (the 'white' of white paint, white paper, and white shoe polish). This company still continues to be successful.

While enjoying a vacation in Florida, Dr. Hauck wondered about the the sand on the beaches where he sat. At night he took a mineral light out to explore and saw an interesting fluorescence. He decided to ship samples off to a lab and discovered it contained important elements for atomic use. He used his connections in Washington, DC to get permission to mine the sands along the east coast of Florida which provided him with hafnium, a metallic element which is used for control rods, the safety valves for nuclear reactors. Others sat on the sand too, but they just didn't ask themselves any questions. Dr. Hauck says he has learned from everyone he has met ... and that is quite a few people in his 100 years. He knew Albert Einstein and Werner von Braun. To be successful, it is important to associate with knowledgeable people and establish friendships.

He believed nothing is ever attained without effort. 'My success wasn't just luck. You have to have energy, optimism, and ambition, but most important you have to have specific knowledge of what you are doing'. He also said, 'Our only limitations are those we set up in our minds. The world does not pay us for what we own; it pays us for what we do and what we induce others to do'. And of course he is an optimist. He said he would have to be since he was expected to die 80 years ago. For all those years his goal was to make the most of the moment, to ask questions of everyone he met, and to treat each day as an opportunity to use his abilities to help others. Dr. Hauck died at the age of 103 in May of 1997, but he left us a wonderful philosophy about living life to the fullest. His involvement with the Sabin Polio Vaccine and his work in recent years to eradicate Alzheimer's disease is just a few of his contributions to the world.

*****

## 18. George Gerpheide – The GlidePoint® Guru

Dr. George E. Gerpheide formed Cirque Corporation in 1991 and its predecessor, Proxima, Inc. in 1988, to further develop and commercialize GlidePoint® technology, which he had previously developed. As founding president, Dr. Gerpheide was the guiding force behind taking Cirque from a small start-up basement business to a respected, multimillion-dollar corporation known throughout the world. He has been responsible for:

- Initially developing GlidePoint → technology on which he holds five patents.
- Assembling and leading a technical team.
- Attracting team members with key financial, sales, and marketing skills.
- Securing over $2 million in private funding.
- Negotiating technology license agreements.
- Formulating corporate strategic and growth planning.

Prior to founding Proxima and Cirque, Dr. Gerpheide founded and operated Quality Microcomputer Instrumentation (QMI), an engineering design firm, and Aquila Instruments, Inc. a geophysical equipment company. He was a Visiting Scientist at MIT's Artificial Intelligence Laboratory, where he was part of a team which developed a dexterous robotics hand. Dr. Gerpheide served as Adjunct Assistant Professor in the Mechanical Engineering Department at the University of Utah, where he specialized in motion control, sensing systems. Dr. Gerpheide initiated and coordinated a research experiment to investigate growth of protein crystals in micro-gravity in conjunction with Utah State University for the Space Shuttle Challenger, Mission 41-B.

Dr. Gerpheide holds a Ph.D. in Computer Science from the University of Utah (1981), where he was a Graduate Research Fellow and IBM Fellow. He also holds a BSEE degree from MIT (1975), where he was a National Merit Scholar. He is a member of the Institute of Electronic Engineers (IEEE). During the startup years, the company was operating in the founder's basement on a shoe string budget, and at times did not have the funds to make the meager payroll. While the inventor saw great potential, the markets need was not yet established. Potential customers were not interested, and most computers did not have a graphical user interface – a Windows operating system.

### The Challenges

Cirque's greatest challenge to date occurred when the company was very small and fragile. A laboratory prototype of the proprietary GlidePoint® touchpad technology had just been developed. This was prototype number 26, following a string of unsuccessful attempts to produce what would be become the first commercially successful touchpad technology.

Operating out of the basement on a shoe-string budget, the company employed several part-time engineers and technicians and had no significant funding behind it. At that time, the technology was visualized for use by manufacturers of notebook computers, who could build it into their keyboards. Another hopeful market was keyboard manufacturers themselves who could build the pointing technology directly into their desktop computer keyboard. Unfortunately, while the inventor saw the potential for this technology, the markets need was not yet established or apparent. Not only that, but the current prototype was a large mass of jumbled wires and circuitry which obviously could not be manufactured at low cost or in the size required for a portable computer.

The company had no success marketing the concept to portable computer manufacturers, who at that time were not even providing Windows operating systems on their computers. There was no money to meet the meager payroll. A keyboard company who had expressed initial interest after evaluating some prototypes had just said no. The founders had just returned from walking the floor at the Comdex trade show exhibiting the large suitcase full of electronics and the demonstration portable computer had just failed. Prospects looked bleak.

## The Successful Solution

The founders persevered. If you play blackjack long enough, you will eventually get the winning hand. In this case, a lucky break came when a very large manufacturer of portable computers finally responded after a long period of silence. The enthusiasm and vision of this first customer lead to initial money for further engineering followed by a significant technology license. This provided the spring board for all of the company's operations which allowed it to go on to become the leading provider of touchpad technology. Cirque created an entirely new category of products in the retail computer market with its line of GlidePoint® pointing devices and keyboards.

From its humble beginnings in 1991 with four employees, Cirque now employs a workforce of 65 and continues the work to improve the technology. Recently named to Inc. magazines '500 Fastest Growing Private Companies' in America, as well as to the 'Utah 100' – the fastest growing public or private companies in the state, Cirque embodies the vision and dedication of the founders to the mission of providing a more 'human approach' to computer interfaces. Determination, perseverance and seed funds from UTFC gave the company needed time. Patented GlidePoint® touchpad technology was to become the first commercially successful technology of its kind, and is now available as both packaged peripheral products to the retail market and modules in component form to mobile computer manufacturers. About one-half of the touchpads found in mobile computers, including those available from dominant market players such as Compaq, NEC, Micron, and Sharp, incorporate Cirque GlidePoint technology.

While the past three years have generally seen few developments in pointing device technologies, Cirque has continued to make advances, improving the sensitivity, responsiveness, and feel of GlidePoint technology. Innovative products and product features have been and will continue to be introduced to meet evolving consumers' needs. With continuing research and development, Cirque Corporation is committed to advancing touchpad technology to the mainstream, and believes that the touchpad will soon become the pointing device of choice for computer users.

## The Vision

The company shares the vision of Bill Gates, Chief Executive Officer of Microsoft, who believes that consumers will be surrounded by 'smart appliances' such as interactive televisions, miniature personal computers, 'smart home' controls, advanced communications products and other home and office technologies with simple, pictorial user interfaces. Dr. Gerpheide believes that touchpad technology will be used to control many of these devices. Cirque shares the ideal pursued by Microsoft, Apple and other industry leaders: Graphical interfaces to simplify the human-to-computer relationship on complex machines. Focusing on the input device, Cirque plans to use its touchpad experience to continue to improve cursor control in the retail and OEM markets.

The management of Cirque Corporation regards the employees more as family members than as '9-5 employees.' As a research and development engineering enterprise, the work requires a level of commitment beyond what is normally expected. Employees are encouraged not only to work hard but also to 'play hard' – take time off to be with family, take an extended vacation after a rigorous project has been completed. Meals are provided for employees who work long into the night on a deadline. Because the work environment is open, friendly, and inspiring, it is a rare weekend or evening when the building is closed and dark. The management team implements unique award systems to acknowledge employees for a job well done, the most interesting being 'The Golden Pig', which is the gold tone plated skull from the luau pig in celebration of the completion of the "Kahuna" project. The previous recipient presents the Golden Pig to an employee who has gone well beyond the call of duty. In addition, the company supports employees with additional or advanced education and flex hours to complete studies.

Even as the inventor and creator of Cirque Corporation and of GlidePoint® technology, Dr. Gerpheide typically resists praise given specifically toward him. During company meetings or announcements, he gives all credit to the employees for their hard work, dedication to task, and commitment to the company's successes. Dr. Gerpheide initiated and coordinated a research experiment to investigate growth of protein crystals in micro-gravity in conjunction with Utah State University for the Space Shuttle Challenger, Mission 41-B, and was present to witness the take-off in Florida. Dr. Gerpheide also spends time each week mentoring grade school children at Eastwood Elementary School.

### QUESTIONS FOR DISCUSSION

1. What advice would you expect Dr. Gerpheide to give potential entrepreneurs who experience failures in starting their business?
2. How would the employees of Cirque probably behave when faced with a problem? Why?
3. What do you think Dr. Gerpheide tells the grade school children that he talks to on a regular basis in Salt Lake City about the relationship of education and success?
4. Why didn't his company succeed at first? What did he do about it?
5. How did Dr. Gerpheide's previous experience lead him to becoming an entrepreneur?

*****

# 19. LABOURER TO MARKET LEADER – KATHURIA

D.N. Kathuria is currently the key Director of M/s. Shivani Locks Pvt. Ltd. located in Faridabad and engaged in the manufacture of latches for years which includes door locks, door stickers, window regulators etc. He commands almost 80 per cent of the national market and has export tie-ups with some of the world's best known brands like Ford and General Motors of USA and Kiekert AG of Germany. His is a very illustrious story of rags to riches.

Kathuria came from Pakistan in 1947 as a result of the partition. Back home his father was a small time worker in NWFP in Pakistan. Upon reaching India, he took up labour work in industrial unit located in Faridabad, completed an ITI Course a few years later. While he was working in American Universal as a small worker, one day he went up to his boss, the owner and expressed his desire to start on his own. Upon the boss's suggestion, an electroplating unit for automobile parts was started in his small house.

A sticker that he was for quality, he soon got orders for precision components for fans and other machinery parts from Khaitan, Escorts and Eicher, some of the best industries in the town. His sincerity and concern for quality brought him into contact with M/s. Maruti Ltd. which was being established in Gurgaon near Faridabad at the behest of M/s. Eicher Ltd. M/s. Maruti gave him components for development as that was the period of indigenization at Maruti. He set up a unit in partnership, M/s. Venus Metals, in Sector 24, this was his first plant for auto components. Soon he had a 500 sq. yards plot in Sector 3.

By 1988, he had indigenization of door latches units in cars. He became a major supplier to TELCO and Eicher and M & M who are the largest manufacturers of automobile in the country.

With liberalization, he came in contact with multi-national companies and entered into a technical collaboration with the biggest German Firm, Keykert AG.

He improved upon the German Technology and then became a vendor for Ford and General Motors. He was approached by MG Howers of UK, one of the biggest names in auto industry in the world and got an order. He improved upon their design and set up R&D Centre with all infrastructures in house. His exports to UK were ₹ 50 crores per year.

Currently at the age of 70, he is planning to set up a large-scale plant. A very ordinary person became a major market supplier and started supplying automobile components in the country and the world only because of his sincerity, hard work, and love for quality.

*****

## 20. Russell Cox – Creating Art Source

Russell Cox dates his entrepreneurial beginnings to when he was 14 years old, and he started a greenhouse business. When he was 17 years old, his parents bought a retail picture frame shop. They had operated a trophy shop in their home, but knew nothing about framing. Russell had an eye for beauty and a gift for working with his hands, however, and he taught himself the business.

Five years later, he was ready to go into business for himself. He had been a B – student at Trinity High School in Euless, Texas. He chose a distributive education (now called marketing education) program at A & M Consolidated, College Station, Texas. 'I think I learned the most from my DE classes when we had open discussion about our jobs'. Russell says. 'I was self-employed, but I learned a lot from fellow students on what not to do as a business owner'.

A self-described natural organizer, Russell held offices in high school and vocational school that taught him how to negotiate and compromise. He was president of Distributive Education Clubs of America (DECA), captain of the gymnastics team, and a candidate for the DECA area presidency.

From these early experiences, Russell learned an important fact about himself. 'A traditional job would not provide me with the independence and financial opportunities that I seek,' he says. And he had observed that other members of his family enjoyed a higher standard of living through owning their own businesses. The frame shop gave him the idea for his own business. 'I moved and started a wholesale version of the same business. In order to reach my goals, I knew that I must serve the larger corporate market. Wholesale can serve a larger market from one location than a retail store,' he explained.

From *Entrepreneur* magazine, he learned creative financing methods and how to draw up a business plan. His accountant helped him prepare a budget. According to industry surveys, there was corporate demand for his type of business. For financing, Russell used personal savings, bank financing, and lease-purchase agreements. He works out of a warehouse with one small office. This arrangement not only keeps down overhead, allowing Russell to price his product competitively and offer volume discounts, but also appeals to his customers. 'Clients seem to like coming out to the warehouse to see other works in progress,' he says.

He stresses the creative side of his business. 'When you supply retailers,' Russell points out,' you must create new designs constantly. I have to produce a number of different designs so that each retailer will have something slightly different than the competition'. 'Buying right is another big part of my business. In order to stay competitive, I must bypass distributors and seek out the manufacturers,' he says.

Besides himself, six people work in Russell Gallery. In the past 3 months, sales were $27,000. Russell put all the profits back into the business. Russell is very precise about his plans for growth. He wants to gross $ 200,000 by the end of this year, and $1 million by the end of 1991. He will expand 'horizontally' into frame molding manufacture, art publishing, and retail sales. He plans to make Russell Gallery into a broad-based wholesale/retail art and framing company.

Being in business for himself has caused Russell to sacrifice material possessions now for future rewards. He knows he works longer and harder than his friends. Some of his hurdles are psychological ... like 'being patient and optimistic when there is little motivation to do so.'

But Russell does not give up. An important failure can deal him a temporary setback, but he bounces back. 'I usually feel down for a day or two before I get my attitude straightened out and come back even stronger,' he says.

## QUESTIONS FOR DISCUSSION

1. What did Russell Cox learn from his early work experience and his family's circumstances?
2. What natural aptitudes and abilities did Russell bring to his parents' framing business?
3. How did the family framing business influence Russell's choice of his own business?
4. Besides high school and vocational school, where did Russell learn the facts and skills that helped him in the business?
5. What advantages does the warehouse operation have over a retail store?

*****

# 21. Professional Entrepreneurship – Vikas Verma

## Angel Investor – Founder – The Colour Factory

Vikas Verma has one of the most interesting profiles you'd come across. From coffee and paints to IT, Media and Entertainment he's seen it all. With over 20 years of experience as an Intrapreneur with the giants of Indian Industry including Asian Paints, Barista, CNBC TV 18 and Marico Industries and as an Entrepreneur himself, Vikas makes it quite difficult to put a finger on what makes him the perfect mentor.

Meet Vikas Verma, the corporate veteran, the Pro-preneur, the Angel Investor, the mentor, as he talks about his latest love, The Colour Factory and shares his valuable insights into the market, MBA, Entrepreneurship and more.

Vikas is an Angel Investor who is very open to investing in new and innovative business ideas of budding Entrepreneurs.

Could you tell us how you started your journey of Entrepreneurship?

I very distinctly remember the birth of my first ever venture of my own. I was then heading the Marketing Department at Bharti BT Internet Ltd. While I enjoyed my work, I just couldn't be satisfied. The urge to have a venture of my own was too strong to be ignored. So khulja simsim opened.

Could you brief us about The Colour Factory Experience? The rainbow times, the dark phase, etc?

Like every entrepreneurial Journey, The Colour Factory also has had very colourful times as well as cloudy days. But the highs certainly outweigh the low tides. The Customer satisfaction has always been our constant motivation and has made our good times good. When we see people enjoying themselves at The Colour factory, it feels really good. There have been times when we have made mistakes, for instance, we moved too fast in expanding geographically without enough support in other areas like logistics. So we had to retract. Customer Delivery logistics was another area which we had some initial hiccups with. But those were also the important points of the learning curve.

— How relevant do you think is a Masters in Management when it comes to real life Entrepreneurship?

MBA doesn't teach you the How's of running a business. It doesn't give you a mathematical formula which you can apply in real life entrepreneurship. But it builds your personality, attitude and moulds you to be an Entrepreneur. It's the discipline, the mindset that it creates which are very valuable. I think a Masters is not necessary but desirable.

— I believe in what I call opportunistic or Seasonal Entrepreneurship. You seem to be a Seasonal Entrepreneur. What's your take on that?

I am what I call a Propreneur. What you call Opportunistic or Seasonal Entrepreneurship, I call Professional Entrepreneurship. Cross Industrial Entrepreneurship involves a lot of effort. The positives include never ending challenges so if you are the kind of person who needs constant challenges then you will enjoy it. It's very stimulating. But like I said before, it's not easy to manage such a switch or expansion. Sometimes it works better to establish oneself in a particular sector and gradually expand over areas that are extensions of your core business.

— How favourable is the Indian climate for young entrepreneurs who start without much experience or financial backing of their own?

It's definitely better than what it was 10 years ago but certainly not what it could be or should be. Encouraging Entrepreneurial activity within the country has to increase at least 10 fold is indispensable for the Indian economy to realize its dreams of International leadership.

— What do you think is the success ratio of Entrepreneurial Ventures by young Entrepreneurs in India?

The success ratio of Entrepreneurial Ventures in India is unfortunately pretty low. The reasons are many. While the number of B-plans I encounter is huge, the percentage of people who are serious about their ventures is again very low.

The Entrepreneurial ecosystem in India has not yet matured, be it access to funding, expert guidance or infrastructure. Some of the existing big players in this arena having their origin in the Silicon Valley are focused on the IT sector. There is a lack of a system that reaches out to the grassroots level Entrepreneurs. With the advent Angel networks, this scenario is changing.

— On Business Incubators in India:

The Business Incubators should go beyond offering space and may be a computer. Their responsibilities must include support in all aspects – legal support, mentorship, networking, access to technology, strategic support. There are issues like copyright and IP rights which are very important but ignored by many entrepreneurs because they don't realize that. The Business Incubators need to offer support in such areas.

— Do you think there is an Entrepreneurs favourite industry?

In India maximum Entrepreneurial activity goes on in the IT industry. The number of start-ups that come up in the IT sector is far higher than those in other sectors. It could be the effect of the popular IT boom.

— Can merging be healthy to a start-up?

Merging can certainly be healthy to a start up but it has to be done after careful and thorough analysis. For instance, a start up can benefit from the technological advantages of the Merger.

But firstly one needs to be very clear about the reasons for merging. Secondly, prepare for the worst; expect dilution and conflicts. One very important factor you should look for in the other company is synergy. If the companies are synergistic the journey will be much smoother.

— Generally, young entrepreneurs are wary of issuing equity to VCs as their financial dependency well as lack of experience renders them insecure. What do you have to say about this? How much do you think is an optimum amount of equity that one can safely part with?

While one should choose a VC who is sensitive to the aspirations of the Entrepreneur, the Entrepreneur himself has to understand that the VC will want return on his investment. This is something that both have to work out. Personally I think one should, if possible, avoid going for VC funding at a very early stage. The amount of equity one needs to part with dependent on the stage of the start up. On the other hand, if the venture is established and demonstrated some amount stabilization and success and seeking financial support for scaling up, then you will be in a good position to negotiate on the equity. You could also consider other options of funding like family and friends.

— In India, Legal awareness among the common mass is low compared to its western counterparts. Legal consulting is also not easily affordable and accessible to all. What are the easily available sources of legal help for young and budding entrepreneurs who start small? What is your advice to young Entrepreneurs like us in this regard?

Legal help is available and affordable, only you need to know where to look for it. I'd recommend you have a mentor who will help you connect with such sources.

— As an investor what do you look for in a start up?

I'd like to offer support to budding entrepreneurial ventures, in terms of seed fund as well as mentorship. What I look for in a start up is the potential of the idea and the commitment level of the team as these define the success of the venture.

*****

# 22. A Nutritious Business

At 17, when most girls of her age were set to go to college for higher studies, Sarala Bastian, now a successful entrepreneur got married. But Sarala Bastian did not wish to just be confined to her house. She wanted to do something on her own. She wanted to be independent and carve out identify for herself.

'My father gave me the initial capital of ₹ 15,000 to start a business in 2004. I started a mushroom farm in my backyard,' says Sarala. There has been no looking back since ..... today, she is a successful entrepreneur in a field not explored by many. It has been an incredible journey for the 32-year-old Sarala.

To add to her glory, she has been short listed for the prestigious Youth Business International (YBI) Entrepreneur of the Year award for 2009. YBI is a UK-based network established by Prince Charles to encourage young entrepreneurs.

Ghada Ba-ageel of Saudi Arabia and Linet Indiazi of Kenya are the other two nominees in the female category for this year's award. The award, to be announced on November 16, will comprise a cash prize of $1,000, a certificate and a medal.

Here's how Sarala transformed herself from a simple housewife into a successful entrepreneur with minimum resources at her disposal and has been facilitating benchmarking for KM adoption to small entrepreneurs.

## The beginning years

She spent her childhood in Coimbatore where her father worked as an auditor in the state co-operative society. In school, she learnt typewriting and shorthand. She was married to Sebastian after passing class 12 exams and so came to Chennai with him. She has two daughters, elder one is 14-years old and seven year old younger daughter is mentally challenged since as a baby, she had brain fever and life changed for the worst because of this.

## Becoming an entrepreneur

There never was any financial difficulty and she was happy with what husband earned. But it was a dream to start something on their own, be independent and offer jobs to other needy women. That is why 95 per cent of employees are women. The dream is to make all women financially independent. The idea to cultivate mushrooms came in mind as she felt it was a very 'nutritious' business and had not been attempted by many.

## Funds to start the business

She got a lot of support from my father who gave the initial capital of ₹ 15,000 to start the business in 2004. She started a mushroom farm in backyard. Before starting mushroom farming, she attended training classes at 11 different places, including the agricultural college in Coimbatore.

## The art of cultivating mushrooms

It was very difficult to get seeds in those days, bought one seed for ₹ 60 and got started. The seeds are kept in a perforated plastic cylinder between layers of cleansed hay. Within 17 days, mushrooms start coming out of the holes in the cylinder. From one cylinder, they get about 2 kg of mushrooms.

## Initial struggles

There was a time when she used to go to the supermarkets and beg them to keep their mushrooms in their shops. They used to reluctantly agree after a lot of persuasion. Today, early in the morning, they call and ask, 'Madam, how many packets would you send today?' It takes time for any business to flourish, but ultimately you succeed. Within 3 months of starting business, they made a profit of ₹ 65,000. Whatever profit have made so far, they have put back into the business. More than making money, the aim is to expand the business. Besides fresh milky and oyster mushrooms, they also sell processed foods like pickles, soup powder, jam, etc. The turnover is around ₹ 2,50,000 every month these days. Now, the aim is to inspire more women. So, she meets many self-help groups and asks them to do something worthwhile.

## Working with jail inmates

Some college students from Oorambakkam (near Chennai) wanted her to teach them mushroom cultivation for a project. Later, she found that the students had adopted a village and they wanted her to teach the villagers too. She decided to teach them free of cost. When these college students were planning to train jail inmates, she went to meet the female inmates of Puzhal prison in Chennai. Initially, though a bit scared she was able to convince them to work hard on their own, after they come out and only after they promised, she agreed to teach them how to cultivate mushrooms. The process is really simple, anyone can do it. She plans to give them regular work, and the process for the same is on.

## International award

It was the Bharatiya Yuva Sakthi Trust that had been helping with lot with business advice from the time she started my enterprise who recommended for her name to the Youth Business International (YBI) Entrepreneur of the Year award for 2009. About 50 names from India had been sent and she is the only Indian short listed from the thousands of names they got from all over the world.

*****

# 23. Dream Houses – Entrepreneurial Journey

Amanora is a new township taking shape few miles away from the humdrum of Pune-Mumbai. It is the brainchild of Aniruddha Deshpande, a man who was known for a long time as someone who brought Motocross to India in the 1980s and a regular participant and winner of the grueling Himalayan car rally. Given this background, it should be no surprise that his plans for Amanora are Himalayan in scale. It is a multi-crores, fully wired, intelligent township that will be controlled by a central data system. All homes will be IT-enabled to monitor everything from the daily vendor system to the security. Every resident will have a portal in the Intranet that will be connected to various vendors. Explains Deshpande: 'You can order anything from any shop or any hotel in the township through this portal. If you are going out of town and need less milk, then some simple clicks on a smart screen will allow you to change your requirement. The laundry, the housekeeping and any other supplier will be connected to this portal'.

Deshpande calculates that one needs 68 such functions or verticals to run a township and the cost of such a data-centre would be ₹ 100 crores. It is not viable to spend this amount for constructing a few thousand houses. But then Deshpande is not setting up a few thousand houses, he is creating a township of 30,000 at which the data-centre becomes very profitable. The centre will be set up by a township management company called City Development Corporation, which is controlled by Deshpande.

In fact, the Amanora concept changes the relationship between the developer and the buyer. You don't get to buy an Amanora property, you lease it for 999 years. Will this be acceptable to buyers? Deshpande's rationale is: 'We will change the customer into a citizen. So we don't sell you the apartment, we give it to you on lease and we provide you water, electricity, education, healthcare, a marketplace, entertainment, gardens, security – everything that you need. We will be able to offer this at a much lower cost and much higher quality because we will be able to negotiate better terms as a bulk buyer of water, electricity and everything else from the suppliers'. He proposes many novel solutions to ensure that Amanora's infrastructure remains top class. One such is a water bank or dam, which he admits is nowhere near being accepted by the government. But, he says, 'The government is short of money for irrigation projects. We are willing to spend money to dam the water and sell it to the Pune Municipal Corporation. We want to be able to sell the surplus water at the rate that the irrigation department sets for water'.

How did Deshpande come into this business and develop these novel ideas, when he is neither an architect nor an engineer? It was – as happens with most entrepreneurs – a matter of chance. 'Both my parents are doctors and nobody in my family is into business. I have been only in the real estate business so far, except for an automobile dealership that I had for a few years till 1988'. That too happened because Deshpande was connected to automobiles in an indirect way. 'I was organizing motor sports in India and was vice-chairman of the Federation of Motor Sports in India for a long time, and then of the Pune Automotive Racing Association. I also used to race and won the Himalayan car rally in 1980-81. I also started the Motocross here in Pune and we even hosted the world championship at the Nehru Stadium. I was the executive chairman of that body for a long time – almost 8-9 years. We had collected ₹ 35 lakh, which was a big amount for a sports body in 1988'. After the world championship was over, there was a lot of infighting and so Deshpande quit. As soon as he resigned in 1988, he stumbled into the real estate business quite by chance.

Deshpande had a friend who had a 5,000 sq ft plot in Bibwewadi in Pune. He asked the friend whether his father would let him develop the plot. He replied, 'I don't think he will, because he is looking for a well-established developer'. Deshpande said, 'If we tie up with an architect and a developer, will he give it to me?' This architect was a member of the racing association. Deshpande also knew a developer who had done construction for 10 years. 'The idea was that the we would take two flats and the developer would sell the remaining six apartments. All of us went to meet my friend's father'. He told them, 'If you three are going to do it, then I am willing to take the risk, I will give you my plot'. The hitch was that the trio had to make a down payment of ₹ 1,20,000 but did not have any money. They suggested that bookings would be announced in 6-8 months and once the cash was raised, they would hand over ₹ 120,000 to the plot-owner. The owner agreed. They completed the project in six months and Deshpande has never looked back ever since. 'We did 10 projects in that area alone. Many people saw the quality of the project and approached us with their plots. All the plots were the same 5,000-sq-ft size. That was how I got into this business.' It was by default.

Building small residential projects is one thing but taking on the task of creating a landmark township on a gigantic scale is quite another. How did Deshpande get involved with Amanora? Before Amanora, he was involved with another unique project, called Lavasa, which is a township atop a hilly area, near Pune. When Deshpande started work on it, it was the most unlikely destination. 'It had no road, no hospitals, no hotels, no communication facilities, no educational facilities, nothing. For the first 1 year, they had to walk for two hours to and fro from the site. No developer would have walked four hours a day to buy land, especially 1 years ago.'

Why did he take the trouble? 'The only reason was that nobody had built a private hill-station after the British left India'. Deshpande bought his quota of land and then applied to start a project under the Maharashtra government's hill-station policy. However, having developed the project up to a point, he has just sold his interest in it to Hindustan Construction Company. Deshpande claims that the Lavasa project was planned very well and has won prizes all over the world for master planning. Deshpande sold out his stake in Lavasa when the project became large and banks insisted on his personal guarantees for loans which were growing too large for comfort.

Apart from Amanora, Deshpande has planned two other townships. The next one is at a lower price point (between ₹ 10 and 20 lakh), deploys a new fabrication technology (consumes less of cement and uses a chemical that expands) to lower the cost and will come up in less than 1,200 days. The township will have all basic facilities including and a transport hub to connect Pune. The third project is a golf estate – a very high-end project with only golf villas. It will have 10-12 towers and will offer an unrestricted view of the golf course. Deshpande has already bought the land and will launch the project before the end of the year. Can Deshpande take his model and learning across the country? No way, he says since 'Real estate in India is not a national game.' It is not easy to buy land if you are not a local developer. If you are doing a joint venture with a local developer, then you are not in control. In any case, for now, Deshpande's hands are full – delivering what is aimed to be a showpiece of India's frenetic real estate development.

*****

## 24. Doctor But Entrepreneur

Dr Sushil Shah, the founder of a chain of pathology labs called Metropolis. Started in 1981, Metropolis now has 50 labs across the country. It also has 17 laboratories abroad – South Africa, Sri Lanka, Dubai, Sharjah, Abu Dhabi, Bahrain. It is also starting some facilities in Thailand and is running a laboratory in Seychelles along with the government there.

What has the journey of this entrepreneur been like? Dr. Shah studied in the Scindia School at Gwalior and graduated from Jai Hind College in Mumbai. His father was a doctor and wanted his son to study medicine. Shah was not keen but agreed. 'At that time, my uncle lived with us and he did not have any children. He had iron-ore mines in five or six other places. I was interested to join him. But my father said that I should do medicine first. And once you get into medicine, you cannot do anything else. The course is so long that, by the time you complete it, you are well set'. Shah completed his MBBS, did his post-graduation in medicine in 1975. After this, he went for a fellowship at Cornell University in the unite a states and, on return, worked in renowned hospitals. He moved to Saifi Hospital in 1981 as the head of the department of pathology and also started Metropolis in that year.

As a pathologist, Dr. Shah was somewhat different. 'Pathologists used to be either in private practice or they were attached to a hospital laboratory. Nobody I knew did both together'. I not only had my own laboratory, Metropolis, but I was attached to three hospitals at a time." As if this were not a plateful, Dr. Shah joined Dr. Reddy's Laboratories (DRL) in 1989 as the executive director of its diagnostics division. He was there until almost 1998. It was as late as 1993 that he really began to think of himself as a serious entrepreneur. 'Doing so many things together – attending to four hospitals, my own lab and Dr. Reddy's in Hyderabad – I was slicing my time too thin. It was time to focus on making Metropolis grow. It took me about 3-4 years to resign from all the places and, from 1998–1999, I focused completely on Metropolis'.

Meanwhile, Dr. Shah had traveled abroad quite a few times, visited some of the large laboratories there and realized that India was very backward in diagnostic support services. 'Clearly, there was scope for setting up a chain of labs in India. The second realization was that there was truly no international chain. All the chains were located in their respective countries. The third thing I noticed was that a lot of our visitors from the US would come to see our lab and say that though we have all the equipment in the laboratory, the layout and systems were poor'. To address all these meant putting together the right team. Though Dr. Shah had some experience with DRL in marketing and administration, he felt this was not good enough. 'So the choice for me was that I hire a team or I take in partners. Initially, I tried hiring but was unsuccessful – either I didn't know how to get work out of them or I chose the wrong people. Whatever the reason, it was a failure and I also lost a lot of money. Then I thought: why not have partners?'

'At that time, we had two labs with local partners outside Mumbai – one in Jaipur and the other in Chennai. The Jaipur lab was not doing well but the Chennai one was. It was run by Shriramchandra group and Dr. GSK Velu was looking after their interest. I knew Velu earlier too, as he was a supplier. He was also running a diagnostics company and I got along well with him. I clearly saw that he can help in networking and growth. I invited him to join the board and support my growth plans. The local partners were only interested in the growth of their own centres, not in the growth of Metropolis. Somewhere along the line, interests used to clash. I decided not to take any more local partners and decided to try to become a national chain. We also got Dr. TK Parthasarthy, who was the vice-chancellor of Sri Ramachandra University, to join the board. He was the man responsible for the tremendous growth of that university. Later, my daughter, who had done her MBA and was, working for Goldman Sachs in the US, came back. We made up the core team and divided our responsibilities. Today, we are a four-people team at the management level who are handling things: Ameera my daughter, Dr. Velu, Ganeshan and I. Ameera looks after the entire Indian operations and marketing. Dr. Velu looks after international operations and business development. Ganeshan, who is a chartered accountant, looks after finance; I look after purchase, quality control and setting up of new labs, because that is my forte and IT'.

Where did he get the initial capital to start with? 'Luckily we had our own nursing home at Opera House in central Mumbai, so I started a lab there and worked there for the first four years. At that time, the lab was very primitive so it didn't cost us too much. In 1985, I shifted the lab to Gamdevi, a few kilometres away, to a 2,000 sq ft space where I remained till 1999. In 2000, we shifted to our current location because we were already starting operations as a national chain. Also, the lab grew with time; so much of the money came from accruals'. Metropolis is now housed in its own three-storied building at Worli, a swank residential and office area in central Mumbai.

Dr. Shah regrets that he waited till 1999 to go full-throttle, though he had started the lab in 1981. That is because he failed to see the difference between the growth of the lab and his personal growth. 'In all the other organizations, I could see that my personal growth was happening – whether in terms of experience or in terms of being well known – but all this did not necessarily translate into the growth of the lab. If I had done what I did in 2000 earlier, probably we would have become 10 times bigger'.

## Growth Model

Metropolis has an interesting revenue model. 'Our kind of laboratory is called a referral laboratory. A small laboratory usually does around 100 to 200 varieties of tests. A lab associated with a hospital carries out around 400 tests. A referral laboratory like ours carries out more than 3,700, including specialized ones. Our customer base is of four types - who walk-in, other laboratories referrals, referrals from clinical trials and referrals for health check-ups from industries. Another avenue they are now looking at is getting samples from abroad to carry out tests'. Metropolis may end March 2009 with a turnover of ₹ 200 crores with an operating margin of 27 per cent and a net margin of 17 per cent. Year-on-year growth is more than 30 per cent.

Major areas of growth in future are: completing the footprint in India, expanding internationally and taking up clinical trials. The global clinical trial market is around $20 billion and is expected to double to $40 billion over the next 5 years. Of this, about 5-10 per cent will be in India, feels Dr Shah. He wants a lot of it to come to Metropolis.

# 25. Essence of Enterprise

Chances are high that the soap, the detergent, the shampoo, the talcum powder, the lipstick, the pan masala and the after-shave lotion you use every day have perfumes and flavours supplied by SH Kelkar. From colognes to room fresheners and mouth fresheners to deodorants and agarbattis, Kelkar's perfumes are in everything that needs fragrance. The entrepreneurial journey of SH Kelkar is neither rags-to-riches nor a new technology creating niche product saga. It is a serious and sharply focused single business stream combined with meticulous execution that has resulted in strong market dominance in fragrances and perfumes.

## Background

SH Kelkar & Company was started in 1922 by two brothers, Sadashiv Haribhau Kelkar, popularly called 'Dadasaheb', and Damodar Haribhau Kelkar, popularly called 'Annasaheb'. It has now grown into a company with ₹ 250 crores of revenues and 500 employees spread across multiple locations. The company is run by Damodar Kelkar's son, Govind Kelkar, who is the chairman and managing director. When Govind Kelkar completed his graduation in chemistry and geology from St Xavier's College, Mumbai in 1952 and joined the business, the firm used to import raw material to manufacture fragrances. That year, the firm decided to set up its own factory in Mulund, a Mumbai suburb, mainly to integrate backward.

## R&D

'In 1952, there was no restriction on imports but my uncle strongly believed that, although raw material is available in plenty, we should manufacture the ingredients ourselves,' recalls Govind Kelkar. 'In those days, there were two products that were very difficult to manufacture – one was hydroxyl citronella and the other was Yara Yara. We had to develop the processes to manufacture these two products ourselves as there was no one to turn to for help in India. We have never bought any know-how or technology from outside. I had Professor Avdhoot Nadkarni – my guru and guide in organic chemistry – and one Mr Bhave who helped me in research. Our customers were able to appreciate our products as our quality was even better than that of products which were imported'. By that time, it was virtually essential for top cosmetics companies to do business with SH Kelkar. Kelkar's top customers were Hindustan Lever and Tata Oil Mills Company (which was later taken over by Hindustan Lever).

One reason for Kelkar's success was investment in top-grade equipment. 'My father was very particular about one thing. Whenever there was any talk of investing in technology, he would insist that we go for the best. For example, we were the first Indian company to have installed a gas chromatograph in perfumery (after Hindustan Lever and Roche)'. Thanks to the top quality of its equipment, Kelkar is able to extract extremely high value for its products. The post-tax return on turnover is as high as 20 per cent.

## Expansion

In the late 1970s, two subsidiaries came up – KV Arochem Pvt Ltd at Vapi (a chemical hub in Gujarat) to manufacture basic raw materials for captive use, as well as for exports, and

Keva Fragrances Pvt Ltd, a 100 per cent export unit for fragrances within the Mulund factory. Kelkar is setting up a factory in Patalganga, near Mumbai where the Mulund factory will be shifted. In 2004, Keva Biotech Pvt Ltd came up to cultivate aromatic plants. 'Through this venture, we are able to pass on the results to farmers with whom we have a buy-back guarantee'. According to Govind Kelkar, the biotech laboratory of the research centre can match international standards. The cultivation of patchouli plant from which oil is extracted was the first successful project. They are also cultivating geranium and vetiver (popularly called as khus) for oil extraction and working on some medicinal plants to be used in Ayurvedic products'.

## Corporate Social Responsibility

Anyone living in Mumbai knows about VG Vaze College/ Kelkar College of Mulund. Kelkar is an old-style business house, aware of its responsibility towards society. It has given back to society in the form of these colleges. The reason for setting up these educational institutions goes deep into family history. Kelkar's belonged to a small village about 12km away from Devgad, a coastal town of Maharashtra. There was no scope for studying after primary education in the vicinity. Since they were lucky to get graduated in science from Fergusson and Wellington Colleges, they believed that education help them prosper. In that spirit, the Kelkar Education Trust was formed, and VG Vaze College started in 1984.

How does an old-style business house deal with today's challenges such as recruiting and retaining staff? They pick up students when they have completed their graduation or post-graduation. Then they are given training for a couple of years and absorbed into the permanent cadre. They do not hire management students; they don't fit into our culture. They prefer science graduates and post-graduates. We are a technologically oriented company and make new products using our in-house research & development facilities. Attrition cannot be stopped but because of training very well they tend to stay for a long time. Kelkar's are not looking to bringing in a strategic investor but is not averse to making a public issue.

*****

# APPENDICES

1. How to Start Small-Scale Industry?
2. Sources of Information: Where? What?
3. Whom to Contact for What Information
4. List of Abbreviations
5. The "Ten Commandments" for the Beginning Entrepreneur
6. Mistakes Entrepreneurs Should NOT Make
7. Model (Review) Questions

# Appendix – I

## How to Start Small-Scale Industry?

The procedure for setting up a small-scale industry is given below:

1. Selection of product and preparation of project profiles.
2. Direct purchase of land or obtaining land in Development Area/Development Plot or obtaining shed in the Industrial Estates or Mini Industrial Estates (through General Manager, District Industries Centre).
3. Registration in case of Formation of Company/Partnership Concern.
4. Agreement with Foreign Collaborator, if any.
5. Obtaining Letter of Intent/DGTD Registration/Provisional SSI Registration as the case may be.
6. Obtaining Foreign Collaboration Approval from Government of India.
7. Preparation of detailed Project Report.
8. Obtaining CG Clearance, Import Licence, etc.
9. Applying for power connection to State Electricity Boards.
10. Sanction by Financial Institutions — start of civil construction after obtaining clearances from local authorities and other statutory organisations.
11. Opening Letter of Credit for imported machinery and equipment, if any.
12. Selection of Personnel — administrative and technical for running the industry.
13. Placement of orders for supply of indigenous machinery.
14. Completion of civil works.
15. Delivery of imported equipment.
16. Delivery of indigenous equipment.
17. Erection of machinery and equipment.
18. Obtaining clearance from the Pollution Control Board.
19. Trial run and commissioning of plant.
20. Start of commercial production.
21. Arrangements for sale of products.
22. Obtain Industrial Licence/DGTD Revalidation/Permanent SSI Registration.

An entrepreneur can obtain the necessary information and guidance from the Governmental Departments, Organization, and Consultant Agencies.

# Appendix – II

## Sources of Information: Where? What?

It is important, for new entrepreneurs to know where to go for a particular information, to avoid running around. For that, they need to know, what they are looking for, as clearly as possible.

Some entrepreneurs may be completely ignorant and some may have knowledge about the marketing, production or finance area, etc. Those who are completely ignorant and do not have any idea about their enterprise will require initial deskwork and personal discussions with knowledgeable persons. This will help them in getting considerable idea about the type of venture they want to undertake.

Those having some knowledge about functional areas like marketing, production or finance will require specific information. For them, it is very useful to list out various activities that require to be completed for setting up their enterprises. By doing this deskwork, they will get clear idea about the assistance and information they need for doing the required activities.

*Agencies to Assist New Entrepreneurs:*

Various developmental agencies to assist entrepreneurs are:

(1) Some agencies provide only general information and the specifics of information must be verified.

(2) Some agencies provide technical/marketing expertise in specialised areas.

(3) Some agencies provide guidance in technical and financial matters and also take up turn-key responsibilities (*i.e.*, implementation assistance).

However, government formalities and procedures will have to be completed in all cases by the entrepreneurs themselves for which they can contact the concerned departments' offices for information.

While collecting such information' from various sources, it is advisable to retain only relevant information. Relevant information, must be filed and kept, at a proper place, so that it is available when required.

The compilation and segregation of information will need table work and the information so compiled should be compared with and ensured whether all necessary data/information has been collected, before commencing the work.

Expert guidance, will help in decision-making process. It will be useful to make personal visits to the institutions, to acquire first hand information and feel, so as to get a clear picture about the ground work to be done.

*Needs and Agencies Classification:* In order to help new entrepreneurs to get right kind of information, Annexure I gives various sources of information at State and National level. Entrepreneurs need not contact all the agencies but can get in touch with relevant ones, depending upon their requirements.

Annexure 1, is followed by various agencies and publications useful for entrepreneurs. It covers:

| | | |
|---|---|---|
| Exhibit I | — | National Laboratories and Institutes. |
| Exhibit II | — | Commodity Boards and Others. |
| Exhibit III | — | Specialised Trade Publications. |
| Exhibit IV | — | Technical Consultancy Organisations. |

# Exhibit – I

## National Laboratories and Institutes

Given below is the list of Institutes in India, who are doing fundamental and applied research. Industry, trade and desirous/aspiring entrepreneurs can benefit from their research and application of scientific knowledge.

| | *Name* | *Location* |
|---|---|---|
| 1. | National Physical Laboratory | New Delhi |
| 2. | National Chemical Laboratory | Pune |
| 3. | Central Fuel Research Institute | Dhandbad – Bihar |
| 4. | Central Glass and Ceramic Research Institute | Jadavpur – Kolkata |
| 5. | Central Food Technological Research Institute | Mysore |
| 6. | National Metallurgical Laboratory | Jamshedpur |
| 7 | Central Drug Research Institute | Lucknow |
| S. | Central Electro-Chemical Research Institute | Kariakudi – Tamil Nadu |
| 9. | Central Building Research Institute | Roorkee |
| 10. | Central Electronics Engineering Research Institute | Pilani – Rajasthan |
| 11. | Central Salt and Marine Chemical Research Institute | Bhavnagar – Gujarat |
| 12. | Central Mining Research Station | Dhanbad – Bihar |
| 13. | Central Leather Research Institute | Chennai |
| 14. | Regional Research Laboratory | Hyderabad, jorhat (Assam) Bhubaneswar |
| 15. | Indian Institute of Experimental Medicine | Kolkata |
| 16. | Regional Research Laboratory | Jammu Tawi (J & K) |
| 17. | Central Mechanical Engineering Research Institute | Durgapur (W. Bengal) |
| 18. | National Environmental Engineering Research Institute | Nagpur |
| 19. | National Aeronautical Laboratory | Bangalore |
| 20. | Central Indian Medical Plants Organisation | Lucknow |
| 21. | Central Scientific Instruments Organisation | Chandigarh |
| 22. | Indian Institute of Petroleum | Dehradun |
| 23. | National Geophysical Research Institute | Hyderabad |
| 24. | Indian National Scientific Documentation Centre | New Delhi |
| 25. | National Institute of Oceanography | Panaji (Goa) |
| 26. | National Register Unit | New Delhi |
| 27. | Central Design and Engineering Research Institute | New Delhi |
| 28. | National Biological Laboratory | New Delhi |
| 29. | Structural Engineering Research Centre | Roorkee |
| 30. | Industrial Toxicological Research Centre | Lucknow |

# Exhibit – II

## Commodity Boards and Others

| | *Commodity Boards* | | *Other Organisations* |
|---|---|---|---|
| 1. | The All India Handicrafts Board, Ramkrishnapuram, New Delhi - 22 | 1. | Jute Commissioner, Kolkata. |
| 2. | Tea Board, 14, Brabourne Road, Kolkata - 1. | 2. | Director of Sugar & Vanaspati, Ministry of Agriculture New Delhi. |
| 3. | Coffee Board 1, Vidhan Veedhi, Bangalore - 1. | 3. | Khadi and Village Industries Commission, 3, Birla Rd, Mumbai. |
| 4. | Coir Board Cochin -16 | 4. | The Chief Controller of Imports & Exports, Ministry of Foreign Trade, Udyog Bhavan, New Delhi - 11. |
| 5. | Central Silk Board 95-B, Marine Drive Mumbai - 2. | 5. | Textile Commissioner, New CGO Building, 48, New Marine Lines, Mumbai - 1. |
| 6. | All India Handloom Board, Mumbai - 20. | 6. | State Bank of India, Overseas Branch, Mumbai - 23. |
| 7. | Rubber Board, M. G. Road, Kottayam, Kerala. | | |
| 8. | Cardamom Board, Chittor Road, Cochin - 16. | | |

# Exhibit – III

## Specialized Trade Publications

| Category | | Publication | Place |
|---|---|---|---|
| 1. Automobile | a. | Automobile India | New Delhi |
| | b. | Upper India Motorist | New Delhi |
| | c. | Auto Spark | Mumbai |
| 2. Ceramics | a. | CGCRI - Bulletin | Kolkata |
| | b. | Indian Ceramics | Kolkata |
| 3. Chemicals | a. | Chemical Age of India | Mumbai |
| | b. | Chemical Weekly | Mumbai |
| | c. | Indian Chemical Engineer | Kolkata |
| 4. Cycle | a. | Cycle Reporter | Kolkata |
| | b. | Cycle Trade | Kanpur |
| 5. Coffee | a. | Indian Coffee | Bangalore |
| 6. Electricals | a. | Electrical India | Mumbai |
| | b. | Electronic Engineer | New Delhi |
| | c. | Electronics For You | New Delhi |
| 7. Engineering | a. | Engineering Profile | Mumbai |
| | b. | Current Engineering Practice | Mumbai |
| | c. | Engineering Times | Kolkata |
| | d. | Journal of the Institute of Consulting Engineers | Kolkata |
| | e. | Industrial Engineering and Management | Mumbai |
| | f. | Indian Engineer | Kolkata |
| 8. Export Import | a. | Ex-Im News | Kolkata |
| | b. | Indian Export Trade Journal | Baroda |

| | | | |
|---|---|---|---|
| | c. | Indian Exporter and Importer | Mumbai |
| 9. Gem | a. | Journal of Gem Industry | Jaipur |
| | b. | Diamond World | Jaipur |
| 10. Leather | a. | Indian Leather | Chennai |
| | b. | Journal of Leather Technologist Association | Kolkata |
| 11. Hosiery | a. | Hosiery and Textile Journal | Ludhiana |
| 12. Hotels | a. | Indian Hotel Keeper and Traveller | Delhi |
| | b. | Hotelier | Bangalore |
| 13. Iron and steel | a. | TISCO | Jamshedpur |
| 14. Machinery and tools | a. | Machine Building Industry | Mumbai |
| | b. | Tool and Alloy Steels | Mumbai |
| 15. Management | a. | Indian Management | New Delhi |
| | b. | Business India | Mumbai |
| | c. | Business Today | Mumbai |
| | d. | Business World | New Delhi |
| | e. | The Director | Kolkata |
| 16. Mining | a. | Indian Mining and Engineering Journal | Mumbai |
| 17. Paints and colour | a. | Colourage | Mumbai |
| 18. Paper and printing | a. | Indian Pulp and Paper | Kolkata |
| | b. | Indian Book Industry | New Delhi |
| | c. | Packaging World | Kolkata |
| 19. Pharmaceuticals | a. | Indian Journal of Pharmacy | Mumbai |
| | b. | Eastern Pharmacist | New Delhi |
| | c. | Indian Pharmaceutical Guide | New Delhi |
| 20. Plastic and rubber | a. | Rubber News | Mumbai |
| | b. | Popular Plastics | Mumbai |
| | c. | Polymer India | Mumbai |
| 21. Radio | a. | Radio Services | Mumbai |
| 22. Silk | a. | Indian Silk | Mumbai |

| | | | | |
|---|---|---|---|---|
| 23. | Shipping | a. | Indian Shipping | Mumbai |
| 24. | Sugar | a. | Co-operative Sugar | New Delhi |
| 25. | Textile | a. | Textile Dyer and Printer | Mumbai |
| | | b. | Textile Industry of India | Kolkata |
| | | c. | Textile Trends | Kolkata |
| | | d. | Textile Magazine | Chennai |
| 26. | Trade and industry | a. | Indian Trade Journal | New Delhi |
| | | b. | Bombay Market | Mumbai |
| | | c. | Industrial India | Mumbai |
| | | d. | The Economic Times | Mumbai |
| | | e. | Financial Express | Mumbai |
| | | f. | SSI Magazine | Mumbai |
| 27. | Wool | a. | Woollens and Worsted of India | Mumbai |
| | | b. | Wool News | Mumbai |

# Exhibit – IV

## Technical Consultancy Organizations

1. Gujarat Industrial and
   Technical Consultancy Org., Ltd.
   Ashram Road,
   Ahmedabad - 9.
2. Technical Consultancy Services
   Org. of Karnataka,
   Nrupatunga Road,
   Bangalore - 2.
3. Orissa Industrial and Technical
   Consultancy Org., Ltd.
   Satyanagar,
   Bhubaneshwar - 7.
4. Madhya Pradesh Consultancy Org., Ltd.
   T. T. Nagar,
   Bhopal - 3.
5. North India Technical Consultancy Org., Ltd.
   Sector 17-C,
   Chandigarh - 17.
6. Industrial and Technical Consultancy
   Org. of Tamil Nadu Ltd.,
   Greams Road,
   Chennai - 6.
7. Kerala Industrial and Technical
   Consultancy Org., Ltd.
   M.G. Road,
   Cochin - 16.
8. North Eastern Industrial and
   Technical Consultancy Org., Ltd.
   Bamuni Maidan,
   Guwahati - 21.

9. Andhra Pradesh Industrial and
Technical Consultancy Org., Ltd.
Basheer Bagh,
Hyderabad - 29.
10. Rajasthan Consultancy Org., Ltd.
Sardar Patel Marg,
Jaipur - 1.
11. J and K Industrial and Consultancy Org., Ltd.
Purani Mandi,
Jammu - 1.
12. U.P. Industrial Consultants Ltd.
G.T. Road,
Kanpur - 2.
13. West Bengal Consultancy Org., Ltd.
Chowringhee Road,
Kolkata - 71.
14. Bihar Industrial and Technical
Consultancy Org., Ltd.
East Gandhi Maidan,
Patna - 4.
15. Maharashtra Industrial & Technical
Consultancy Org., Ltd.
Pune Vidhyapeth Rasta,
Pune - 7.
16. Himachal Consultancy Org., Ltd.
The Mall,
Simla - l.
17. Haryana Industrial Consultancy Ltd.
Sector - 14,
Sonepat - 1.

# Appendix – III

## Whom to Contact for What Information

| | *Area of Assistance* | **State Level* | **National Level* |
|---|---|---|---|
| 1. | For selection of a project | SISI, DIC, IDCs, IICs, TCOs, SFCs, SIC, IC, IEB, PTC | CB, SIDO, CSIR, DEP, IIC, IFCI, IPB, NRDC, EDI. |
| 2. | Registration and licences | CIF, DDCA, DIC, EB, GMD, SIC, WPCB, IC, LA, STC, TC. | CECD, CCIE, ISI, IDC, MID, NSIC, RC, RT, SC, DGTD. |
| 3. | Finance | DIC, Banks, SFC, SIC, IICs, IDCs. | CB, CEC, ICICI, IDBI, IFCI, NSIC,, SBI, DIC |
| 4. | Technical DJCII, TCOs, | DDCA, DIC, IIFT, MRDC, NSIC, GMD. | CIPET, CSIR, IIC, RT, SBI, SISI, CITD, ICMR. |
| 5. | Training | EDPs, SISI, TCOs, DICs. | SBI, CB, CIPET, IRL, NISIET, IITs, NIESBUD, EDI |
| 6. | Infrastructure facilities | DIC, EB, IDC, LA. | |
| 7. | Raw materials | DIC, MID, MDC, SIC, IC, STC. | CCIE, MMTC, MDC, SPF |
| 8. | Plant and machinery | DIC, IIC, SFC, SEC, IC, IEB. | CCIE, NSIC, SISI. |
| 9. | Marketing information | DIC, TCOs, SEC, SIC, RIMCO | DEP, DGSD, CCIE, IIFT, MID, SIC, ICMR, ICAR |
| 10. | Product standardization, inventions and quality marks | DIC, IC, IRL, TRL, IITs, or Technical Colleges. | IPB, ISI, RT, SISI, CITD, ICMR. |

*For abbreviations details, refer Appendix- IV.

# Appendix – IV

## List of Abbreviations

| | | |
|---|---|---|
| 1. | CB | Commercial Bank |
| 2. | CECD | Central Excise and Customs Department |
| 3. | CIPET | Central Institute of Plastic and Engineering Tools |
| 4. | CSIR | Council of Scientific and Industrial Research |
| 5. | CCIE | Chief Controller of Imports and Exports |
| 6. | CITD | Central Institute of Tool Design |
| 7. | CIF | Chief Inspector of Factories |
| 8. | DEP | Directorate of Export Promotion |
| 9. | DGSD | Director General of Supplies and Disposal |
| 10. | DDCA | Directorate of Drugs Control Administration |
| 11. | EB | Electricity Board |
| 12. | EDI | Entrepreneurship Development Institute of India |
| 13. | EDP | Entrepreneurship Development Programmes |
| 14. | EPC | Export Promotion Council |
| 15. | GMD | Geology and Mining Department |
| 16. | ICICI | Industrial Credit and Investment Corporation of India |
| 17. | IDBI | Industrial Development Bank of India |
| 18. | IIC | Indian Investment Centre |
| 19. | IIFT | Indian Institute of Foreign Trade |
| 20. | IFCI | Industrial Finance Corporation of India |
| 21. | IPB | Invention Promotion Board |
| 22. | ISI | Indian Standard Institute |
| 23. | IDCs | Industrial Development Corporations (State level) |
| 24. | IICs | Industrial Investment Corporations (State level) |
| 25. | IC | Industries Commissioner |
| 26. | IEB | Industrial Extension Bureau (State level co-ordinating agencies) |
| 27. | IRL | Industrial Research Laboratory |
| 28. | ICAR | Indian Council of Agricultural Research |
| 29. | ICMR | Indian Council of Medical Research |
| 30. | LA | Local Authorities — Municipal Councils, Panchayat, etc. |
| 31. | LC | Leasing Companies |

| | | |
|---|---|---|
| 32. | MID | Ministry of Industrial Development |
| 33. | MMTC | Minerals and Metal Trading Corporation |
| 34. | MDC | Mineral Development Corporation |
| 35. | NIESBUD | National Institute of Entrepreneurship and Small Business Development |
| 36. | NRDC | National Research and Development Corporation |
| 37. | NISIET | National Institute of Small Industry Extension Training |
| 38. | NIDC | National Institute Development Corporation |
| 39. | NSIC | National Small Industries Corporation |
| 40. | PTC | Polytechnology Transfer Centres |
| 41. | RIMCO | Rural Industries and Marketing Corporation |
| 42. | RC | Registrar of Companies |
| 43. | RTM | Registrar of Trade Marks |
| 44. | SBI | State Bank of India |
| 45. | SIDO | Small Industries Development Organisation |
| 46. | SISI | Small Industries Service Institute |
| 47. | SC | Office of Salt Commissioner |
| 48. | SPC | State Chemicals and Pharmaceuticals Organisation of India |
| 49. | SEC | State Export Corporation |
| 50. | SFC | State Finance Corporation |
| 51. | SIC | State Small Industries Corporation |
| 52. | STC | State Trading Corporation |
| 53. | TC | Textile Commissioner |
| 54. | TCO | Technical Consultancy Organisation of the State |
| 55. | TRL | Technical Research Laboratories |
| 56. | WPCB | Water Pollution Control Board |

# Appendix – V

## The "Ten Commandments" for the Beginning Entrepreneur

### 1. Raise Capital When You Don't Need It

A typical entrepreneur is always in a constant race in search of financing sources. The right time to look for new finance is at the beginning of each step, while there are still some cash reserves. Otherwise, he may find himself in a constant chase of cash flow and interim finance, which will prevent him from performing his role as an entrepreneur within his organization.

### 2. Focus on a Well-Defined Limited Business Field/Niche

Entrepreneurs often make the mistake of trying to cover too many subjects at the same time. Many of the entrepreneurial companies try too often to develop a relatively large number of new products simultaneously, or as a variation of the above, try to develop new products, and at the same time, do sub-contracting or consulting work. This is a sure-fire recipe for failure.

### 3. Listen to Expert Advice and Don't Hesitate to Pay for Professional Services

Entrepreneurs tend to think they "know it all." They think that since they possess a wide technical knowledge, all other complementary areas, such as marketing, financing and organization are "child's play" that they can offhandedly master. Furthermore, entrepreneurs tend to think that they know better than specialists and thus refuse to allocate funds for professional advice. These "savings" eventually end up costing the company large sums of money, and sometimes, its very existence.

### 4. Choose a Team of Professionals and Don't Compromise on the Quality of Manpower

In any organization, and especially in those that are high-tech based, the most valued assets are its human resources. The entrepreneur should therefore, from the start, select a professional team that would complement him and shouldn't compromise on the quality of the people around him. The task of locating key personnel in Israel is easier, due to its smaller size.

### 5. Don't "Argue" with the Market

Many entrepreneurs think they know better what the market's demands are, because they think that "there is no way the market wouldn't want my invention." Such reasoning, which stems from a technology-driven attitude, is quickly proven wrong, the result being money and efforts spent in vain.

### 6. Develop a Strategic Business Vision as Early as Possible and Learn from Your Own Mistakes

Developing such a vision would enable the entrepreneur to have an overall view of the political, business and economical impacts of the environment on his business, and will enable him to plan ahead in a way that would minimize his chances of a loss. The other part of this vision is a candid (and sometimes very painful) examination of past mistakes and drawing the applicable conclusions.

## 7. Enlist the Support of Your Family and Friends

An entrepreneur tends to work long hours, to see very little of his family, and at certain times, to fail to bring sufficient income for his family. Field studies have shown that entrepreneurs who fail to receive the full support of their families and close friends tend to "break" at critical times and abandon their entrepreneurial activities.

## 8. Define Correctly the Comparative Advantage of Your Product from the User's Standpoint

The typical Israeli entrepreneur tends to believe that he represents the familiar combination of "better and cheaper." In most cases, this is insufficient to draw the attention of the potential buyer. The right way to approach the potential buyer would be to point out the benefits and advantages of the product or service from the buyer's point of view.

## 9. Stay in Touch and Learn from Other Entrepreneurs — Network

"It's lonely at the top" is a saying often associated with entrepreneurship, which is an activity encompassing loneliness and individual struggle. It is, therefore, important to develop a support network of entrepreneurs that have already experienced different entrepreneurial stages and have been exposed to successes and failures in order to enlist their support in the difficult moments that each entrepreneur faces.

## 10. Learn About the "Life Cycles" of the Entrepreneur and the Business

There is one embedded conflict in entrepreneurship. The turning point, in which the entrepreneurship succeeds, the business develops, sells on a large scale, and its various departments institutionalize, is exactly the point at which the entrepreneur should leave the business and concentrate on what he's really good at — starting other new businesses. Most entrepreneurs find it hard to make the transition and they tend to remain in the business they've started and "rest on their laurels." In theory, as well as in reality, only very few entrepreneurs succeed in becoming good managers. The rest finally fail the companies they have invested so much effort in building up.

# Appendix – VI

## Mistakes Entrepreneurs Should NOT Make

### 1. "The Product will sell itself"

If you believe this, and don't do the required marketing — at the right time, in the right way, on a regular basis — the probability is very high that you will fail.

### 2. "We will raise the money later"

Don't be sure that you can raise it later. Markets change, investor interest changes, new competitors appear. So, when you have the chance for an investment, take the money and run.

### 3. "Why do we need a lawyer/accountant/consultant, etc.?"

You need the best possible professional help you can get, to prevent the mistakes that can destroy your business, and to give you the best chance to succeed. You may think professionals are too expensive, but, it is much more expensive in the long run without them.

### 4. "We will make the decisions informally. No need to put anything on paper."

Write everything down, at least in draft form, so when people remember things differently, you have a document that you can refer to.

### 5. "Tell the customer it will take a week, and then we'll see what we can do."

Don't make promises to customers that you can't keep. Develop a reputation for credibility and reliability. If you can't meet a tight schedule, be honest about it. Build your customer base to last. Build long-term relationships. Don't see them as one-time buyers; you need them to come back again and again and to recommend you to others.

### 6. "The customer will take care of the adjustments."

The customer does not understand your product the way you do. Don't make him struggle with it; help him by offering easily accessible, professional support.

### 7. "Competition? What competition?"

Don't assume that you have no competition, or that it is not serious. There are lots of people in your field, in many parts of the world, who may be designing a product that is just as good or better than yours, or that is being introduced to the market before yours is ready. Be aware and make plans accordingly.

### 8. "Clearer than this ...."

You designed and developed your product. Everything is clear to you. Remember that the customer needs very clear, explicit, simple documentation. Have a technical writer, mother-tongue English if possible, prepare high-level material.

## 9. "No need for written agreements; we're old buddies."

Write everything down and get everyone to sign. People can easily forget or choose to forget what was agreed. People outside the immediate circle will soon join you, and they need to know exactly what agreements are in place. Friendships don't last forever, especially when money — or the lack of it — is involved.

## 10. "They are really getting on our nerves, these investors."

Investors have put a lot of money into your company, taken a big risk, and stand to lose everything if you don't make it. They have every right to receive regular, honest reports, and to have their advice at least listened to seriously.

# Appendix – VII

## Model (Review) Questions

## Section A:

**(Answers to be written in about 50 words. Each question usually carries three or four marks)**

1. Who is an entrepreneur?
2. What is an entrepreneur?
3. What is Entrepreneurship development program?
4. Define small scale industry.
5. What is a 'Project'?
6. Define market research.
7. Define industrial sickness.
8. What is project appraisal?
9. Define entrepreneurship.
10. What is an ancillary unit?
11. State objectives of industrial estates.
12. What is a feasibility report?
13. Mention the qualities of entrepreneurs.
14. Mention the objectives of national small industries corporation (NSIC).
15. State attitudinal factors influencing entrepreneurship.
16. Define 'Tiny Sector.'
17. Mention problems of SSI.
18. State the need for entrepreneurial development.
19. Mention six acts regulating SSI.
20. State the types of entrepreneurs.
21. What are the external causes of industrial sickness?
22. What is an export house?
23. Mention the types of industrial estates.
24. What is 'soft loan'?
25. What is 'cottage Industry'?
26. Write short notes on:
    (1) Cottage industries.
    (2) Ancillary industries.
    (3) Village industries.
    (4) Tiny Sector.
    (5) Rural industry.

(6) National small industries corporation (NSIC).
(7) Small industries development organisation (SIDO).
(8) Minimum wages.
(9) Commodity boards.
(10) Routing.
(11) Inspection.
(12) Scheduling.
(13) Production planning control (PPC).
(14) Inventory management.
(15) Industrial designing.
(16) Prototype development centre (PDC).
(17) Industrial estate.
(18) Entrepreneur, entrepreneurship, enterprise.
(19) Intrepreneurs.
(20) Fabian entrepreneur.
(21) Economic viability.
(22) EDP.
(23) Innovation.
(24) Functions of entrepreneur.
(25) Industrial sickness.
(26) Rural entrepreneur
(27) Sustainable entrepreneurship.
(28) Knowledge management.
(29) Strategic framework.
(30) International entrepreneur.
(31) Brainstorming.
(32) Creativity.
(33) Problem solving.
(34) Social entrepreneur.
(35) Service enterprise.

## Section B:

**(Answers to be written in about 250 words each. Question usually carries six or eight marks)**

1. Discuss the factors influencing entrepreneurship.
2. Discuss the role of SIDO in promoting small industries in India.
3. Explain briefly the problems faced by small-scale industries in India.
4. What is Marketing Information? What are the sources of market information available to an entrepreneur?
5. Analyse the causes for sickness in small-scale units.
6. Compare and contrast entrepreneur with entrepreneurship.
7. Explain the factors influencing the birth of an entrepreneur.
8. Analyse the role of the "National Small Industries Corporation" for the growth and development of SSI.
9. Explain the remedial measures for the revival of sick units.
10. Describe the procedure for estimating the financial needs of a small manufacturing unit.
11. "Small is Beautiful." Do you agree? Substantiate.
12. "Sickness in small sector is something which can be prevented." Do you agree? Substantiate.
13. What are the essential qualities of a successful entrepreneur?
14. What are the guidelines for measuring the financial viability of a new project?
15. What is a market survey? What steps are involved in conducting a market survey for a small soap manufacturing unit?
16. Analyse the contributory role of small-scale industry in our economy.
17. Discuss the importance of entrepreneurship development.
18. Explain the legal formalities to be observed while starting a small-scale unit.
19. What is the role of an entrepreneur in economic development?
20. Explain the functions of an entrepreneur.
21. Briefly discuss the importance of personality factors in entrepreneurial development:
22. What are the phases in entrepreneurship development?
23. Explain the need for entrepreneurship development programme.
24. Analyse the concept of women entrepreneurship.
25. Explain project appraisal.

## Section C:

**(Essay Type answers to be written in about thousand words *i.e.,* three or four pages of normal handwriting. Question usually carries 15 or 17 marks)**

1. Discuss the importance of an entrepreneur in a developing economy, with special reference to Indian conditions.
2. Elaborate on the Government policies and measures towards promotion of entrepreneurship in India.
3. What is entrepreneurship? Discuss the need for entrepreneurship development. How is it done?
4. "Entrepreneur is a doer not a dreamer." Comment and explain the characteristics of an entrepreneur.
5. Discuss the factors which inhibit the growth of entrepreneurship.
6. Explain the phases of entrepreneurship development.
7. Discuss the important functions of an entrepreneur.
8. "Entrepreneurs are made, not born," comment and justify your view.
9. Discuss the trends in the development of women entrepreneurship.
10. Explain the various aspects of project appraisal.
11. Prepare a project report for starting a small scale leather industry.
12. Explain the role and significance of small scale industry.
13. Discuss the procedure for setting-up of SSI.
14. Explain the causes of sickness in SSI. Discuss the remedies also.
15. Explain the procedure of/and the documents to be furnished while starting SSI.
16. Discuss the various factors influencing location of SSI.
17. What is a market survey? What are the steps involved in conducting a market survey for a small industry?
18. Explain the organization and functioning of:
    - *(a)* Small Industries Service Institute (SISI).
    - *(b)* State Financial Corporation (SFC).
    - *(c)* Industrial Development Bank of India (IDBI).
    - *(d)* Industrial Credit Investment Corporation of India (ICICI).
    - *(e)* Commercial Banks.
19. Give a brief account of important institutions and agencies engaged in the promotion and development of SSI in India.
20. Discuss the steps in obtaining Finance/Advances from:
    - *(a)* Industrial Finance Corporation of India (IFC).
    - *(b)* National Small Industries Corporation (NSIC).
    - *(c)* Industrial Development Bank of India (IDBI).

21. "Sickness in small sector can be prevented." Do you agree? Analyse the causes for and remedies to industrial sickness.
22. "Small is Beautiful." Do you agree? Discuss the strengths and weaknesses of small industrial sector in our country.
23. What are the guidelines for measuring the technical feasibility and financial viability of a new project?
24. What is an 'Industrial Estate'? What are the objectives of establishing Industrial Estate? Review whether the objectives of establishing Industrial Estates in India have been achieved.
25. Discuss the importance. of marketing and problems of marketing in SSI.

*****

# Additional Reading


Acs Z, Audretsch D. (1990). Innovation and Small Firms, Cambridge, MA: MIT Press.

John Kao (1991). The Entrepreneur, Englewood Cliffs, New Jersy: Prentice-Hall.

*Tarun Khanna (2008). Billions of Entrepreneurs: How China and India are Reshaping Their Futures –and Yours. Boston, MA: Harvard Business School Press.*

Jeffry A. Timmons (1989). The Entrepreneurial Mind Andover, MA: Brick House Publishing.

Amar V. Bhide (2000). The Origin and Evolution of New Businesses, New York, NY: Oxford University Press.

Michael A. Hitt (2002). Strategic Entrepreneurship: Creating a New Mindset, Wiley-Blackwell.

Morris, S.; R. Basant; K. Das; K. Ramachandran; and A. Koshy (2001). The Growth and Transformation of Small Firms in India, New Delhi, Oxford University Press.

Jane Applegate (1992). Succeeding in Small Business: The 101 Toughest Problems and How to Solve Them, Plume/Penguin.

David H. Bangs, Jr. (1992). The Business Planning Guide: Creating a Plan for Success in Your Own Business, 6th edition, Upstart. 1992 (comes with a CD-ROM).

Gordon B. Baty (1990). Entrepreneurship for the Nineties, Prentice-Hall.

Roger Bel Air (1988). How to Borrow Money from a Banker: A Business Owner's Guide, AMACOM.

Tim Burns (1999). Break the Curve: The Entrepreneur's Blueprint for Small Business Success, International Thomson Business Press.

Lawrence Finley (1994). Entrepreneurial Strategies: Text and Cases, PWS-Kent Publishing.

David Gladstone (1998). Venture Capital Handbook, new and revised edition, Prentice-Hall.

David E. Gumpert (1990). How to Create a Successful Business Plan, Inc. Publishing.

Craig Hall (2001). The Responsible Entrepreneur: How to Make Money and Make a Difference, Career Press.

*Robert D. Hisrich and Michael P. Peters (1995). Entrepreneurship: Starting, Developing, and Managing a New Enterprise, 3rd edition, Irwin.*

Jay Conrad Levinson (1997). The Way of the Guerrilla: Achieving Success and Balance as an Entrepreneur in the 21st Century, Houghton Mifflin.

Charles P. Lickson (1994). A Legal Guide for Small Business: How to Do It Right the First Time, Crisp Publications.

Bill Meyer (1998). Cash Flow: A Practical Guide for the Entrepreneur, Perc Press.

Robert Ronstadt (1998). Entrepreneurial Finance: Taking Control of Your Financial Decision Making, Lord Publishing.

Eric S. Siegel, Brian R. Ford, and Jay M. Borstein (1993). The Ernst & Young Business Plan Guide, 2nd edition, Wiley.

Karl H. Vesper (1990). New Venture Strategies, Revised Edition, Prentice-Hall.

Parrish, B.D., Tilley, F. (2009). Sustainability Entrepreneurship: Charting a Field in Emergence In: Schaper, M. (Ed.), Making Ecopreneurs: Developing Sustainable Entrepreneurship. Gower, Aldershot, UK.

Alter, Sutia Kim (2000). Managing the Double Bottom Line: A Business Planning Guide for Social Enterprises. Washington, D.C.: Save The Children.

Austin, James E. (2000). The Collaboration Challenge: How Non-Profits and Businesses Succeed Through Strategic Alliances. San Francisco: Jossey-Bass Publishers.

Barker, Joel Arthur (1992). Paradigms: The Business of Discovering the Future. New York: Harper Business, A Division of HarperCollins Publishers.

Boschee, Jerr (2001). The Social Enterprise Sourcebook. Minneapolis: Northland Institute.

Brinckerhoff, Peter C. (2000). Social Entrepreneurship: The Art of Mission-Based Venture Development. New York, John Wiley & Sons, Inc.

Bygrave, William D. (2003). The Portable MBA in Entrepreneurship, 3rd Edition. New York, John Wiley & Sons, Inc.

Dees, J. Gregory, Jed Emerson, Peter Economy (2001). Enterprising Non-Profits: A Toolkit for Social Entrepreneurs. New York, John Wiley & Sons, Inc.

Hawken, Paul (1988). Growing a Business. New York, Simon & Schuster.

Kotler, Philip, Alan R. Andreasen (2002). Strategic Marketing for Non-Profit Organizations (Sixth Edition). New York, Prentice-Hall, Inc.

Frame, J. Davidson (2003). Managing Projects in Organizations: How to Make the Best Use of Time, Techniques, and People[* | In-line.WMF *], 3rd edition, Jossey-Bass.

Kerzner, Harold (2009). Project Management: Project Management: A Systems Approach to Planning, Scheduling, and Controlling[* | In-line.WMF *], 10th edition, Wiley.

Lewis, James (2006). The Project Manager's Desk Reference, 3rd edition, McGraw-Hill.

Meredith, R. Jack and Mantel, Jr., Samuel J. (2008). Project Management: A Managerial Approach[* | In-line.WMF *], 7th edition, Wiley.

*Weiss, Joseph and Wysocki, Robert (1992). Five-Phase Project Management: A Practical Planning and Implementation Guide, Basic Books.*

*Vasant Desai (2000). Small-Scale Enterprises (Set of XII Volumes), Himalaya Publishing House.*

## Useful Websites

*http://msme.gov.in/ and http://www.laghu-udyog.com/ - The Ministry of Micro, Small and Medium Enterprises lists various government schemes for entrepreneurs*

http://www.techno-preneur.net/ - The Technology Innovation Management and Entrepreneurship Information Service assists techno-preneurs in finding technologies, projects, funding options and information on policy environment, incentive schemes and industrial infrastructure availablein the country, covering central and state governments.

http://www.sidbi.in/ - The Small Industrial Development Bank of India works towards empowering Micro, Small and Medium Enterprises.

http://dst.gov.in/scientific-programme/t-d-tdb.htm - The Technology Development Board is the first organization of its kind within the Government framework with the sole objective of translating the fruits of indigenous research into commercial products or services.

http://www.dsir.nic.in/tpdup/tepp/tepp.htm - The Technopreneur Promotion Programme is run by Department of Scientific & Industrial Research.

http://www.indiavca.org/ - The Indian Venture Capital and Private Equity Association (IVCA) is a member based national organization that represents venture capital and private equity firms.

http://www.indianangelnetwork.com/ - The Indian Angel Network (IAN) is India's first and largest Angel network with successful entrepreneurs and high profile CEOs.

http://www.thenetworkenterprisesfund.in/ - The Network Enterprises Fund is an equity fund that invests in commercially viable, sustainable enterprises in sectors impacting low-income households.

http://www.nenonline.org/ - The National Entrepreneurship Network (NEN).

http://www.tie.org/ - The Indus Entrepreneurs, also known as Talent Ideas and Enterprise is spread across 11 countries, fostering entrepreneurship globally through mentoring, networking, and education.

http://www.bystonline.org/ - The Bharat Yuva Shakti Trust works with young people in the age group of 18 - 35, who are either unemployed or underemployed, providing financial and mentoring support to establish their own ventures.

http://www.ediindia.org/ - The Entrepreneurship Development Institute of India (EDI), fosters entrepreneurship through various programmes and courses.

http://www.niesbud.org/ - An apex body established by Ministry of Industries, Govt. of India for coordinating, training and overseeing the activities of various institutions/ agencies engaged in Entrepreneurship Development, particularly in the area of small industry and small business.